46386

THE MEXICAN INQUISITION
OF THE SIXTEENTH CENTURY

Manuscript page with the seal of office of Diego de Mayorga, Secretary and Apostolic Notary of the Holy Office 1536-1543

THE MEXICAN INQUISITION OF THE SIXTEENTH CENTURY

Richard E. Greenleaf

ALBUQUERQUE
UNIVERSITY OF NEW MEXICO PRESS

© University of New Mexico Press 1969. All rights reserved.
Manufactured in the United States of America by the
University of New Mexico Printing Plant, Albuquerque.
Library of Congress Catalog Card No. 77-78553, SBN 8263-0130-4.
First Edition.

For
FRANCE VINTON SCHOLES
El Decano de los Investigadores

PREFACE

MANY YEARS AGO the director of the Archivo General de la Nación told a young investigator in the Ramo de la Inquisición, "In these *legajos* you will find the social and intellectual history of colonial Mexico." France V. Scholes immersed himself in the manuscripts and he learned to use the *procesos* as solid foundations for studies of seventeenth-century New Mexico and colonial Yucatán.

Because the conventional documentary sources had been destroyed in the Pueblo Rebellion and the Spanish retreat from Santa Fé in the 1680's, many scholars felt it was impossible to write primary history of the New Mexico colony. Dr. Scholes proved otherwise in his two volumes on Church and State in New Mexico. By extracting data from Inquisition trials sent to Mexico City prior to the rebellion, he was able to reconstruct a century of important borderlands history.

Professor Scholes communicated his enthusiasm for Inquisition sources to me, and he also taught me the paleography and the archival techniques necessary to follow in the Scholes tradition of historical research. His scholarly example, his friendship and his guidance have inspired me for fifteen years. This book is dedicated to him.

Quite a number of individuals have contributed to my study of the Mexican Inquisition of the sixteenth century. During fourteen years of research in and out of the Mexican archives, members of the staff have been kind and helpful. Don Jorge Ignacio Rubio

Mañé never failed to give me encouragement. Sra. María de la Luz Viamonte and Sra. Carmela Camacho lightened my task with their courteous, professional help.

Without the guidance of my friend Don Miguel Saldaña, who has spent fifty years as a paleographer and investigator in the archive, my work could not have progressed. I am obligated to Eleanor B. Adams, Lewis Hanke and F. Benedict Warren for advice and support. They, along with France Scholes, have helped me surmount the obstacles to research and publication inherent in the administrative life. Professors Scholes and Warren shared with me documentary sources from their own research. Miss Patricia Núñez, my secretary, has contributed far more than her secretarial skills to this book. In a real sense she has helped me push it through to completion.

Richard E. Greenleaf
México, D.F.
1969

CONTENTS

Preface	vii
Introduction	1
Chapter One: The First Decade of the Mexican Inquisition, 1522-1532	7
I The First Inquisitors, 1519-1526	7
II Betanzos and the Blasphemers	11
III Rodrigo Rengel: Horrifying Blashemy, 1527	19
IV The Auto de Fé of October 1528	26
V Epilogue	37
Chapter Two: The Inquisition in Michoacán, 1536-1537	45
I The Career of Gonzalo Gómez to 1537	46
II The Denunciation of Gonzalo Gómez, September 1536-June 1537	50
III The Defense of Gonzalo Gómez, June-July 1537	55
IV Litigation and Recriminations, July-October 1537	59
V Climax, November 1537	65
VI Aftermath: 1572	70
Chapter Three: The Episcopal Inquisition in Mexico, 1535-1571	74
I The Indian Inquisition of Tello de Sandoval, 1544-1547	75
II The Holy Office and Protestantism, 1543-1569	81
III Faith and Morals in the Colony	99

IV	The Inquisition and the Medical Profession, 1551-1570	103
V	Judaizantes, 1558-1564	107
VI	Usury	111

Chapter Four: The Montúfar Inquisition and the Mexican Clergy, 1555-1571 — 116

Chapter Five: The Tribunal of the Holy Office, 1571-1601 — 158
   I Corsairs and Judaizantes — 162
   II Faith and Morals in the Colony, 1571-1601 — 172
   III Conflicts of Jurisdiction and Politics — 174
   IV Books and Men — 182

Chapter Six: The Mexican Inquisition and the Calvinists, 1598-1601 — 191
   I The Evidence Against Simón de Santiago — 192
   II Inquisitorial Proceedings — 198
   III Indictment and Judicial Torture — 201
   IV Climax — 203
   V The Other Flamencos, 1598-1601 — 206

Chapter Seven: Conclusions — 211

Bibliography — 215

Index — 233

INTRODUCTION

THE HOLY OFFICE of the Inquisition in Mexico had as its purpose the defense of Spanish religion and Spanish-Catholic culture against individuals who held heretical views and people who showed lack of respect for religious principles. Inquisition documents always contain social and intellectual history. They reflect the lives of the people and colonial mentality at any given time. When studied *en masse* the records provide an overview of colonial life not available from other sources. Perhaps a society is best known through its heretics and dissenters. The way in which social institutions react to the rebel, the nonconformist, the argumentative and the intellectually combative yields all manner of data on heresy and tradition, and the reaction helps to measure social and ideological change.

I

Inquisition trials illuminate more than religious practice in the punishment of unorthodoxy. They are concerned less with the psychopaths of the Mexican colony than with the security of religion within the social structure. Kinship and family life show through the procedural apparatus, and patterns of speech and behavior reveal the folk culture. The colloquial language of humble people paints vibrant pictures of lower-echelon Spanish and mestizo society. Glimpses of daily life, devotion and recreation emerge from the documents. The anarchism of the Spanish character comes out in the blasphemy and bigamy prosecutions. Common profanity indicates a familiar dichotomy of reverence and mocking, of belief and agnosticism, of subservience and resentment, of conformity and alienation of the individual. More often than not, those entrusted with the enforcement of orthodoxy among the masses were surprisingly tolerant, perhaps because they understood this anarchy of character and viewed a certain amount of irreverence as healthy, a safety valve which gave acceptable relief to the volatile personality.

Meanings of blasphemy are difficult to translate and to relate to the times. For instance, the foremost expletive used by the sixteenth-century settler was "Pese a Dios," "May it spite God." But of course "Pese a Dios" really had a more colloquial meaning, something like "God damn." Obviously it is difficult to visualize a mule driver kicking a donkey and saying "May it spite God." Formal piety and everyday speech were two different things. The Inquisition seemed to understand this.

During the sixteenth century one special function of the Holy Office was the enforcement of orthodox conduct and belief among the recently converted Indian population. Trials of Indians show that religious syncretism was the primary concern of the Mexican church in its first century. In many areas the natives developed a religion which was Catholic in form but pagan in substance. The Inquisition procesos reveal fascinating data for the ethnohistorian and the ethnologist, information preserved only in specific documents in Mexico and Spain. Where else can one investigate from primary sources native religion at the time of contact with the Spaniard? Where else does one get eyewitness accounts of post-conquest idolatry and sacrifice, burial rites, native dances and ceremonies? The procesos often contain clues to indigenous genealogy and social organization, as well as living testimony to culture shock as two civilizations collided.

The real heretics of the Mexican colony were usually non-Spanish subjects of Charles V, corsairs in the era of Philip II, and peninsular Jews who had fled Spain or Portugal for a variety of

INTRODUCTION 3

reasons. Investigation in depth in the Inquisition archive leads one to believe that there were many more Protestants and Jews in sixteenth-century Mexico than is commonly supposed, and the documents hint that only a small number of these ever came before the Holy Office. Both groups constituted a nebulous subculture in the early colony, lending variety to the social scene and the intellectual milieu. Except when they challenged the Church or Spanish authority in an open manner or when they particularly rankled the peninsular Spaniard as a business competitor or a political rival, these heretics did not appear in the halls of the Inquisition. When they were indeed tried for heresy, their cases help exemplify the ambivalence of tolerance and rigidity in the social structure.

Anti-Semitism and prejudice against the foreigner on the part of some colonists are evident from the earliest years of the conquest. But since a sizable number of the settlers came from questionable backgrounds, the total picture probably was one of tolerance—at least until the Counter Reformation reached Mexico. For example, the word *marrano* (pig) was not used in sixteenth-century Mexico to refer to *Judaizantes* (Judaizing Christians). More formal, less emotionally charged words are used to characterize these "New Christians" who had converted from Judaism but who still practiced the old religion in private.[1]

A most absorbing dimension of the Holy Office's activities in its first century was the preoccupation with clerical morality. Clerical life, intellect and mentality are illustrated in the trials by the attitudes of those who were subjected to prosecution and those who conducted the proceedings. The posture of orthodoxy was on the one hand self-righteous and inflexible; on the other hand it was permissive until the regular clergy were identified with Protestantism by the Counter Reformation seculars and the Jesuits. The Holy Office acted as a clearinghouse for clerical ideas, old and new. The conflict between the regulars and the hierarchy clergy over the mission of the Church added volumes of documents to the Inquisition archive. Certainly the investigations by the Holy Office are a gauge of ideological change in sixteenth-century Mexico.

While many authorities have stressed the apocalyptic medieval world view of the clergy, the "spiritual conquest" of Mexico was surely grounded in the Renaissance. But the Inquisition documents show the ascendancy of the Counter Reformation mentality by the middle of the century, and they provide the key to the development of baroque intellect at the turn of the seventeenth century.

The administrative records of the tribunal of the Holy Office show that within the framework of its procedure the Inquisition rarely acted in an arbitrary way but in a very orderly manner. Twentieth-century scholars have a difficult time evaluating the procedures of the Holy Office unless they judge them fairly according to the judicial system and ideological structure of sixteenth-century Catholicism. The administrative documents confirm that the inquisitors acted with zeal but with fairness in the vast majority of cases. Economic data in the archive confirm that the responsible bureaucracy of the tribunal administered with scrupulous honesty the properties and fines of those who were censured. Volumes of inventories of estates, accounts of the debts and profits of those tried, of the expenses of attorneys, judges and the Inquisition jail, are meticulous in their detail. Documents of administrative litigation involving the Inquisition, especially cases of competency and conflict of jurisdiction, offer some of the most valuable insights into the history of the Mexican Holy Office, for only through disputes of this nature can one see the Inquisition as a viable institution at all levels of colonial society.

Studies of the Holy Office of the Inquisition in Mexico lack depth and perceptive analysis, despite the extremely valuable efforts of pioneer scholars José Toribio Medina, Henry C. Lea and Luis González Obregón, in the sections of their works which deal with the sixteenth century. A reason for this shortcoming is the tabulative approach. Counting of heretics does not produce knowledge about heresy, and reliance upon abstracts of trials rather than the complete records nets little substantial information. Stress on descriptions of crimes and punishments has led many to ignore the intellectual content and social data in the

INTRODUCTION 5

documents. Rarely does the statistical method relate the prosecutions of the Holy Office to prevailing social, political and ideological currents. Contemporary historians have the lamentable tendency to recapitulate the first generation of Mexican Inquisition studies without breaking any new ground and to tabulate crimes and sentences from the Inquisition Index without reading the actual procesos. Only Julio Jiménez Rueda has tried to relate heresy to colonial intellect. If one is to interpret and to theorize about the Mexican Inquisition as an institution, a painstaking investigation of hundreds of actual trials must precede any generalizations.

II

The purpose of these historical essays is to probe various facets of sixteenth-century Inquisition activity in the Mexican colony. In this respect the book is not a history but rather an attempt to place an institution in a historical setting. A general theme of all of the essays is the involvement of the Holy Office in political controversy, and the effort, not always successful, to keep the Inquisition aloof from nonreligious disputes.

Chapter One examines heresy in the first decade of the conquest and looks at the Holy Office as a weapon used against the Cortés faction. Chapter Two deals with the Inquisition in a provincial setting and stresses local politics and economic rivalries as reasons for denunciation of heretics. Chapter Three surveys the episcopal Inquisition during 1535 to 1571 and focuses on faith and morals among the colonists and the Indians. It also views the inception of Counter Reformation activity against the foreigner. Chapter Four investigates inquisitorial activity within the clerical establishment and relates the Holy Office with diocesan politics, the struggle between regular and secular clergy and the conflict between the Renaissance and the Counter Reformation in New Spain. Chapter Five narrates the administrative history of the tribunal of the Holy Office in Mexico from

1571 to 1601 as the Counter Reformation became articulate. Chapter Six details the flurry of Protestant prosecutions between 1598 and 1601 which culminated in the greatest of the Counter Reformation *autos de fé* in March 1601. Most of the documents used in these essays have not been examined or analyzed by previous authors.

Note

[1] An extremely useful etymological study of the word *marrano* is contained in Yakov Malkiel, "Hispano-Arabic *Marrano* and Its Hispano-Latin Homophone," *Journal of the American Oriental Society*, Vol. 68 (1948), pp. 175-184.

Chapter One

THE FIRST DECADE OF THE MEXICAN INQUISITION
1522-1532

AFTER THE MILITARY CONQUEST of the Aztec Empire in 1521, the Spanish government and the Spanish church saw the necessity to present the Indians of Mesoamerica with proper examples of Christian conduct and to insure that the newly discovered lands were not populated with heretics. Because the humanistic ideals of the clergy and the materialism of the colonist often collided when it came to treatment of the Indian and because there was no adequate administrative machinery in the primitive church for the enforcement of orthodoxy, the clergy had to rely upon the civil authority to help preserve the faith during the first years of the Spanish occupation of Mexico. Co-operation of Church and State in the exercise of inquisitorial functions led to political involvement of the Holy Office of the Inquisition in the contest for political and economic lordship of the colony, and the inquisitors often took a partisan stand in the struggle.

I

The First Inquisitors, 1519-1526

Where formal tribunals of the Inquisition did not exist, bishops in portfolio of ecclesiastical judge ordinary had responsibility for enforcement of faith and morals in the diocese. But in the early years of the Mexican conquest there were neither Inquisition tribunals nor bishops to exercise this function. Instead, a monastic Inquisition in which friar-inquisitors assumed episcopal powers operated in Mexico from 1522 until Bishop Juan de Zumárraga finally received his bulls of consecration and went through the formal ceremony of consecration on his return visit to Spain in 1532.[1] Because there was a shortage of secular clergy to carry on the spiritual conquest of new lands, the Pope gave special faculties to the regular clergy in bulls of 1521 *(Alias felices)* and 1522 *(Exponi nobis),* and empowered their prelates to perform almost all episcopal functions, except ordination, where there were no bishops or where the see was two days distant.[2] Thus the first Franciscan and Dominican prelates in Mexico acted as ecclesiastical judges ordinary under the 1522 bull, known in the Spanish world as the *Omnímoda,* and assumed inquisitorial functions until more formalized Holy Office machinery was provided by the Church and the State in the decade of the 1530's.

To safeguard their authority from any future episcopacy, the Spanish inquisitors general between 1517 and 1519 delegated their functions in the Indies to bishops and prelates there; and the bishop of Puerto Rico, Alonso Manso, and the vice-provincial of the Dominican order in the Indies, Fray Pedro de Córdoba, were empowered to establish Inquisitions.[3] The Dominican chronicler Antonio de Remesal contended that Pedro de Córdoba in turn delegated his inquisitorial authority to the Franciscan Martín de Valencia when the famous "Los Doce" of the Franciscans passed through Santo Domingo on their way to Mexico in 1524. Remesal contended that Córdoba specified that the delegation of authority was valid only until there should be a Dominican prelate in Mexico.[4] Records in the Mexican Inquisition archive indicate that activities against heretics began in Mexico in 1522, two years before the arrival of Fray Martín de Valencia, and presumably under authority of friar-inquisitors empowered by the papal bulls. When Pedro de Córdoba died,

THE FIRST DECADE

probably on June 30, 1525, the *audiencia* of Santo Domingo and the inquisitor general in Spain made another delegation of power to the new Dominican Prelate Tomás Ortíz who arrived in Mexico from Santo Domingo in 1526. After a brief period in Mexico, where he became involved in some volatile political controversies with Hernán Cortés, Prelate Ortíz turned his office over to the newly elected prelate of the Dominicans in Mexico, Domingo de Betanzos, who assumed quasi-episcopal functions under the Omnímoda, including the jurisdiction over heresy.[5]

The civil government in New Spain continued to discipline heretics and blasphemers during the first decade of the Inquisition. Often the extant records of the civil jurisdiction place inquisitorial procedures in a more meaningful context. Cortés initiated the movement to punish blasphemers in 1520 with a stern ordinance. After he recounted the many blessings bestowed upon the conquerors by God and the Holy Mother, the conqueror charged that many were blaspheming in Mexico in such a way as to insult or express ingratitude to the deity, and he placed a caveat on such expressions as "No creo en Dios, ni pese, ni reniego, ni del Cielo, ni no ha poder en Dios" and other sayings. Cortés warned that Spanish legal punishments prescribed for blasphemers would be enforced, and those guilty were to be fined fifteen *castellanos de oro*. The fine was to be shared in equal parts by the Cofradía de Nuestra Señora, the royal treasury and the sentencing judge.[6]

Two edicts against heretics in 1523, directed against Jews and "all people who by word or deed did things that seemed sinful," were no doubt cooperative ventures between Church and State to curb blasphemy.[7] The proceedings of the *alcalde mayor* of Tenochtitlán against Diego de Morales for blasphemy in 1524 and 1525 emanated from the decrees of both religious and civil authority. Had not a fragment of the alcalde's trial been preserved in the Inquisition archive, no adequate documentation for the mysterious auto de fé of the Santa María Inquisition of October 1528 would exist. Even after the monastic Inquisition ceased, from 1528 to 1532, the civil authority continued its jurisdiction over heresy and immorality, as evidenced in the Nuño de Guzmán trial of the Caltzontzin of the Tarascans for idolatry, sacrifice and sodomy in 1530.[8] Civil intervention in Inquisition matters, and the reverse, continued well into the 1560's.[9]

It appears that the first mendicant orders that came to Mexico with Cortés carried with them inquisitorial powers. Whether the faculty to act as inquisitors came as a delegation of authority from a Cuban churchman is not known. It is possible that Pope Leo X's bull of April 10, 1521, which granted the Franciscans episcopal powers where there were no hierarchy clergy in the New World, established the jurisdiction. But it is not known whether the Franciscans initiated the first trial of the Mexican Inquisition, that of an Indian, Marcos of Acolhuacán, for the crime of concubinage in 1522. It is probable that the Franciscans participated in the framing of the two edicts against heretics in 1523, but these documents along with the 1522 trial have disappeared from the Mexican archives.[10] Whether Fray Martín de Valencia extirpated heresy under the aegis of the Omnímoda, or by faculties delegated to him by the Dominican Vice-Provincial Pedro de Córdoba, he did engage in Inquisition-like functions in 1524 in Tlaxcala, and in 1525 in Mexico City. He appeared to have had a free hand in the Tlaxcala province, where he executed four Indians for idolatry and sacrifice.[11] The inquisitorial activities of Fray Martín in the metropolitan area were concerned more with jurisdictional competency than with punishment of heretics. From March through July of 1525, the Franciscans had an altercation with the *cabildo* of Mexico City over interpretation of the jurisdiction inherent in the Bull Omnímoda and the royal *pase* of the papal document giving them episcopal powers.

Cabildo records show that Fray Martín de Valencia tried to assume civil and criminal jurisdiction in addition to the quasi-episcopal faculties granted by the Pope.[12] On March 9, 1525, Prelate Valencia presented his bulls to the cabildo and demanded obedience to his instructions. He designated Fray Toribio de Motolinía his deputy in matters of civil and ecclesiastical jurisdiction. The *regidores* of the cabildo spent many weeks studying the bulls, and they actually incorporated the documents into the municipal records. On July 28, 1525, the scribe of the cabildo, Diego de Ocaña, summoned Motolinía to appear before that body and to bring all credentials with him. In a courteous manner the aldermen told Motolinía that they respected the briefs of the Pope, and they were disposed to obey all commands of the King, but they could find no grant of authority in the documents empowering the Franciscans with civil and criminal jurisdiction. Motolinía was charged to refrain from the use of that authority until he had a specific mandate from the crown. Fray Toribio suggested that the attorneys of the cabildo analyze the documents before any action was taken, but he was informed that lawyers Juan de Ortega and Alonso Pérez already had given their opinions on the matter. The regidores were firm in this decision.

Despite the initial conflict over jurisdiction, the Franciscan order and the Cortés government got along very well in furthering the missionary and economic motives of empire. Very soon, however, the function of inquisitor passed over to the Dominican prelates Tomás Ortíz (1526), Domingo de Betanzos (1527-1528) and Vicente de Santa María (1528). The Dominican order controlled the Mexican Inquisition until the Franciscan Bishop Juan de Zumárraga took over the function as ordinary in 1532. Zumárraga became apostolic inquisitor in 1535. It seems as if the Inquisition of the Dominicans made a political alliance with the anti-Cortés faction after 1526. The resultant controversies between the Dominican inquisitors and the Cortés supporters are most difficult to place in the proper perspective.

II

Betanzos and the Blasphemers

During his short inquisitorial ministry (May 1527 to September 1528), Domingo de Betanzos concluded blasphemy trials of some twenty *conquistadores,* and he began to gather information leading to celebrated trials of Judaizers by his successor. The problem of defining orthodox dogmatic belief and determining heretical conduct was a difficult one for the friar-inquisitor in the 1520's. The rough-and-ready swashbuckling character of the conqueror and his earthy mentality often led to a confused image of heresy. No clear definition of heresy as opposed to blasphemy evolved during the first decade of the Mexican Inquisition, and one suspects that broad terms like "blasphemy" covered up a large amount of heresy, especially in relation to Jews. Neither the inquisitors nor the colonists had a sophisticated view of Judaism, and proceso data on baptism, diet and covert social behavior of suspects often was misunderstood and misinterpreted by responsible officials. After 1528, the same problems were manifest in the Inquisition's dealings with Protestants.

As the Dominican friar-inquisitors began to try blasphemy cases, many Cortés supporters came under fire. In particular cases one wonders about the political implications of the trial, and whether or not the analagous anti-Cortés conquistador was also subject to the Inquisition's wrath. One of the frequent rebuttals made by soldiers who were tried was that remarks had been taken out of context, and denunciations had been made out of malice. It is well established that obscenity was a soldierly trait during the Mexican conquest and that blasphemy was a characteristic of Spanish Renaissance culture. Henry C. Lea, in his monumental study of the Spanish Inquisition, came to this conclusion and asserted that:

> the Spaniard was choleric, and not especially nice in his choice of words when moved by wrath; gambling was an almost universal passion and, in all lands and ages, nothing has been more provocative of ejaculations and expletives than the vicissitudes of cards and dice.[13]

The expletives were irreverent and indecent but not necessarily heretical.[14] Civil law provided penalties ranging from imprisonment and fines to piercing of the tongue for repeated offenses.

Betanzos' *fiscal* initiated the first blasphemy trial by the Dominicans on May 20, 1527 when he asked for the arrest of Juan Bello of Ciudad Rodrigo.[15] Bello had come to New Spain with Juan de Grijalva and later had returned with the Pánfilo de Narvaéz expedition of 1520. He became a staunch supporter of Hernán Cortés after the Cortés-Narvaéz struggle was resolved, and he participated in the reconquest of Tenochtitlán in 1521. He accompanied Cortés on the Honduras expedition and later campaigned against the Indians in Pánuco and in the Chontal area.[16] During 1525 Bello had helped to counteract the Chirinos and Salazar stories that Cortés was dead, and he had served as a steward at the controversial dinner which Cortés gave for the Visitor Luis Ponce in 1526.[17] The Dominican Prelate Tomás Ortíz spread the story that Ponce was poisoned at the meal and died from poison some weeks later.[18] Bello had been given an *encomienda* in Ixmiquilpan. His daughter married Gil González Benavides, who succeeded to the encomienda when her father died.[19]

The trial record indicates that Juan Bello had been penanced for blasphemy at an earlier time but had relapsed into obscene language such as "Pese a Dios," "No creo en Dios" and other blasphemies. Betanzos made Bello appear before him to answer the charges and to enter a plea. Presumably Bello presented himself within the four-day limit prescribed by the judge and admitted his guilt. He went to jail until he paid a fine of twelve *pesos de oro,* and upon his release he was required to make a pilgrimage to the shrine of Our Lady of Victory. Betanzos made the prisoner pay the costs of the trial. After Juan Bello had fulfilled Betanzos' sentence he was absolved of guilt. From the political standpoint it is noteworthy that the first blasphemer tried by Betanzos bore such a close relationship to the Cortés partisans of the 1524-1526 period. Notary records show that Bello was prepared for trouble with the Inquisition and that he had given power of attorney to his relatives, presumably to avoid property embargo by Betanzos.[20]

Blasphemy prosecutions of other conquistadores follow the format of the Bello trial and tend to show the Dominican Inquisition as a political instrument against the Cortés faction. On May 21, 1527 Betanzos moved against the famous Cortés cohort Gil González de Benavides, whose son was executed in the Avila-Cortés conspiracy of the 1560's.[21] González de Benavides had already been jailed for two weeks before Betanzos wrote the proceso. Betanzos sentenced him to pay the costs of the trial and three pesos de oro, as well as to make two trips barefoot to the shrine of Our Lady of Victory. If he did not fulfill the sentence within three days of his release from prison, Inquisitor Betanzos ordered that he would pay an additional ten pesos fine. Presumably González de Benavides paid the fine and suffered the public humiliations with candor and good grace, because his political career continued to advance. In the 1528 notary records he appears as alcalde of the capital in June, and the late 1527 records show him to have been economically active in the cattle and wheat business after the Inquisition's censures.[22]

As the Cortés followers gradually left military careers for economic pursuits and political offices after 1526, many of them fell prey to the Betanzos Inquisition. Hernando de Escalona was one of these who decided to center his enterprises in Veracruz.[23] Fiscal Arriaga had him appear before Betanzos on May 22, 1527 to answer blasphemy charges. The fragmentary trial record indicates that Motolinía had penanced him previously for the same crime. Francisco González, the *pregonero* (town crier) of Veracruz and of Cortés' cabildo of Tenochtitlán in the crucial years 1526-1529, was another Betanzos target.[24] González was fined six pesos de oro and costs of the trial, but he also had to stand barefoot in church during mass with a candle in his hand as a sign of penitence. As the audiencia began to absorb Cortés' power in the late 1520's, and after the conqueror went to Spain, Francisco González decided to leave central Mexico to participate in the conquest of Nueva Galicia—far from the inquisitor's grasp.[25]

Juan Martín Berenjel, a merchant in the Veracruz trade with the central valley of Mexico, traveled extensively; while he was in the capital, Betanzos caught him for repeated use of "pese" and other blasphemies.[26] The inquisitor was lenient with Berenjel, requiring only that he make a pilgrimage on foot to a nearby church. Diego García was another Veracruz merchant who ran afoul of the Holy Office because of uncouth speech.[27] On July 10, 1527 Betanzos acted harshly; he sentenced García to make two penitential pilgrimages to the shrine of Nuestra Señora de los Remedios, to eat only bread and water on seven successive Fridays, to stand without shoes with a candle in his hand while three masses were said and to deliver three pounds of white wax to the Remedios Church.

The relationship between the Núñez families of Salamanca and Hernán Cortés is well known. The exact connection between a Francisco Núñez whom Betanzos tried for blasphemy in 1527 and Cortés is not documented. This Francisco Núñez was involved in the Rodrigo de Paz affair of 1525, and he was one of the Paz heirs.[28] In June of 1527, Francisco Núñez ran into trouble with the Inquisition. Fiscal Arriaga and Inquisitor Betanzos charged Núñez with blasphemy and indecent language and sentenced him to make a pilgrimage to the Remedios shrine.[29] One can only assume than Betanzos wanted to make public example of a Cortés aide.

During the two days of June 26-27, 1527 the blasphemy trial of Alonso de Espinosa was brought to a close by the Betanzos Inquisition.[30] Espinosa had migrated to Cuba from Palos and had participated in the original conquest expedition into the Mexican interior. He had gone to Honduras and Nicaragua in 1524,[31] but had returned to open an inn in the Texcoco area by the time of his Inquisition trial in 1527. Betanzos sentenced Espinosa to thirty days in jail or the payment of six *pesos de oro de minas*. In addition he had to walk to los Remedios to hear mass, barefoot and with a candle in his hand, in the same manner as the other blasphemers. Sometime after August 28, 1528 when he purchased a slave in Mexico City for thirty-nine pesos de oro,[32] Alonso de Espinosa moved to Zacatula.

Two members of the pro-Cortés faction were tried by Betanzos as blasphemers during July 1527. Cristóbal Díaz, then a resident of Mexico before he moved to Coatzalcoalcos, was sentenced on July 1, 1527 and fined four pesos de oro.[33] He did spiritual penances as well. Díaz had signed several of the petitions asking that Charles V appoint Cortés as captain general of New Spain in 1522.[34] Gregorio de Monjarrás was arraigned by Fiscal Arriaga on July 29, and sentenced by Betanzos on July 30, 1527.[35] Monjarrás had been a loyal Cortés lieutenant from 1521 and he already had an encomienda grant in Coatlán.[36] Through the difficult years when Chirinos and Salazar tried to take over the colony while Cortés was on the Honduras expedition, Monjarrás actively supported the Cortés agents in Mexico even after they were jailed by Chirinos and Salazar, and Monjarrás had conspired to set them free.[37]

Bartolomé Quemado was a wealthy entrepreneur in New Spain during the years 1525-1528 when he came to the attention of the Dominican inquisitors. He bought and sold horses frequently, and he invested in real estate and slaves for the mines. His name was linked with other soldier-*encomenderos* in the economic life of the early colony, especially with the blasphemer Juan Rodríguez de Villafuerte and the Judaizer Bartolomé de Morales, who was later burned at the stake.[38] Betanzos sentenced Quemado as a simple blasphemer on August 3, 1527.[39] He was fined the stiff sum of 4,000 *maravedís* and had to sell most of his property to meet the obligation.[40] Perhaps Betanzos suspected Quemado of being a Jew; the fine seems to indicate that this was the case.

One of the most complete trials, from the standpoint of records kept by Betanzos, was that of Diego Núñez. Although the suspect was tried for blasphemy, the inquisitor made a searching investigation of his background to ascertain whether or not he could be indicted as a Judaizante.[41] Whether this Diego Núñez was a relative of Francisco Núñez, Cortés' attorney, and the *Licenciado* Diego Núñez, companion of Nuño de Guzmán,[42] is not clear from the trial record. It appears that they were all related. What concerned the Holy Office most in the accusations against Núñez was that he had used a cross as a target for rock throwing, and he had thrown several stones before battering it to pieces. After arresting Núñez and embargoing his property on August 2, 1527, Sebastián de Arriaga called four conquistadores as witnesses for the prosecution.

They introduced circumstantial evidence pointing to the probable *converso* parentage of Núñez in his home city of Gibraltar and testified about his blasphemies and lack of respect for religious observances. None of them had seen him go to church or practice the precept of abstinence on Fridays or during Lent. It was on a trip to Michoacán, in the village of Chilapa, that Fernando Damian and Juan Guisado witnessed the breaking of the cross. Damian told the Betanzos Inquisition that he knew there were many conversos in Mexico, implying that Diego Núñez was one of them, and that he had watched autos de fé of reconciliation in Sevilla as well as burnings of Jews. One gets the impression that Damian was mouthing the words of Guisado, who turned out to be an untrustworthy character, and that Damian was an unctuous do-gooder. Guisado accused Núñez of concubinage among other things.

Juan Torres de Villafranca defended Núñez in the trial, and he called four witnesses who testified to Diego's character and *limpieza de sangre*. On August 26, 1527 Gaspar Ramírez swore that he had known Diego Núñez for nine years in Gibraltar and Mexico. Diego's parents had been good Christians, as had all of his relatives, and Diego himself was a practicing Catholic. Ramírez related that Diego's father was a responsible citizen of Gibraltar, serving as alcalde and regidor for many years. Juan Díaz de Real, Francisco de Terrazas and Pedro Arvallos testified that Núñez was a good Christian and a practicing Catholic. They had heard of the destruction of the cross through rumor and gossip, but their testimonies tended to weaken the charges against Diego.

On September 3, 1527 Diego Núñez gave testimony before Betanzos. He indicated that he was a baptized Catholic and had been confirmed by a bishop in the Canary Islands when he accompanied his father there on business. His godfather was Alonso Sánchez of the Canaries. He described for Betanzos the bishop's confirmation and the use of the chrism (consecrated oil) in the ceremony. Núñez told the inquisitor that his brother Juan was a priest in minor orders in Gibraltar. Diego said he came to Mexico in 1519. Other sources say he came to Veracruz from Florida while

Cortés was headquartered in Texcoco.[43] Diego claimed that he received the sacraments regularly and that he had gone to confession in Honduras. Although he denied ever having performed any Hebrew rites, he did admit to blasphemy and eating meat on Fridays when he had no choice in the matter. He related quite a different story of the Chilapa incident, claiming he tossed the rocks at a fire in the *brasero* and hit the cross by accident. Without knowing his accusers, he singled out Juan Guisado as an enemy who bore him ill will because he had testified against Guisado when the latter hanged an Indian servant. He discredited the Guisado testimony in a straightforward way, and on September 12, 1527 Villafranca, his attorney, charged that the prosecution had failed to offer trustworthy proof against Núñez. On the same day Betanzos passed his sentence and released Diego Núñez from the ecclesiastical jail. He dismissed the fiscal's charge relating to desecration of the cross but found Núñez guilty of blasphemy. Diego was sentenced to thirty days in jail or payment of costs of the trial coupled with a spiritual penance. The trial record bore no signs of political malice against Diego Núñez. His exoneration after meticulous investigation was the only such case among the two score of blasphemers tried by the Dominicans during the first decade of the Mexican Inquisition.

Alonso de Carrión, a tailor and cloth merchant in the Mexican capital, was tried for blasphemy by Betanzos between July 29 and August 20, 1527.[44] Apparently Carrión foresaw trouble with the Holy Office, because the notary records are full of acknowledgments of debts to friends, grants of power of attorney and sale of slaves during the month of July 1527.[45] Carrión was a servant of the Cortés household *(criado del gobernador)* who uttered many blasphemies and other uncouth words while gambling. The final page of the proceso is no longer extant, but it is justifiable to conclude that Hernán Cortés' servant was punished by Betanzos in the same manner as other blasphemers.

One of Cortés' captains, Juan Rodríguez de Villafuerte, who had participated in the naval operations in the reconquest of Tenochtitlán and who had become a loyal partisan of Don Fernando during the Salazar-Chirinos usurpation of power in 1525-1526, was tried as a blasphemer by Betanzos on August 30, 1527.[46] Rodríguez de Villafuerte defended Cortés against charges by the *residencia* judge Ponce and the criticisms of Dominican Prelate Tomás Ortíz. He had been imprisoned by Chirinos and Salazar and kept in a cage during Cortés' foray into Honduras, and he was released only after Cortés returned to Mexico City.[47] Betanzos sentenced Rodríguez de Villafuerte to twenty days in jail and costs of the trial as well as a fine of twenty-five pounds of wax for the church. Rodríguez consented to the sentence without complaint and went back to his shipbuilding activities in league with Cortés in Zacatula.[48]

Much less is known from the cryptic trial records of seven other blasphemers tried by Betanzos in 1527. Some of the procesos are incomplete. Several of the culprits, notably Juan de Cuevas,[49] an official of the mint, were members of the Cortés faction. Fines and public humiliation similar to the sentences of the other blasphemers were meted out to Diego Cortés,[50] Rodrigo Rodríguez,[51] Reinaldo de Luna,[52] Lucas Gallego,[53] Alonso Corellana,[54] and Hernando García Sarmiento.[55]

III

Rodrigo Rengel: Horrifying Blasphemy, 1527

The most spectacular blasphemy case of Betanzos' inquisitorial ministry was that of Cortés' camp master, Rodrigo Rengel, who served as alcalde in Veracruz and Pánuco and was a regidor of the city of Mexico. On May 1, 1527 Betanzos arrested Rodrigo Rengel for being "a horrifying blasphemer."[56] There were obvious political overtones in the Rengel prosecution, but it was certainly true that he had been the most blatant blasphemer in the colony during the 1519-1526 period. Many reports in civil and administrative documents make mention of Rengel's violation of the Cortés ordinances against indecent language.[57] But there is no question that Rengel's close association with Cortés and his involvement in the controversies and conspiracies of the 1520's netted him powerful enemies among the civil population and the clergy. The May 1527 introduction to the Rengel proceso makes passing reference to a denunciation of Don Rodrigo by the Dominican Prelate Tomás Ortíz in 1526.

Fiscal Sebastián de Arriaga pressed serious charges against Rengel. He said the accused could not even lay claim to the designation of "Christian" because he had committed so many heresies, and he had uttered so many "abominable blasphemies" as to preclude any faith in God. Arriaga pictured Rodrigo Rengel as a dirty old man.[58] This characterization was undoubtedly fair in light of the testimonies gathered from hostile witnesses. Rengel's supporters did little more than attempt to find excuses for his conduct. The fiscal accused Rengel of blasphemy and heresy on twenty-nine separate counts. Among the most horrifying, other than the usual "peses," "reniegos," and "válgames," were his denial of the virginity of Mary and his charge that she was a *puta* (whore). He had blasphemed against Saint Anne, the grandmother of Christ. When he was ill, or drunk and gambling, he used obscene and lascivious language. When the pain from the syphilis which had attacked his nervous system (probably a form of paresis) became unbearable, Rengel shouted that God did not have the power to cure illness or cleanse the sins of man. From his bed he spat upon images and did dirty things with crucifixes. When well, he was an inveterate gambler, and he raced horses calling upon the Devil for assistance in winning. Frequently he incorporated blasphemy into songs, taking time while singing them to spit toward Heaven and to threaten God.

Still other statements and actions by Rengel were shocking. He saw no reason why the Indians should not be allowed to practice idolatry as a harmless pastime. He expressed his doubts about the sacrament of marriage, and he had lived with other men's wives while the husbands were away. It was alleged that he had desecrated churches in Pánuco and elsewhere. There were evidences of cruelties, if not sexual perversion, in Rengel's treatment of his slaves and others.[59] Thus Arriaga established the picture of a reprobate, heretic, possible Judaizante and dirty old man.

When Rengel answered the fiscal's accusation, he was a humble and repentant man. He admitted that under great mental strain, and many times, he had blasphemed. He contended that circumstances of "excessive work, almost inhuman tasks in the conquest and pacification" of New Spain had led him to blaspheme, and that he had been gravely ill and in great pain from *bubas* (syphilis) during the six years when he continued to work for Cortés.[60] "Many times I was out of my mind and any natural understanding," he said, "and it is public and notorious that I said bad things against our Lord God and his Glorious Mother and the blessed Saints." He confessed that he was very guilty, but said that he didn't even remember some of the things he was reputed to have said.

Rengel contended that heresy never permeated his thoughts or actions and he had never left the faith. Since his whole family for generations had been Christians *(cristianos viejos)*, and in view of his contrition, he begged the inquisitor for an appropriate and wholesome *(saludable)* penance to expiate his sins. On June 28, 1527, fearing the worst, he wrote another confession and presented it to Betanzos in the office of the governor of New Spain. The record does not specify whether Cortés was present, but presumably there was good reason to present the confession at the governor's house with his subordinate administrators as witnesses.

Fiscal Arriaga and Betanzos subpoenaed an impressive list of witnesses against Rengel. Much of the sworn testimony was taken in April 1527 before the Holy Office moved against the accused. It was required that each witness swear that he was not motivated by hate or economic reasons for giving testimony. The first witness was Juan Bello, who was also tried for blasphemy six weeks later. He swore on April 1, 1527 that Rodrigo Rengel was a very blasphemous man *(hombre muy blasfemador)*. Bello did not know if the Rengel family had Jewish ancestry, but he related the oft-told tale that Rengel claimed that his sister was as pure as Saint Anne. Antonio de Torres quoted Rengel as saying that God had no power to cure the ill, and the brothers Gonzalo and Francisco de Solís, who had campaigned in the Zapoteca with Rengel, testified to his indecent language. Many clergy were asked to give sworn testimony. A Fray Gonzalo, novitiate in the Dominican order, related what he had heard over the last three years about Rengel's blasphemies and the obscene stories he habitually told. Another Dominican novice, Fray Diego Hinojosa, told of the blasphemous songs Rengel sang and the disgusting things he did with crucifixes. Fray Luis de Fuensalida, guardian of the Franciscan Convent in Mexico City, told what he knew of Rengel's indecorous language and repeated a story told him by Fray Juan Suárez, that Rengel allowed his Indians to shoot arrows at the friars when they came to preach in his village and to take away the idols the natives had hidden there.

Many of the twenty-eight witnesses called by Arriaga related the story that Rengel, as alcalde of Pánuco, after he had assisted Gonzalo de Sandoval in the pacification, had annulled the marriage of a woman with a silversmith so that she could become his concubine. Alonso Ortíz de Zúñiga, who testified on April 5, 1527, quoted Rengel's indecent remarks about Saint Anne and the Virgin Mary. An especially damaging witness against Rengel was Juan Tirado, a violent foe of Cortés.[61] On April 6, 1527 Tirado told the Holy Office that he had known Rodrigo Rengel for eight years and that he considered him "a public and notorious blasphemer and a bad Christian." Tirado said he had heard that Rengel was of converso lineage on the side of his father and that his grandfather had been reconciled or burnt by the Inquisition in Toledo. Tirado told the Betanzos tribunal that Rengel had desecrated churches and had expostulated at length about the nonvirginity of the Mother of Christ. Tirado claimed that a lot of his information on Rengel came from a man who had died in Honduras, one Ovejón de Lovera, who had written to the Sevillian inquisitors about Rengel. Tirado himself had given all these data to Dominican Prelate Ortíz in 1526, and he indicated that a Fray Melchor had reprimanded Rodrigo Rengel from the pulpit as a result of his *denuncia*. It appears that Tirado struck a blow for the anti-Cortés

THE FIRST DECADE 23

faction when he gave this testimony. Perhaps the judges realized that this was the case, since Tirado's data were largely discounted in the final deliberations on the Rengel case.

Many of the witnesses came from Pánuco or Veracruz. Obviously several of them had grudges against Rengel because of his actions as alcalde. One such person was Bartolomé de Porras, who testified on April 6, 1527. Porras had been acquainted with Rengel for seven years and called him a converso, blasphemer, defamer of women and an obscene man who insisted he was a bishop who could perform and annul marriages. Juan Bolante of Veracruz related that Rengel "when he was ill said things so horrendous that it was fearful to hear them." On April 9, 1527 a political note pervaded the testimonies when Diego Ramírez quoted Rengel vis-a-vis the Cortés controversy: "If anyone said that the servants of the Governor were not as good as God, he [Rengel] would put them to death."

On July 31, 1527 Rodrigo Rengel and his attorney Gaspar de la Plaza started a defensive action.[62] On that day Plaza appeared before the alcalde *ordinario* of Mexico City, Juan de la Torre, and began a *probanza* on Rodrigo Rengel's ancestry and his good reputation. It is very revealing that Plaza initiated proceedings in a civil court under the jurisdiction of Governor Cortés rather than in the ecclesiastical tribunal where Rengel was on trial. By this action, and most likely with the governor's permission, Plaza was able to use the civil jurisdiction as a lever against the Dominican Inquisition. As will be seen in the final sentence of the Holy Office, Plaza's maneuver was clever and partially successful. Gaspar de la Plaza received the alcalde's permission to frame an interrogatory and to present testimony on Rengel's ancestry, background, religious life and state of health. A preview of Plaza's line of defense was Question Four of the interrogatory, which asked witnesses whether Rengel was known to have been seriously ill and delirious from "rheumatism" for the past five years, and whether they knew that for the last three years he had been paralyzed, crippled and tormented, and was so weak that he could not get out of bed.

Sworn testimony in answer to Plaza's interrogatory was taken from three people who had known Rodrigo Rengel and his family for at least thirty years. The fourth witness was the governor and captain general of New Spain, Don Fernando Cortés. Baltazar de Mendoza, Violánte Rodríguez, the wife of Diego de Soria, and Pedro de Orozco related that they had known Rengel and his family for some three decades in the Villa of Medellín, Spain, and in Mexico. They attested to the fact that Rodrigo's parents had been old Christians and of noble lineage *(hijos dalgo)*. Never had the family been touched by heresy or tried by the Spanish Inquisition. They pronounced Rodrigo to have been a man of great honor *(mucha honra)* until his debilitating illness.

Governor Fernando Cortés gave strong support to Plaza's defense. The governor testified that he had known Rengel's family for thirty years as good Christians[63] and persons of gentle birth. Cortés said it was public knowledge that for the last five years Rodrigo Rengel had been crippled and weakened by bubas. This section of testimony does not bear the Cortés rubric but the scribe and notary who made the clean copies of the testimony for the Inquisition authenticated the document. Escribano Diego de Corona delivered the probanza to the Holy Office.

As early as July 1, 1527 the Dominican Inquisitor Domingo de Betanzos was beginning to feel pressures in the Rodrigo Rengel case. Betanzos and Fiscal Arriaga interviewed the accused, who was "hospitalized" in the *posada* of Gonzalo de Sandoval on that day. Presumably it was about this time that Attorney Plaza and Governor Cortés decided to make an issue of the affair. On July 1 Rodrigo Rengel repeated his "voluntary confession" and asked for a "wholesome" sentence. The deposition was full of guilt and remorse. Whether Betanzos had to absent himself from the case because of pressing problems in his capacity as Dominican prelate, or whether the politics of the case were getting too volatile, is a matter of conjecture. At any rate, almost precipitately, the Dominican prelate abdicated jurisdiction in the Rengel trial and the Franciscan order assumed jurisdiction.

On September 2, 1527 Fray Luis de Fuensalida, guardian of the

Monastery of San Francisco and custodian of the Franciscan province, wrote an interesting letter of commission to Fray Toribio de Benavente Motolinía, who was then guardian of the Convent of San Antonio in Texcoco.[64] Fuensalida recapitulated the history of the Rodrigo Rengel prosecution by Betanzos. He then told Motolinía that Betanzos had remanded the entire trial proceedings to him for study. He informed his colleague that he had assumed responsibility for the conclusion of the trial and he delegated his authority to Motolinía, "trusting in your discretion, knowledge and conscience" in passing sentence and seeing to its execution. Rather than specify that the Dominicans had relinquished jurisdiction in the Rengel case, Prelate Fuensalida told Motolinía he was being empowered with apostolic faculties by virtue of the papal bulls of Leo X (April 10, 1521, which gave quasi-episcopal powers to the Franciscans) and Adrian VI (May 10, 1522, known as the Omnímoda).

Fray Toribio de Motolinía passed sentence on Rodrigo Rengel on September 3, 1527. Before reading the sentence, Motolinía delineated his rationale for the penalties. He said that even though God had been gravely offended by Rengel's blasphemies, the offenses were diminished in Motolinía's eyes because of the mitigating circumstances of his illness and his "spontaneous confession." Fray Toribio took into account Renegel's lineage of old Christians, his noble ancestry and his services in the conquest. However, the sentence was far from lenient. Rodrigo Rengel was to demonstrate his remorse publicly by standing during mass with a candle in his hand. He was to be incarcerated in a monastery for a five-month period so that he could consider his sins and do penance. He was ordered to provide food for five poor people for an indeterminate time and he was fined five hundred pesos de oro de minas to be used for pious works. Of this sum eight ounces of gold *(un marco de oro)* was to be given to the Monastery of Santo Domingo to purchase a silver chalice. The church in Veracruz, which Rengel was supposed to have desecrated, was to receive ten marcos de oro and a silver chalice, and ten pesos each were to be contributed to the confraternities of Our Lady of Los Angeles and Our Lady of the Cross.

The remainder of the fine was earmarked for the Monastery of Santa Clara for the care of orphans and the poor. Finally, Motolinía required Rodrigo Rengel to use his Indians to construct a hermitage in Tacuba, and to provide the Franciscan Monastery of Mexico City with three dozen tables to be used in its religious activities.

Presumably Rengel was able to raise the considerable sum of five hundred pesos rapidly. He delivered the money in installments beginning September 10, 1527. He was well enough to stand with a candle in his hand during mass on the appointed day of January 7, 1528. The notary archives record the sale of his urban real estate in October 1528.[65]

IV

The Auto de Fé of October 1528

On the margin of a routine notary document on October 17, 1528 the scribe made the following comment:

> On this day Hernando Alonso, blacksmith, and Gonzalo de Morales were burned for heresy. Diego de Ocaña was reconciled, and Diego de Morales and another foreigner were paraded in penitential garb. May it please our Lord God, and his glorious Mother, that their holy catholic faith has been uplifted.

This description of the controversial auto de fé of 1528 was not unearthed until 1945, and until that time the actual date of the burnings was not known.[66] The only date available to the late sixteenth-century inquisitors, who were curious about the burnings of two "Jews" in 1528, seemed to be a series of testimonies taken by the tribunal of the Holy Office in 1574. These testimonies have served as equivocal documentation for the little we know of the first decade of the Mexican Inquisition.[67] In reality there were documents available in the archives of the ordinary Inquisition that shed considerable light on the October 1528 proceedings,

THE FIRST DECADE

but they were not employed in 1574, and they have not been studied until the present time.

From the civil and Inquisition records of the trials of Diego de Morales, November 1524 to October 1528, most of which are extant, it is possible to reconstruct the events surrounding the burnings of Diego de Morales' brother Gonzalo de Morales and Hernando Alonso in 1528, both for being Judaizantes. The 1574 investigation of the auto de fé of October 1528 did not avail itself of indexed lists of trials with short bio-theological descriptions provided by an *abecedario* (alphabetical listing by year) compiled by an unknown Inquisition clerk in 1571.[68] The list specified the burnings of Gonzalo de Morales and Alonso in 1528 as well as the reconciliation of another Judaizer, Diego de Ocaña, and it contained data on four separate trials of Diego de Morales between 1524 and 1558. Presumably the civil investigation of Diego de Morales, 1524-1525, had its genesis in the Cortés blasphemy ordinances and the 1523 decrees. Betanzos tried Morales as a blasphemer and suspected heretic in 1528, and the ordinary in Oaxaca tried him for Judaism and made him abjure his Hebrew beliefs and practices in a 1538 prosecution. From Oaxaca he migrated to Guatemala where the abecedario informs us that Bishop Marroquín prosecuted him once again in 1558 for being a Judaizante.[69]

From the very beginning the Diego de Morales trials make it clear that he was some kind of nonconformist Jew. The fragmentary investigations of the alcalde of Mexico City, Leonel de Cervantes, in 1524 and 1525 provide the first clues.[70] *Alguacil-Fiscal* Diego de Marmolejo demanded that Cervantes punish Diego de Morales for blasphemy, renunciation of God and the chrism, and for taking a cross between his feet and stepping on it. The attorney claimed he had evidence that these things were done in Morales' home in November 1524 in the presence of Juan de Guzmán Ballesto, and he presented other data on Diego's blasphemies and heresies in other places. After Morales was jailed, sometime in 1525 (the records are torn and almost illegible), he replied to the charges in a plea directed to Alcalde Cervantes from the jail.

Morales denied that Marmolejo had offered any reliable proof of his accusations or that the fiscal had carried on proper investigations to substantiate the charges. Diego proclaimed that he was innocent. While he might have "cursed" at times, he had always been "a good Christian, fearful of God . . . and had lived a clean life." Morales summarized testimony on his behalf by Pedro de Vergara, García Hernández, Iñigo Pérez and others who had known him a long time, and who had given character references. He spent considerable time attacking the testimony of the Guzmán family who, he said, hated him and were his major enemies in New Spain. He claimed that the father, Juan de Guzmán, who helped frame Marmolejo's denuncia, was a rapacious, crooked gambler who was "working to destroy me." Morales went to great length to paint a picture of Juan de Guzmán as a cardsharp who was frequently in jail for cheating and playing games prohibited by law. Morales took pains to point out that Guzmán's headquarters was a house owned by Governor Cortés where gambling habitually took place.[71] Morales said Guzmán was a blasphemer who masqueraded in the habit of a friar, and that he often uttered sexual obscenities in public. He said Juan de Guzmán hated him because he thought Morales had robbed him of an hacienda which had been entrusted to Diego as a real estate agent. As for the son of Guzmán, Diego de Guzmán, Morales said the father's hate had spread to the boy who, in any event, was under the mandatory twenty-five years of age required for witnesses. When it came to the wife, María Morales de Guzmán, Diego was brutal in his attack. He charged that she was a public whore whom Juan had won in a card game in Castilla.

Diego de Morales challenged the validity of the other witnesses in a like manner. He singled out Francisco de la Palma Zapata as another cheating gambler who got so intoxicated that he went out of his mind. Morales claimed he threw Palma out of his house bodily, and before witnesses, for uncouth conduct. Because the records are incomplete, there are gaps in the story. From an appeal which he made to Lt. Governor Alonso Canseco it appears that

Diego was convicted and subjected to torture. In the 1528 proceedings more is recorded about the 1525 sentence. From July 13, 1528 until September 12, 1528, Inquisitor Vicente de Santa María, O.P., conducted the first of the Inquisition trials of Diego de Morales.[72] Juan de Rebollo, the apostolic notary, made the denunciation. Hernando de Santillana, who had testified against Morales in 1525, told Santa María that Notary Pedro del Castillo had in his possession records of the Cervantes investigation of three years earlier, and that Diego de Morales had "renounced God and all of His apostles." On July 20, 1528 Martín de Berri gave testimony that Morales was the son of converso Jews from Sevilla, and that Diego blasphemed and flogged crucifixes. Francisco de la Palma, also a hostile witness in 1525, substantiated the other witnesses, as did others subpoenaed by Santa María.

Then came a startling piece of testimony. María de Morales, the wife of Juan de Guzmán, whom Diego had attacked as a prostitute in the 1525 proceedings, related that she had known Diego for several years as a converso, this by his own admission. Whether Mrs. Guzmán was retaliating for the 1525 abuse heaped on her by Morales, or whether Diego had tried to undermine her testimony in advance, is a moot point. María Morales de Guzmán said Diego's family came from a town some two leagues from Sevilla and that his father had been reconciled as a Judaizante. When Diego moved to Sevilla, she claimed, people laughed at him for being a son of a *reconciliado*. María proceeded to inform the Inquisition of Diego's arrest in Cuba as a blasphemer, and to document the fact that Diego was the brother of Gonzalo de Morales, whom the inquisitors later burned as a Jew in October 1528.

Other witnesses expanded on what María had said. Alonso de Espinosa, himself tried for blasphemy in 1527 by Betanzos, related that some eight months earlier when Diego de Morales was in San Juan de Puerto Rico, he had been jailed by the bishop there. Doña Leonor de Cervantes said that while her husband was alcalde of Mexico, Diego de Morales was tried for blasphemy before Hernán

Pérez and was sentenced to be tortured. Then she remembered that Diego had appealed the case to Licenciado Sauzo, who upheld the sentence. Even though Morales was on the rack and the cords were tightened on his body, he confessed to no more than saying "Pese a Dios" and "No creo en Dios." Doña Leonor recalled that he was fined 4,000 maravedís.

With these bits of testimony out of the way, Santa María proceeded to embargo the Diego de Morales properties. The inventory showed him to be still a wealthy man with considerable refined gold and gold dust in his possession. In addition to the bullion, the inventory showed long lists of silk and other fine textiles, gloves, *marfil* rosaries, large amounts of foodstuffs, preserved meats and much more. Notary records of this time showed the extent of his dealings in slaves and merchandise. He had a whole legajo of powers of attorney given him by clients.[73]

On July 24, 1528 Fray Vicente de Santa María called Diego de Morales before him to testify. The prisoner told the court he was thirty years of age, born in Sevilla, the son of Hernando de Morales and Leonor Marquéz. He did not remember when he was baptized because he was so young at the time. When interrogated about whether he came from converso lineage, Diego told Santa María that his father had said to him many years ago, "My son, for this you should thank God Our Lord because your grandfather is from the mountain country, and neither he nor I were ever jailed or reconciled by the Inquisition." Diego related that his father had told him his grandmother was an Indian (presumably from India) but that she had converted to Catholicism when she married. Diego told Santa María of his career as a merchant and hosier in Cuba. He denied any trouble with the law other than having been in a debtors' jail and having been tried for blasphemy in Mexico three years before. For blasphemy he had served a thirty-day jail sentence and paid a fine of 4,000 maravedís. He denied that any parent or grandparent of his had ever been tried as a heretic, Judaizante or *Morisco* (a converted Moor who had lapsed into infidelity).

Then Diego de Morales began the tricky part of his testimony.

THE FIRST DECADE

A wrong maneuver might well have caused his death at the stake alongside his brother. He told Santa María that on the island of San Juan de Puerto Rico he had heard of a man named Palma and another called Morales, who had taken a crucifix and done very dirty things to it. He had known Palma and they had been friends. When he was in Santo Domingo, Diego de Morales said Bishop Alonso Manso had questioned him about Palma and Morales. Manso had asked him if his *brother* Gonzalo de Morales was a heretic or a bad Christian. He told Manso that he knew little about his brother Gonzalo but considered him a good Christian. Later Diego said he had sent a letter to Gonzalo in the care of his partner Anton Ruíz, telling him that Palma had been burned by the Inquisition. Diego de Morales reaffirmed to Santa María that he didn't doubt any article of the faith and that he had never had anything to do with suspect people. He admitted only the crime of blasphemy, for which he had been punished. When it came to the charge that he had flogged a cross, Morales modified the story somewhat. Actually, he said, he had "touched" the cross on the table in Guzmán's presence, and he had sworn upon it.

On August 31, 1528 the trial record made note of the fact that Diego de Morales was ill. By September 5, he had thrown himself on the mercy of the court and had asked for a lenient sentence because of his family obligations. It is remarkable, especially in light of Diego's subsequent trials for Judaizing in Oaxaca and Guatemala, that the Santa María Inquisition accepted his story and tried him on the blasphemy count alone. Perhaps two conjectures are in order. Maybe Santa María agreed to the blasphemy charge in Diego's case in exchange for incriminating data about his brother Gonzalo. It is equally possible that politics played a part and Diego de Morales' anti-Cortés sentiments swayed the judges. There certainly were political reasons for the reconciliation of Diego de Ocaña, who was tried along with Diego's brother.

Diego de Morales' sentence as a convicted blasphemer was very lenient. On three successive Sundays he had to stand in the chorus of the church, barefoot, gagged and with a candle in his hand. Each Sunday he was required to give alms to two poor people, and he was fined fifty pesos de oro. He also paid the costs of the trial. Thus ended the prosecution of Diego de Morales, who walked in penitential garb as a blasphemer in the same auto de fé where his brother was burned at the stake as a Judaizante.

Most of the data on the October 17, 1528 burnings derives from testimonies taken by the Inquisition tribunal in 1574. The records of the archive of the episcopal Inquisition were incomplete, and the penitential garb that had been displayed in the cathedral for the 1520's and 1530's had disappeared. Accordingly, in June of 1574, the tribunal of the Holy Office began to interrogate old settlers and senior clergy who had been in Mexico four or five decades. Elderly friars from the Franciscan and Dominican houses in the viceregal capital were summoned to give testimony and to speculate about possible sources of information about missing procesos.[74] While the data collected on the auto de fé of October 1528 was hazy when it came to the biographical notes and heresies of the three relaxed heretics, the memories of witnesses were more or less consistent.

Other than the trial of his brother Diego, there is little extant information on the history and the heresies of Gonzalo de Morales. On June 16, 1574 Fray Vicente de las Casas, a seventy-three-year-old member of the Dominican order in Mexico, gave his recollections of the auto de fé of 1528 in which Gonzalo de Morales and Hernando Alonso were burned as heretics.[75] Fray Vicente had witnessed the burnings near the church of Tlaltelolco, and he could remember the illustrious persons who attended—the Inquisitor Fray Vicente de Santa María, Licenciado Altamirano (Cortés' agent) and Governor Alonso de Estrada. Fray Vicente de las Casas had heard Fray Pedro de Contreras preach a sermon at the auto, and Contreras had recounted the heresies of the condemned as part of the ceremony. The *sanbenitos* (penitential garb) were hung in the Cathedral of Mexico, but Las Casas had no idea what happened to them in later years.

According to Las Casas' reminiscences in 1574, Gonzalo de Morales had been tried for concubinage prior to his prosecution as a Judaizante. Other witnesses related that Anton Ruíz had denounced Gonzalo de Morales as a Jew—this was the same Anton Ruíz who was a business partner of Diego Morales and the courier who carried letters between the two Morales brothers. Inquisitor Santa María had received a letter from Bishop Alonso de Puerto Rico stating that Morales' sister had been burned as a Judaizante in Santo Domingo. The sister had inculpated her brother during the trial: they had placed a crucifix on a door latch and had flogged it.

More information was obtained from Gonzalo de Morales during Santa María's trial. He admitted flogging a crucifix and then urinating on it in the company of the mysterious Palma mentioned in Diego de Morales' interview with Bishop Manso in Santo Domingo. Palma had placed the crucifix upside down and put his feet on the arms of the cross, and Morales had said "that was the way the cross deserved to be held." Fray Vicente de las Casas said Gonzalo de Morales had confessed to Santa María, "and thus they burned him as a Jew as he had admitted." Fray Vicente told the investigators in 1574 that Gonzalo de Morales had confessed too late to avoid the stake. Vicente and other witnesses related that Gonzalo de Morales had a brother who had also been tried by the Inquisition, and who went to Oaxaca after he was reconciled.

We know considerably more about the other condemned Jew, Hernando Alonso.[76] He was born *circa* 1460 in the Condado de Niebla, Spain. He had come to Mexico from Cuba with Pánfilo de Narvaez in April 1520, joining the Cortés army after Narvaez' defeat. He was nearly sixty years old when he made the *Noche Triste* retreat and later helped Cortés recapture Tenochtitlán. Alonso was an ironsmith and carpenter by trade. He proved a useful aide to Cortés, with whom he had become acquainted in Cuba in 1516. He helped Martín López build the famous brigantines on Lake Texcoco which were launched in the final phases of the reconquest of Mexico City in 1521.[77] After the subjugation of the Aztecs, Alonso was rewarded by Cortés with land grants and encomiendas in Actópan.[78] He became an important entrepreneur in the Mexican colony of the 1520's. As a wealthy miner, meat merchant, buyer and seller of slaves and investor in Michoacán enterprises, Hernando Alonso's name appears often in the records of the cabildo and in the notary archives.[79] He continued his military career in the early years of the decade, campaigning with Gonzalo de Sandoval in the Pánuco area.

Hernando Alonso was married in the early 1520's to Beatriz de Ordaz, who probably was the sister of Cortés' lieutenant, Diego de Ordaz. He was said to be a close friend of Alonso de Estrada, the acting governor of the colony in 1527 and 1528, and he remained a stout supporter of Cortés throughout the troubled years of 1524 and 1528. After the death of Beatriz de Ordaz, Alonso married twice. His last wife, Isabel Ruíz de Aguilar, and a daughter survived him after 1528, and they returned to Spain, according to the 1574 testimonies. The 1574 testimonies point to the fact that Hernando Alonso was related to the Contreras family in Mexico City, and it appears that the Alonso and Morales families had intermarried. The notary documents indicate that Alonso's businesses were bound up with the Morales concerns. It was reported that one of the Alonso children had married into the Núñez family of Sevilla. Hernando Alonso was probably related to many of the people tried by the Mexican Inquisition for blasphemy and heresy in 1527 and 1528.

Whether or not Hernando Alonso was a Jew is debatable. Orthodox Jews who have studied Alfonso Toro's transcripts of the 1574 testimonies contend that none of the evidence proved that he was a Jew, nor were the so-called "Jewish ceremonies" he performed really Hebrew rites.[80] However, the testimonies inform us that Alonso confessed to practicing Jewish rites, and Fray Vicente de Santa María charged him with being a Judaizante.[81] The major charge against Alonso was that in Santo Domingo he baptized a child twice—once in the church and once in his home. In the private ceremony, Alonso, Palma and the guests placed the infant in a basin, poured wine over its head, and the wine that ran down its body and dripped from its genitals was gathered into a cup and drunk by those present while they danced around the basin and sang what the witnesses called "Jewish songs," especially "Dominus Deus Israel Egipto," or as they said, "something similar to that

[song]." Other witnesses said Hernando Alonso forbade his wife Isabel de Aguilar to go to mass during her menstrual period, "in observance of the Law of Moses." Seventy-year-old Pedro Vásquez de Vergara, on July 7, 1574 told the investigators he had heard Isabel tell her husband "that this was an old Jewish custom that they no longer observed since they were Christians."[82]

When the Santa María Inquisition interrogated Hernando Alonso about these practices in 1528, and took him to the torture chamber as part of the proceedings, the 1574 witnesses said Alonso confessed to being a Jew and that the "rebaptism" was a "Jewish ceremony" performed in mockery of the sacrament of baptism. Other testimonies indicated that Alonso had his own Christian son baptized twice.[83] Some witnesses connected Gonzalo de Morales with the Santo Domingo incident but the accounts were inconsistent on this point. Perhaps after some forty-six years the stories of what they had heard about Hernando Alonso and Gonzalo de Morales had become confused.

Diego de Ocaña, the third man tried as a Judaizante in 1528, was reconciled, and he escaped the death penalty because of political influence. Ocaña was a native of Sevilla and had migrated from Santo Domingo to Mexico City in June of 1525,[84] where he was licensed by the cabildo of Mexico as a notary. By November 13, 1525, he bore the title of *escribano público y de gobernación*.[85] Contemporary documents, and his will executed in 1533, indicate that his daughter Leonor Suárez de Ocaña and his son Hernán García Suárez lived with him in Mexico.[86] The notary records relate that on February 6, 1527 Ocaña was given a house on Huitzilopochtli Street in Mexico City in recognition of his services as scribe to the cabildo.[87] Ocaña had aided the cabildo in the struggle with Motolinía over the use of civil and criminal jurisdiction in 1525.[88] He joined the anti-Cortés faction in the power struggle going on in the colony and he wrote a series of letters to the Casa de Contratación in Sevilla denouncing Hernando Cortés' greed and dishonesty in the administration of New Spain.[89] He was a business partner of the Martín de Berri who had testified against Diego de Morales in the blasphemy trial.[90]

Ocaña's trouble with the Inquisition really started with the edict against the Jews in 1523, and when Charles V decreed that all new Christians had to leave the Indies Diego had paid a fee to be permitted to stay.[91] He was even allowed to remain in Mexico after the cabildo's order of May 17, 1527 that all new Christians were to arrange passage back to Spain immediately on pain of loss of all their properties if they failed to do so.[92] No doubt Diego de Ocaña was exempted from these decrees because he was the valued secretary of the treasurer of New Spain, Gonzalo de Salazar. The witnesses of 1574 did not give details on Ocaña's crimes against the faith. He was described as "an old man who was a scribe," and a converso who was jailed for Jewish practices. He wore a "very long robe" in public and "a round black hat," looking "very Jewish" *(muy ajudiado)*. The testimonies said Ocaña killed chickens in the Jewish manner and ate meat on Fridays, while on other days "he ate shark and other fish prepared in the Jewish manner."[93] Apparently the witnesses and the inquisitors were unaware that shark and other scale fish were not kosher. Except for his dietary habits the testimonies said nothing about Ocaña's religion except that he performed Jewish ceremonies and followed the Law of Moses. Gonzalo de Morales, who was in the cell next to Ocaña, reported to the inquisitors some of Ocaña's mumblings "that all of the witnesses were dead." That there were other serious charges against Ocaña seemed evident from the testimonies.

The Franciscan Prelate Fray Antonio Roldán, who had seen the stakes where the other "Jews" were burned, speculated in July 1574 that Diego de Ocaña had escaped the death penalty because of Gonzalo de Salazar's pressure on the Santa María Inquisition. Roldán believed that Salazar kept the Ocaña sanbenito from being placed in the cathedral.[94] Fray Vicente de las Casas testified that Ocaña wore the penitential garb for six months and that he heard Ocaña go through a ceremony of abjuration of error. After the six-month sentence of penitential garb, Ocaña was banished from New Spain and all his properties were confiscated. Because his son, Hernán Suárez, refused to recognize his father in the sanbenito, Ocaña disinherited him. Bernal Díaz del Castillo reported that

THE FIRST DECADE

Diego de Ocaña secured a license in Spain to return to Mexico. In his 1533 will, Ocaña contended that he had never been a heretic, and he charged his heirs to continue to press suit before the inquisitor general so that his name might be cleared.[95]

The circumstances of the 1528 auto de fé and the mysterious lack of contemporary documents caused great consternation in the tribunal of the Holy Office of the Inquisition in the 1570's. Those who testified in 1574 reported that Sebastían Ramírez de Fuenleal, president of the second audiencia, had questioned whether the 1528 Judaizantes had received due process, and he had remarked on the harshness of Santa María's punishments. He was told that Hernando Alonso and Gonzalo de Morales had confessed "too late" to avoid the death penalty.[96]

In point of time the closest mention of the unjustness of the 1528 burnings was the 1536 Inquisition trial of Juan Franco by Zumárraga.[97] Franco contended that Hernando Alonso had been condemned without cause. The tribunal of the Holy Office went to great lengths to uncover records of the 1528 affair and charged the prior of the Monastery of Santo Domingo, Fray Bartolomé de Ledesma, to search the conventual archives for the papers of Fray Vicente de Santa María. Ledesma reported that he could find no pertinent documents of the Dominican Inquisition of the 1520's. Melchor de Legazpi, son of the Inquisition secretary Miguel López de Legazpi during the Zumárraga period (1536-1543), was called to testify about any papers that his father, who had departed for the Philippines, had left in his private archive. Legazpi the younger testified that his father's agent, Licenciado Salcedo, had handed all the papers over to the tribunal of the Inquisition. A document in the Inquisition archive attests to the fact that this was done.[98]

V

Epilogue

In his cryptic description of the October 17, 1528 auto de fé the notary made intriguing reference "to another foreigner" reconciled along with Ocaña and Diego de Morales. It is probable that the third reconciliado was a Greek named Andreas of Rhodes, or Andrés Griego, as he was called by the Santa María Inquisition. On September 15, 1528 the Greek was tried for heretical comments on the Eucharist.[99] Gabriel de Luque told the Inquisition that some ten years ago in Santiago de Cuba, Andrés had laughed at "the little bit of bread and wine" that some people thought so important. Other witnesses confirmed the story before Santa María required Andreas of Rhodes to testify on September 24, 1528. At the time Andrés was a shipwright at Zacatula.[100] He informed that he had always been a sailor and that he had come to New Spain with Juan de Grijalva, later joining the Cortés army. The Greek had been born in the city of Coron on the island of Rhodes. His parents George and Anastasia had baptized him at a very early age in the Church of Saint Andrew on the island. He had taken communion from the age of eight years forward and he said he usually went to confession. He claimed that no member of his family had ever been investigated by the Inquisition. He knew considerable about the dogma of the Church in the Greek tongue but his exposition of the ideas in Spanish was fuzzy. Andreas of Rhodes denied that he had ridiculed the bread and wine in the Eucharist and affirmed that he believed them to be the body and blood of Christ.

After Inquisitor Santa María required Andreas to search his memory, on September 30, 1528 Andreas admitted the substance of the denunciation but qualified the circumstances. He made his statement because in Greece the host was consecrated differently, "while the bread was rising." Santa María ordered Andreas ridden through the streets of the parish on a burro without a shirt and with a gag in his mouth. He was fined the costs of the trial and was incarcerated in a monastery for a month so that he could study Catholic dogma. Presumably it was he who donned penitential garb and marched as a reconciled heretic in the same auto de fé of the Morales brothers and Ocaña.

During the proceedings that led to the controversial auto de fé of October 1528, the Santa María Inquisition tried four other

THE FIRST DECADE   39

heretics for diverse crimes. Francisco de Agreda was a recurrent blasphemer who had his tongue split in Cuba as punishment. In New Spain he continued to use blasphemous and obscene language. Santa María tried him in October 1528 and sentenced him to public humiliation and thirty days in jail.[101] Juan de Jaén was a wealthy merchant who was discovered having an affair with his *comadre* (he was the godfather of her child). Santa María meted out a harsh punishment. Jaén was fined seventy pesos de oro and had to perform public penances.[102] The two scribes who held secretarial and notary positions in the civil government of the colony—Pedro del Castillo and Juan Fernández del Castillo—were tried by Santa María in 1528. The denunciation against Fernández del Castillo charged him with encouraging the Indians to practice idolatry, but no details are given.[103]

Pedro del Castillo had been the custodian of the Diego de Morales civil trial documents in 1525 and 1526. He was reported to be incarcerated for blasphemy during March 1528. The cabildo records show that he escaped from jail on April 24, 1528.[104] To what extent the escribanos were the victims of the political side of the inquisitorial process is not clear. Both men had been partisans of Cortés in the disputes of the 1524-1526 period.

Mexican Inquisition trials during the first decade of the activities of the Holy Office must be seen against a complex background of the struggle between Cortés and his enemies, between Church and State, and the rivalry between the Dominican and Franciscan orders. At its inception the Mexican Inquisition became involved in a political struggle which conditioned its development, a situation which had to be remedied by Inquisitor Zumárraga in the following decades. Many responsible officials questioned the harshness of the burnings of Alonso and Morales in 1528. It seemed strange that the Cortés supporters were burned by the Dominican inquisitors while the Cortés critics were reconciled. Perhaps the Dominican Inquisition was the first agency which tried to limit Cortés' economic and political lordship of New Spain in the 1520's, anticipatory of the first and second audiencias.

After October 1528, about the time that Cortés began to lose much of his power, the Holy Office became moribund. Some credence may be given to the view that the burnings of 1528 placed the Dominican Inquisition in a bad light, and as a result Santa María had his inquisitorial faculties revoked. It is more likely that Bishop Juan de Zumárraga's appointment to the Mexican see in December 1527 removed the Inquisition from control of the Dominican prelates and vested it in Zumárraga as ecclesiastical judge ordinary.

It may be true that for the years 1528-1532 there were no trials because Zumárraga had left Spain without the bulls of consecration. Only two trials were carried on during the period 1528-1534. Ruy Díaz, a mule skinner, was tried for blasphemy in Oaxaca in 1532 by Judge Juan de Valdivieso,[105] and Zumárraga's first case as ordinary was a bigamy and concubinage trial in 1534.[106] It appears that Dominican and Franciscan Inquisition judges withdrew from any political alliances in the difficult era of the Nuño de Guzmán—Zumárraga conflict of 1529-1531. Perhaps the Holy Office's activities under Dominican prelates Ortíz, Betanzos and Santa María in the 1526-1528 era revealed that the Holy Office, if it was to fulfill its true ministry, had to remain aloof from political controversies.

Notes

[1] See Richard E. Greenleaf, *Zumárraga and the Mexican Inquisition, 1536-1543* (Washington, D.C., 1962), pp. 3-25, for a brief treatment of the organization of the Inquisition in Mexico.

[2] See José Toribio Medina, *La Primitiva Inquisición Americana 1493-1569* (2 vols., Santiago de Chile, 1914), Vol. II, ff. 74-79, 83-92, for the bulls.

[3] *Ibid.*, Vol. II, ff. 69-70. Cf. Greenleaf, *Zumárraga*, p. 9.

[4] Antonio de Remesal, *Historia de la Provincia de San Vicente de Chyapa* (Guatemala, 1932), Lib. II, Cap. II.

[5] Medina, *Primitiva Inquisición*, Vol. I, ff. 115-117.

[6] Archivo General de la Nación (México), Hospital de Jesús, Leg. 271, exp. 11; (hereafter cited as AGN). See also *Escritos Sueltos de Hernán Cortés* (México, 1871), pp. 16-17. See Greenleaf, *Zumárraga*, pp. 100-110, for the nature of early blasphemy in Mexico.

[7] AGN, Inquisición, Tomo 1, exps. 2, 3. (The decrees are no longer extant.)

THE FIRST DECADE   41

[8] France V. Scholes and Eleanor B. Adams, eds., *Proceso contra Tzintzicha Tangaxoan el Caltzontzin formado por Nuño de Guzmán, Año de 1530* (México, 1952).
[9] Greenleaf, *Zumárraga*, pp. 17-18.
[10] AGN, Inquisición, Tomo 1, exp. 1. (The decree is no longer extant.)
[11] Charles Gibson, *Tlaxcala in the Sixteenth Century* (New Haven, 1952), pp. 34-37; Joaquín García Icazbalceta, *Bibliografía Mexicana del Siglo XVI* (México, 1954), p. 452.
[12] *Primer Libro de las Actas del Cabildo de la Ciudad de México* (México, 1889), ff. 49-50.
[13] Henry C. Lea, *A History of the Inquisition of Spain* (4 vols., New York, 1908), Vol. IV, p. 330.
[14] *Ibid.*, p. 331; Lea defines the nature of blasphemy.
[15] AGN, Inquisición, Tomo 1, exp. 8.
[16] Francisco A. Icaza, *Diccionario Autobiográfico de Conquistadores y Pobladores de Nueva España* (2 vols., Madrid, 1923), Vol. I, p. 35.
[17] *Colección de Documentos Inéditos Relativos al Descubrimiento, Conquista y Colonización de las Posesiones Españolas en América y Oceanía, Sacados de los Archivos del Reino, y muy especialmente del de Indias* (42 vols., Madrid 1864-1884), Vol. 26, p. 210; Vol. 28, p. 260. (Hereafter cited as DII.)
[18] Francisco López de Gómara, *Cortés, The Life of the Conqueror By His Secretary*, Lesley B. Simpson, translator and editor (Berkeley and Los Angeles, 1964), pp. 30, 382.
[19] France V. Scholes and Eleanor B. Adams, eds., *Relación de las Encomiendas de Indios hechas en Nueva España a los Conquistadores y Pobladores de ella, Año de 1564* (México, 1955), p. 23.
[20] Agustín Millares Carlo and J. I. Mantecón, *Indice y Extractos de los Protocolos del Archivo de Notarías* (2 vols., México, 1945), Vol. I, p. 107, extract of Notary Book II, ff. 45 r.v.
[21] AGN, Inquisición, Tomo 1, exp. 9.
[22] Millares Carlo and Mantecón, Vol. I, p. 226, extract of Notary Book III, ff. 64r.v. See also DII, Vol. 16, p. 389; Vol. 27, pp. 6, 73, 242, 550; and Scholes and Adams, *Relación de las Encomiendas*, p. 29.
[23] AGN, Inquisición, Tomo 1, exp. 7a.
[24] *Ibid.*, exp. 10b. See also DII, Vol. 26, pp. 58, 79, 224.
[25] Icaza, Vol. II, p. 51.
[26] AGN, Inquisición, Tomo 1, exp. 9b.
[27] *Ibid.*, exp. 10c.
[28] Millares Carlo and Mantecón, Vol. I, p. 49, extract of Notary Book I, ff. 102v. and 103r.

In October 1524 when Hernán Cortés set out on his famous expedition to Honduras, he left his cousin Rodrigo de Paz as major-domo of his estates and as his official representative in Mexico City. Paz was already high bailiff and alderman of the city. In 1525 after Cortés was well on his way south, his enemies, especially Gonzalo de Salazar and Pedro Almindez de Chirinos, assumed political control of the colony. They imprisoned Rodrigo de Paz, and he was brutally tortured. They roasted his feet over a fire until his toes fell off and his feet were burned off to the ankles, thus hoping to force Paz to reveal the storehouses of Cortés' treasure. Unsuccessful, they finally hanged him. Francisco Nuñez tried in vain to save Paz's life.

The intrigues against Cortés and the politics and personalities of the strife-ridden colony during the years 1524-1527 can best be examined in Hubert H. Bancroft, *History of Mexico* (6 vols., San Francisco, 1883-1889), Vol. II, pp. 193-253.

[29] AGN, Inquisición, Tomo 1, exp. 10d.
[30] *Ibid.*, exp. 9e.
[31] Icaza, Vol. I, p. 175.
[32] Millares Carlo and Mantecón, Vol. I, p. 305, extract of Notary Book III, f. 423r.
[33] AGN, Inquisición, Tomo 1, exp. 9c; Icaza, Vol. II, p. 78.
[34] DII, Vol. 28, p. 493, *passim.*
[35] AGN, Inquisición, Tomo 1, exp. 10e.
[36] DII, Vol. 9, p. 216.
[37] DII, Vol. 29, p. 63.
[38] Millares Carlo and Mantecón, Vol. I, pp. 89, 260, 276.
[39] AGN, Inquisición, Tomo 1, exp. 9d.
[40] See Millares Carlo and Mantecón, Vol. I, p. 362, extract of Notary Book III, ff. 662v., 663r., in which Juan Pérez and Marcos de Medina buy at public auction "todos los esclavos indios, con sus herramientas y botas, que pertenecieron a Fernando Alonso y Bartolomé Quemado."
[41] AGN, Inquisición, Tomo 1, exp. 7. (The folios in the trial are bound out of order.) See also Icaza, Vol. II, p. 96.
[42] Icaza, Vol. II, p. 37; DII, Vol. 13, p. 367.
[43] Icaza, Vol. II, p. 96.
[44] AGN, Inquisición, Tomo 1, exp. f. 10.
[45] Millares Carlo and Mantecón, Vol. I, pp. 153, 159, 163, 166, 167, 217, extracts of Notary Book II, ff. 268r.v., 305-06r.v., 311v.-312r.; Notary Book III, f. 19r.v.
[46] AGN, Inquisición, Tomo 1, exp. 9a. DII, Vol. 26, p. 406; Vol. 35, p. 442.
[47] DII, Vol. 13, p. 398; Vol. 27, pp. 51, 420; Vol. 28, p. 325.
[48] For additional data on Juan Rodríguez de Villafuerte, see the treatment of C. Harvey Gardiner, *Naval Power in the Conquest of Mexico* (Austin, 1956), pp. 211-212. See DII, Vol. 15, p. 344, for Villafuerte's activities in Zacatula as late as 1540.
[49] AGN, Inquisición, Tomo 1A, exp. 15. (This annex of documents to Inquisición, Tomo 1, is no longer extant. Fortunately there are microfilm copies of Inquisición, Tomo 1A in the AGN, the private collections of Professor France V. Scholes and the author. For additional data on Juan de Cuevas, see Icaza, Vol. I, p. 200; and Scholes and Adams, *Relación de las Encomiendas*, p. 16.
[50] AGN, Inquisición, Tomo 1, f. 53. (An incomplete trial.)
[51] *Ibid.*, f. 54. (A fragment of the trial.)
[52] *Ibid.*, Tomo, 1A, exp. 14.
[53] *Ibid.*, exp. 17.
[54] *Ibid.*, exp. 16.
[55] *Ibid.*, Tomo 14, exp. 2a.
[56] *Ibid.*, Tomo 1, exp. 10.

THE FIRST DECADE   43

[57] DII, Vol. 26, pp. 92-93, 406, 458; Vol. 27, p. 31; Vol. 28, p. 367; Vol. 35, p. 442.

[58] The accusations of Fiscal Sebastian de Arriaga were extracted in Greenleaf, *Zumárraga,* pp. 102-103, as an introduction to the Zumárraga campaign against the blasphemers in the 1530's.

[59] "Yten. Digo que el dicho Rengel as hombre cruel y sin piedad y se deleita en hacer crueldades sin causa y razón por que muchas vezes por su deleite y pasatiempo haze desnudar a los muchachos y muchachas Judios, Esclavos y esclavas, y los haze muy cruelmente e azotar y pingar en su presencia teniendo esto por pasatiempo . . . como hombre enemigo de la naturaleza humana y de las criaturas criadas a imagen y semejanza de Dios." AGN, Inquisición, Tomo 1, exp. 10, f. 58.

[60] The substantiation of Rengel's "illness" is made by Cortés himself in a special deposition apart from the Inquisition record. *Ibid.,* f. 85.

[61] Juan Tirado was a vocal leader of the anti-Cortés faction from 1526-1529. See his activities as documented by G. R. G. Conway, "Hernando Alonso, a Jewish Conquistador with Cortés in México," *Publications of the American Jewish Historical Society,* Vol. XXXI (1928), p. 11.

[62] Gaspar de la Plaza also had trouble with the Inquisition. Zumárraga tried him three times in the 1536-1543 period. AGN, Inquisición, Tomo 2, exp. 6; Tomo 1, exp. 10a. Cf. Greenleaf, *Zumárraga,* p. 87.

[63] ". . . por buenos cristianos no torcidos ni maculados en las cosas de Nuestra Santa Fe," AGN, Inquisición, Tomo 1, exp. 10, ff. 85.

[64] *Ibid.,* f. 86.

[65] Millares Carlo and Mantecón, Vol. I, p. 355, extract of Notary Book III, f. 637r.v. Cf. Greenleaf, *Zumárraga,* p. 103.

[66] Millares Carlo and Mantecón, Vol. p. 355, extract of Notary Book III, f. 637r.v.

[67] G. R. G. Conway first studied the 1574 testimonies on sanbenitos in his article "Hernando Alonso," pp. 9-31. Alfonso Toro reproduced the testimonies in *Los Judíos en la Nueva España* (México, 1932), pp. 20-32. The Toro transcriptions have been used as the primary sources in Arnold Wiznitzer, "Crypto-Jews in Mexico During the Sixteenth Century," *American Jewish Historical Quarterly* (1962), Vol. 41, pp. 168-173, and by Seymour B. Liebman, "Hernando Alonso: First Jew on the North American Continent," *Journal of Inter-American Studies* (1963), Vol. 5, pp. 291-296. All four studies suffer from the failure to study corollary documentation in the Mexican Inquisition archives.

[68] AGN, Inquisición, Tomo 223, ff. 711-739. Addenda to the list were added at intervals after 1571.

[69] *Ibid.,* f. 718.

[70] *Ibid.,* Tomo 1, ff. 93-134. The author wishes to express his gratitude to don Miguel Saldaña of the Archivo General de la Nación for help in deciphering the almost impossible paleography. Many folios are torn and missing. Others are blurred and faded.

[71] *Ibid.,* f. 102v., ". . . en casa del señor gobernador donde acostumbran jugar."

[72] *Ibid.,* exp. 6.

[73] Millares Carlo and Mantecón, Vol. I, ff. 29, 38, 150, 160, *passim.*

[74] Toro, *Los Judíos*, pp. 20-32.
[75] *Ibid.*, pp. 20-23.
[76] Conway, "Hernando Alonso"; Liebman, "Hernando Alonso"; Toro, *Los Judíos*, pp. 20-32, *passim*.
[77] Gardiner, pp. 121-128; Conway, "Hernando Alonso," pp. 11, 12, 25.
[78] Greenleaf, *Zumárraga*, pp. 90, 90n, 91.
[79] Millares Carlo and Mantecón, Vol. I, Nos. 31, 250, 299, 300, 474, 572, *passim*.
[80] Wiznitzer, pp. 171-173.
[81] Testimony of Fray Vicente de Las Casas in Toro, *Los Judíos*, p. 21.
[82] Testimony of Pedro Vásquez de Vergara in Toro, *Los Judíos*, pp. 31, 32.
[83] *Ibid.*, p. 33.
[84] *Primer Libro de Actas del Cabildo*, p. 44.
[85] Archivo General de Indias (Sevilla), Patronato, Leg. 54, exp. 2; hereafter cited as AGI.
[86] The Ocaña will of 1533 is published in Publicaciones del Archivo General de la Nación, *La Vida Colonial* (México, 1923), pp. 1-8.
[87] Millares Carlo and Mantecón, Vol. I, p. 102, extract of Notary Book II, f. 24r.
[88] *Primer Libro de Actas del Cabildo*, pp. 49-50.
[89] DII, Vol. 13, pp. 348-356, 393-406. Cf. Joaquín García Icazbalceta, *Colección de Documentos para la Historia de México* (México, 1858), Vol. I, pp. 524-537.
[90] Millares Carlo and Mantecón, Vol. I, p. 278, extract of Notary Book III, ff. 312r.v.
[91] Wiznitzer, p. 172.
[92] *Primer Libro de Actas del Cabildo*, p. 132.
[93] Toro, *Los Judíos*, p. 23, *passim*.
[94] *Ibid.*, pp. 36-37.
[95] *La Vida Colonial*, pp. 1-8.
[96] Toro, *Los Judíos*, p. 33.
[97] AGN, Inquisición, Tomo 38, exp. 1.
[98] Toro, *Los Judíos*, p. 45. See the document on the López de Legazpi papers in AGN, Inquisición, Tomo 72, exp. 32.
[99] AGN, Inquisición, Tomo 1, ff. 141-146.
[100] Millares Carlo and Mantecón, Vol. I, p. 275; Gardiner, pp. 64, 91, 95-96. (Andreas was also known as Antón.)
[101] AGN, Inquisición, Tomo 1, ff. 151-154.
[102] *Ibid.*, Tomo 42, exp. 13.
[103] *Ibid.*, Tomo 40, exp. 3-bis-a.
[104] *Primer Libro de Actas del Cabildo*, pp. 69, 162, 167.
[105] AGN, Inquisición, Tomo 14, exp. 1.
[106] *Ibid.*, Tomo 36, exp. 1.

Chapter Two

THE INQUISITION IN MICHOACAN
1536-1537

AS THE MEXICAN CONQUEST spread into the northwest country in the decade from 1521 to 1531, many of the more ambitious colonizers went into Michoacán to gain the economic and political power which Hernán Cortés had denied them in the valley of Mexico. Mining activities, cattle and sheep ranching and abundant Indian labor made exploitation of the Tarascan area second in wealth only to the riches gleaned from the Aztec Confederacy.

There were bitter enmities and savage competition between settlers in this developing area. There was also a large measure of autonomy in political administration and business affairs. The Franciscan "conquest" of Michoacán took place between 1525 and 1530, but formal diocesan organization waited until the appointment of Quiroga as the first bishop in 1537. Before that time, Licenciado Vasco de Quiroga, as *oidor* of the second audiencia in Mexico City, developed a lasting interest in Michoacán.[1]

Economic activities of Mexico City merchants in Michoacán are well known from the notary protocols during the era 1524-1528. Hernando Alonso and Gonzalo de Morales and their kin, whose families had intermarried, were active entrepreneurs in the post-conquest Tarascan area. After these men were executed in the auto de fé of October 1528 their properties were dispersed, but one suspects from the notary records that relatives assumed control of the Alonso-Morales investments in Michoacán.[2] Members of the Núñez clan, who were implicated in the Betanzos blasphemy trials of 1527-1528 in Mexico City, also had Michoacán property. Whether the Núñezes were "new Christians" rather than blasphemers is an apt speculation.[3] Illustrative of the rapacity of the Michoacán conquest were the activities of Nuño de Guzmán. As he left his post as president of the first audiencia to reconnoiter the Tarascan area in 1529, the tempo of conflict over the economic spoils of empire intensified. Guzmán's trial and torture of the Caltzontzin of the Tarascans in 1530, in order to learn where the treasure was stored, and the subsequent inquiries about the disposition of the loot, are but case studies of the crass opportunism of the Michoacán colonization.[4]

As soldier-encomenderos assumed political office in the new province, often to insure their own economic holdings, rivalries intensified, and the partisans were not above the use of false testimony, conspiracy and other underhanded tactics to combat their enemies. One way to seek revenge and to reduce one's economic competitors was to denounce them to the Holy Office of the Inquisition as heretics or Jews. Such was the case when Cristóbal de Valderrama denounced Gonzalo Gómez, former alcalde mayor of Michoacán and a prominent encomendero, in 1536.[5]

I

The Career of Gonzalo Gómez to 1537

From the lengthy Inquisition proceso against Gonzalo Gómez and from lawsuits in the Spanish archives, it is possible to compose a sketch of his life. In June 1537, when the Apostolic Inquisitor Juan de Zumárraga tried him for heresy, Gonzalo Gómez was about forty-seven years old.[6] He claimed to have been a native of Sevilla, where his family had migrated from his birthplace in Castilla when he was nine years old (*circa* 1499). Later, as the Inquisition trial progressed, Gómez had to abandon the story of his Castilian ancestry and he admitted to having been born in the *barrio* of Santa Cruz in Sevilla. The accused pled scant knowledge of his grandparents since his family had left their village when he was only a child. He had been told that his paternal grandfather was a farmer who had been killed in a dispute over title to some land. Gonzalo also knew by family tradition that his father's parents were devout Christians and that they had never been in any trouble with the Holy Office. As for his own parents, Juan and Beatriz Gómez, Gonzalo told Inquisitor Zumárraga that he had never heard anything about their being reconciled heretics or descendants of heretics until the current denunciations were made against him.

As Gonzalo Gómez described his family's travels, he was careful to stress that they returned to Castilla at intervals after the grandparents were deceased. When they settled in Sevilla in 1499, they remained for three years before Gonzalo's father took him to the Indies. He was twelve years old when they arrived in Española, presumably in the Ovando expedition in 1502.[7] He said they remained in Santo Domingo for four years before returning to "Castilla," where they stayed some thirty to forty days before again setting sail for the new world. The movements of the family suggest that Juan Gómez and his son were merchants, although Gonzalo remained vague on this point. After another ten years of residence in Santo Domingo, Gonzalo Gómez made a second trip to Spain (1516). After a short while he journeyed to Darién, on the Isthmus of Panama, where he was associated with Pedrarias Dávila. Soon thereafter he proceeded to Cuba and then back to Española. In the islands Gonzalo said he had worked with Licenciado Alonso Zuazo.[8]

In 1537 Gonzalo Gómez swore that he had been in New Spain some thirteen years. After arriving in Mexico City (1524) he had traveled widely in the central valley, Michoacán, and on the Pacific Coast around Zacatula. In mid-1531 he founded an hacienda at Guayangareo, later Valladolid-Morelia.

Just why Gonzalo Gómez settled in Michoacán is not clear, but one suspects that he wished to be away from the jurisdiction of the Mexico City audiencia. By his own testimony Gómez informed that he had been thrown in jail by Oidor Juan Ortíz de Matienzo —judge on the first audiencia from December 1528 to July 1530. Gómez claimed Ortíz de Matienzo arrested him for having sold Indian slaves from Michoacán, and Ortíz had told him that he was "one of those prohibited from being in these parts." This last caveat almost certainly referred to Gómez' Jewish ancestry, even though Gómez interpreted it to Zumárraga in terms of Ortíz de Matienzo's desire to keep him out of Michoacán.

There is little doubt that a fragmentary document in the Inquisition archive written around 1530 put the finger on Gómez as a Judaizante. Alonso de Carrión, who later testified in the Inquisition trial, gave Oidor Licenciado Delgadillo data on one Juan Gómez Pacholero, a reconciliado from Sevilla, who had two sons living in New Spain. These, said Carrión in 1530, were Gonzalo Gómez and Melchor Gómez.[9] It appears as if Gómez went to jail for a short stretch after this denunciation. Then he went to Michoacán to live. Had Bishop Juan de Zumárraga not been engaged in a celebrated fight with the first audiencia during 1529-1531, it is clear that Gómez would have had trouble with ecclesiastical authority over his ancestry and residence in New Spain. It is fair to speculate that Ortíz de Matienzo may have jailed Gómez on orders of President Nuño de Guzmán because the two were competitors in Michoacán developments.

When did Gonzalo Gómez serve as alcalde mayor of Michoacán? He implied that it was during the mid-1520's, because in 1553 he testified that "thirty years ago this witness went to the Province of Michoacán as Alcalde Mayor."[10] In March 1532, Gómez was listed as "Alcalde" when he testified before Licenciado Cristóbal de Benavente regarding villages that Juan Infante was trying to take over in Michoacán, and when Gómez fought an accusation that he was illegally in possession of a pueblo that belonged to the city of Michoacán (Tzintzuntzan).[11] By February 15, 1532, however, the second audiencia had appointed Benavente *corregidor* of the city of Michoacán and alcalde mayor of the province. By November

INQUISITION IN MICHOACAN

1532, the second audiencia had sent Licenciado Vasco de Quiroga as *visitador* of Michoacán, and by August of 1533 he had restructured the administration of the province.[12] It is entirely possible that Quiroga reappointed Gonzalo Gómez as alcalde mayor during his visitation. It is more probable that Quiroga appointed him alcalde ordinario of the city of Michoacán at that time. Gómez continued as alcalde ordinario of the city of Michoacán after the Inquisition trial, and in 1538 Bishop Vasco de Quiroga presented an interrogatory before Gómez as alcalde ordinario.[13] In 1540 Gómez continued to aid Licenciado Cristóbal Benavente in the complicated land and tribute litigations between the crown and Juan Infante, and he continued to use the title of alcalde ordinario.[14]

There is no doubt that Gonzalo Gómez participated in the economic exploitation of the Michoacán province from 1525 onward. He was the original encomendero of the pueblo of Yztapa.[15] Perhaps this was the same encomienda mentioned by Gómez in March 1532 as Ytacaro,[16] and by Icaza as Iztepec, which had been given Gómez in a 1528 *"cédula* of Treasurer Alonso de Estrada."[17] In March 1532 Gómez claimed he had been in the Morelia-Pátzcuaro area for seven years, *i.e.* since 1525. The confusion over Gonzalo Gómez' encomienda at Yztapa is typical of the state of early Michoacán encomienda history.

> Encomiendas distributed by one group in power would be cancelled and redistributed by those who followed them. Out of this arose many lawsuits, some of which continued during the whole lifetime of the encomenderos. Some of these lawsuits ... indicate that certain pueblos changed hands as often as three times during the first ten years after they had been distributed.[18]

This description by Warren explains the reason for the conflict over the title to Gómez' encomienda and it helps to explain why Juan de Ortega's *visita* record in 1528 recorded Gonzalo Gómez as encomendero of Yztapa, and other sources declared Cristóbal de Valderrama as the holder of the encomienda.[19]

During the troubled years of 1528 to 1532, Gonzalo Gómez became an important political figure in Michoacán and a very wealthy man. In 1531 he established himself at Guayangareo, the site of the modern city of Morelia. There, situated at the crossroads of Michoacán commerce, Gómez expanded his business to include the manufacture and sale of cotton and woolen cloth, and he founded one of the first *obrajes* (cloth mills) in New Spain.[20] From the ranch Gómez directed his other businesses, mostly mining and land speculation,[21] and he traveled back and forth to Mexico City and to Tzintzuntzan and Pátzcuaro to exercise his duties as alcalde ordinario. Apparently his success in business and the nature of his political functions netted him few friends and made him many enemies.

During 1532 the story of Gómez' imprisonment by the first audiencia again cropped up, and it seems as if he was jailed in Michoacán as a result of the same charges during the same year. This time the matter went directly to the King, and Charles V instructed the audiencia of México in a cédula of 1534 to require the corregidor of Michoacán to prove charges that Gómez was a bad Christian or to absolve him of any guilt. The audiencia ordered the corregidor to obey the cédula on December 5, 1534.[22] Perhaps the animosity between Gonzalo Gómez and Cristóbal de Valderrama over the encomienda of Yztapa led Valderrama to renew the charge a third time in 1536, when he denounced his old rival to the Inquisition as a heretic and a Judaizante.

II

The Denunciation of Gonzalo Gómez
September 1536-June 1537

On September 19, 1536 Apostolic Inquisitor Juan de Zumárraga heard Cristóbal de Valderrama of Michoacán make formal denunciation of Gonzalo Gómez as the son of a reconciled heretic. The Inquisition secretary, Martín de Campos, recorded testimony given by Valderrama that Gómez was well known as a heretic in Mexico and in Michoacán; "that he observed Saturdays and worked on Sundays;" that he had mocked the sacrament of baptism by entering an Indian village and performing the ceremony on a dying child as though he were a priest, saying, "I baptize you in the name of the Father, the Son and the Holy Ghost."

Valderrama told Zumárraga there were witnesses to the baptism and the other allegations contained in his denunciation. He swore that he made his statement in order to rid his conscience of guilt and that he bore Gonzalo Gómez no hatred or jealousy. Since Gómez and Valderrama were competitors in Michoacán, and because of the fact that they had both claimed the encomienda of Yztapa, the trial began on a sour note. Already in the Inquisition archive was a September 14, 1530 statement given by Alonso de Carrión to Oidor Delgadillo in which Carrión claimed that Gonzalo Gómez was the son of Juan Gómez Pacheco, a Sevillian reconciliado.[23]

It is to the credit of the Zumárraga tribunal that a year of careful investigation preceded the Inquisition trial. On May 21, 1537 Zumárraga summoned the three major witnesses mentioned by Valderrama in his accusation. Gregorio Gallego testified that he knew Gonzalo Gómez, rancher of Guayangareo, Michoacán, and he had heard that Gómez had been jailed in New Spain because he was the son of a reconciled heretic. Gallego did not consider Gómez to be an exemplary Christian because he worked his employees and his Indian charges on Sundays and feast days. Pedro de Sosa had told Gallego about Gómez' often quoted statement that he neither wished to see God nor to have God see him, preferring as he did to remain at the ranch rather than go into Tzintzuntzan to hear mass and to partake of the other sacraments. Gallego related a story of Gonzalo Gómez' baptism of an Indian child, joking as he did it. The witness also repeated Gómez' commentaries on a painting of the Last Judgment in Uruápan. He said Gómez called the work fanciful and contrived. Gallego ended his remarks before Zumárraga testifying that it was public knowledge in Michoacán that Gómez was a bad Christian and a heretic. Gómez never went to mass or observed religious holidays, and he had a broken crucifix on an arch at his ranch. Gallego said Gómez had another cross under the roof of one of the buildings in his patio, saying he kept it there so that people would not step on the shadows it cast.

Martín de Aranda claimed to have known Gonzalo Gómez some thirteen years, and he had stayed as a guest on the Gómez ranch during his travels in Michoacán. Aranda repeated the stories about Gómez' reconciliado lineage, the baptism incident and other matters mentioned in the previous testimonies. Martín Jofre, an employee of one Bocanegra, swore that he had known Gonzalo Gómez for nine years. Gómez had discussed with Jofre the Uruápan painting and one in Toluca, and he had opined, rather cynically, that Dominicans and Franciscans would have painted the same view of Judgment Day in two different ways, each giving its own order the most importance. Gómez had also said to Lope de Sayavedra, the corregidor of Michoacán, that animals such as mules and donkeys would be resurrected as part of the Last Judgment. Pedro de Sosa, who had known Gonzalo for sixteen years, told Zumárraga he had no knowledge of Gómez' ancestry but he did remember that the Auditor Rodrigo de Albornoz had ordered Gómez jailed for some kind of violation of the law. Sosa repeated Gómez' remarks about going to mass in league with such people as his Michoacán neighbors, whom Gonzalo apparently despised. Sosa makes first mention of a chapel on the Guayangareo ranch which had fallen into disuse. He said Gómez kept the place very dirty and that it was infested with lice.

Pedro de Sosa recounted many of Gonzalo Gómez' vitriolic sayings when people criticized his conduct. If anyone chastised him for making the Indians work on Sunday, Gómez said, "Let them go to the Devil where he can take care of them." While riding his horse on the way to Mexico City, Gonzalo stared toward Heaven and uttered, apparently to Christ, "I deny that you were sent from the body of God." Sosa claimed that Gómez' brother, Francisco Gómez of the city of Puebla de los Angeles, could give further statements about Gonzalo's conduct—because he had heard Francisco say that Gonzalo ought to be burned as a heretic. According to Pedro de Sosa all of this was common knowledge—that Gómez was an unchristian man; that he worked his servants every day like animals; that he had broken the arms of a cross on the ranch and then had joked about it; and much more.

Diego Hernández knew a great deal of the gossip on Gonzalo Gómez' ranch. He said it was suspected Gómez tore the arms off crosses on the ranch on Holy Thursday or Good Friday to show his contempt for the holy days. Hernández said Gonzalo once took an oath with his hand upon "this stick that was a cross." Hernández related a conversation he had with Gonzalo Gómez' servants when he found them hard at work on a feast day. They told him they had to work because their master was not a Christian. However, there was no evidence of Gonzalo Gómez' engaging in "Jewish ceremonies," and therefore Hernández was unable to present any clue to Gómez' "Jewishness." Juan López, a merchant who had been associated with Gómez nine years, told Zumárraga of a dispute between Gonzalo and Fray Diego Velásquez, of the town of Colima. It concerned some Indian boys who had been sent into Gómez' ranch for baptism. Gómez likened baptism in this case, and others, to the baptizing of donkeys, since the Indians did not wish the sacrament and they did not know the Pater Noster. It was López who first made the charge against Gonzalo Gómez that he used the chapel on his ranch as a dormitory for visitors and a rendezvous for fornication, and that he used crosses as drying racks for his chili peppers.

On the same day these testimonies were entered in evidence, May 21, 1537, Apostolic Inquisitor Zumárraga took the first round of evidence from Antonio de Godoy, former alcalde mayor of Michoacán and Gómez' old enemy. In this appearance before the Inquisition, Godoy gave restrained testimony. He swore that in the presence of Sosa and Gallego at Guayangareo, he had heard Gonzalo Gómez proclaim his views on the painting of the Last Judgment; that he knew of Gómez' practice of working his Indians on days of religious obligation as well as the fact that Gonzalo used the ranch chapel as an inn for itinerant merchants; and that Gómez used crosses on the ranch to dry chili peppers. On May 29, 1537 Zumárraga recalled Godoy to testify in more detail. In this session Godoy related personal knowledge that Gómez was not a practicing Catholic and refused to go to mass. Perhaps in anticipation of a charge that Antonio de Godoy was a hostile witness, Inquisitor Zumárraga required him to swear that his testimony was not motivated by hatred or any other animosity.

On this same day a Portuguese merchant who had lived at the Gómez ranch two and a half years testified. Francisco Arías spoke of Gonzalo's maltreatment of crosses and related that some people from the area considered Gómez to be a bad Christian and a Jew. It later developed that Arías was an employee of Vasco de Quiroga. Zumárraga continued the investigation on June 1, 1537 when Dominican Friar Diego Pérez, who had known Gonzalo Gómez seven or eight years, repeated the tale heard from others about Gómez and the baptism of a dying Indian.

Finally Gonzalo de Riobo y Sotomayor was called to give evidence on June 1. Riobo had known Gómez for "nearly thirty years in these parts and on the Island of Española." Riobo had heard Gonzalo's discourses on religious paintings, and he knew that Gómez had dismantled the crosses on his ranch save for two at the roadway entrance to the property. When Zumárraga asked Riobo specifically whether Gómez had performed any Jewish rites, the witness replied that the Guayangareo Indians worked on Sundays and feast days, and that Gonzalo Gómez always "changed into clean clothes on Saturdays," but in other ways lived like a heathen without going to church. Riobo commented on the sad condition of the chapel on the ranch, which was "very dirty and filled with grain and beds for migrants... birds roosted on the altar, and many men slept there with their concubines." Riobo gave much more testimony about Gómez' blasphemies and desecration of crosses and he swore he had heard Gonzalo say "Pese a Dios" and "No creo en Dios," but Riobo said this was to be expected from one who had the notorious reputation as a "son of a reconciliado or a *quemado*." As a postscript to his statement, Riobo added that Francisco de Arias had told him of Gonzalo Gómez' travel habits. He journeyed on Friday, rested on Saturday, and resumed the travels on Sunday.

III

The Defense of Gonzalo Gómez, June-July 1537

Because of a curious circumstance which will be discussed later, the Inquisition trial record does not contain Zumárraga's order for the arrest of Gonzalo Gómez and the embargo of his properties. This part of the record shows up in the 1572 Inquisition investigation provoked by Gómez' children.[24]

On June 1, 1537 Apostolic Inquisitor Juan de Zumárraga instructed the alguacil mayor of the Holy Office of the Inquisition, Pedro de Mendinilla, to proceed to arrest Gonzalo Gómez at Guayangareo, Michoacán, and to sequester all his properties and wealth. The alguacil was cautioned to look for any writings and papers, "especially any Jewish ones," and to make a thorough search of the ranch for any crucifixes which had been mistreated. Zumárraga continued his orders: "You are to inform us about the person of Gonzalo Gómez and his manner of living, and any excesses and heresies he has committed and any suspicious books which he might have...." Mendinilla was to deliver the prisoner and his liquid assets to the Mexico City offices of the Inquisition within two weeks. If he was unable to arrest Gonzalo Gómez for any reason, he was still to embargo and sequester the property.

We do not know whether Alguacil Pedro de Mendinilla served the warrant of arrest. The Inquisition proceso resumes on June 12, 1537 when Gonzalo Gómez appeared before Zumárraga to make a statement. Apparently of his own free will, Gómez said he had heard about the charges they were making against him in the Holy Office of the Inquisition and that everyone in Michoacán knew about the case against him. He had learned the details from Francisco Ruíz, a Michoacán settler, who had written about it. When Zumárraga pressed Gómez for a detailed statement, Gonzalo admitted that he had received another letter three weeks before from Alonso de Avila. After this first interview with the apostolic inquisitor, Gonzalo Gómez went to jail and formal embargo of his property took place.

On Friday, June 15, 1537 Zumárraga interrogated Gómez for the first time. The accused admitted that he was a native of Sevilla and that his parents Juan and Beatriz Gómez were dead. His grandparents were from Castilla, where Gonzalo claimed to have been born, but his parents had left the ancestral village when he was so young that he remembered nothing about them. Gonzalo denied that either his parents or grandparents were of Jewish or heretic lineage. He admitted having been jailed in New Spain because he was "prohibited from being there," but Gómez attributed his arrest to the death of an Indian, and to his slaving activities in Michoacán. He gave Zumárraga rather full details about his life in the Indies since 1502, when his father brought him to Española. Zumárraga questioned him very closely about his alleged statements regarding the baptism of Indians. Gómez said he had acquired his views from Fray Alonso de Herrera, a Franciscan father from the monastery in Cuernavaca. Herrera had told Gómez that unless the Indians understood things of the faith and unless they asked to be baptized, the sacrament in itself meant nothing,[25] and one might as well baptize animals. Later on, at a ford in the River Yupelcingo in Michoacán, Gómez had repeated these views when a dying Indian was brought to him so that he could arrange for baptism. He had repeated the words that priests use in the sacrament of baptism but denied there was anything irreverent or joking about it.

Meticulous questioning about crosses and crucifixes on the Guayangareo ranch followed the testimony on baptism. Gómez told Zumárraga that it was true he had taken a cross from the patio of his ranch and he had placed it instead over the roof of his warehouse. This he had done because Licenciado Quiroga suggested that it was irreverent and bad form for people to pass back and forth stepping on the shadow cast by the cross in the patio. Later on Gómez moved the cross and affixed it to a wall where it was charred in a fire which broke out while he was away from the ranch. He declared he had no knowledge that the cross had been used as a drying rack for chilies. Gómez denied that he or any of his people had broken the arms off crosses on Holy Thursday or

INQUISITION IN MICHOACAN

Good Friday. He specified that there was a cross on the road about one-half league from his *estancia* and that it had neither arms nor feet. Then Gómez admitted he had given a traveler directions to go down the highway "where you will find a post which used to be a cross." He claimed there was nothing irreverent in what he had said.

Gonzalo Gómez gave quite a different account than his accusers had given of his statements about the painting dealing with Judgment Day. He admitted that he had said the painting was fanciful and highly subjective. But he contended that when he and Francisco de Villegas, Pedro de Sosa, and others were looking at the picture, he had said obviously it was a matter of point of view. For instance in this work the Franciscans were pictured as rescuing more souls from the sea than the Dominicans—but how would it look if a Dominican had painted it?

Zumárraga spent considerable time probing Gonzalo Gómez' views on Christianity in general. He asked him if he had ever made the statement that he did not wish to go to mass or to see God in all of his life. Gómez tried to put the answer to the question in its proper framework, or so he claimed. What had happened was that one day some two years earlier Gómez had been at home on the ranch when Antonio de Godoy, Francisco de Villegas and Pedro de Sosa tried to get him to go into the city of Michoacán with them "because they ought to go to church." Gómez replied, acidly, that he preferred to worship God at home rather than among the gossiping and mischievous people in the town. Gómez claimed he had said no more than this to Antonio de Godoy and the others, and Godoy was misrepresenting the matter. From that time onward, Gonzalo said he had gone to mass and observed the days of obligation in Cinapécuaro and Uruápan.

Then Zumárraga and Gómez discussed the subject of the chapel on his ranch. Gonzalo maintained that until there was a fire on the premises he had kept the chapel clean and in perfect condition. The fire had burned the guestrooms on the ranch and part of the chapel. Before the disaster no one had used the church as a dormitory, but afterward Gómez had had to open the room to travelers who often brought their women with them. But Gómez said by that time he had moved all objects of religious worship to his own home.

Finally, point by point, Gonzalo Gómez denied the blasphemies attributed to him by the denuncia, and he denied that he observed Saturdays rather than Sundays and other holy days. He related the times and places where he had heard mass and where he had confessed and had taken communion during the last year and especially during the lenten season. As a seemingly irrelevant part of Zumárraga's questioning, he asked Gómez for the location of his father's parish, and Gonzalo replied that it had been Santa Cruz and San Salvador in Sevilla. These of course were enclaves of Jews. As a last question, Zumárraga demanded of Gómez whether he was circumcised, and Gonzalo maintained that he was not.

During the Friday, June 15, session of Zumárraga's court, Francisco Gómez, brother of the accused, was interrogated. Francisco Gómez had the same father as Gonzalo, but they had different mothers. When the inquisitor demanded why Francisco on many occasions publicly declared his brother ought to be burned as a heretic, the witness said he was scandalized by his brother's use of the ranch chapel as a place of business and a dormitory, and he disapproved of the way Gonzalo had treated the cross in the patio of the ranch yard. Zumárraga was unable to draw Francisco Gómez out on any Jewish background of the family.

By June 19, 1537 the Holy Office was attempting to determine how the news of Gonzalo Gómez' denunciation, a supposedly private matter, had spread all over Michoacán. Alonso de Avila was forced to admit that he had heard the story from Gregorio Gallego and Antonio de Godoy on the Mexico City Zócalo. Hoping to encourage Gonzalo Gómez to come to the viceregal capital to clear his reputation, Avila said he wrote him the entire story. Avila said many people in Michoacán knew that Gallego and Aranda were coming to the capital for the express purpose of denouncing Gómez to the Holy Office.

On June 2, 1537 Dr. Rafael de Cervanes, prosecuting attorney of the Inquisition, presented twelve formal charges against Gon-

INQUISITION IN MICHOACAN

zalo Gómez, indicting him as a heretic and a blasphemer. The accusation, based on testimonies of ten reliable witnesses, ended with the demand that Zumárraga punish Gómez as a "New Christian who was prohibited from being in New Spain," and if necessary relinquish him to the secular arm for burning at the stake. Gonzalo Gómez appointed three famous lawyers to frame his defense —Licenciado Vincencio de Riverol and Licenciado Francisco Téllez in Mexico City and Licenciado Cristóbal de Benavente in Michoacán.

As he answered the testimony of his accusers, Gómez reiterated the statements he had made to Zumárraga regarding baptism, the painting of the Last Judgment, and his life on the Michoacán ranch. He claimed that the denunciation and charges had taken his words out of context, whereas he had said nothing irreverent or reprehensible in the eyes of the Church. Riverol and Téllez gave special attention to defending Gómez against charges that he had "observed Saturdays as a Jewish ceremony" and that he had not been a practicing Catholic. On both counts they produced evidence to the contrary. Gómez went into detail about his own baptism by a Reverend Torres in the Church of San Gil in Sevilla, and about the fact that neither of his parents ever had any difficulty with the Inquisition. Prior to complicated and prolonged litigation, Gómez' lawyers tried to get him released from prison on bail. Zumárraga refused the plea, but since Gonzalo was ill he was allowed to go free of the chains and manacles which he had been wearing.

IV

Litigation and Recriminations, July-October 1537

As the first week of July 1537 passed, the Gómez lawyers were busily amassing evidence for Gonzalo's acquittal. Gómez entered testimony about the good treatment and religious education of the Indians in his encomienda. His attorneys framed an interrogatory consisting of thirty-two items to be used in gathering testimony that would substantiate his innocence. Some of the questions bring out interesting data about Corregidor Lope de Sayavedra's intrigues against Gómez and the corregidor's refusal to let Gómez enter the city of Michoacán. It was Sayavedra who had imprisoned Gómez in 1532 when he sought the aid of the crown in securing his vindication. Many of the questions were designed to prove that Gómez had been a practicing Catholic and that his parents had been known as good Christians in Sevilla.

In all, twenty-three witnesses were summoned to answer each of the thirty-two questions. Without exception the men who testified said they had known Gonzalo Gómez for two to three decades —in Sevilla, Española and Mexico. They attested to his Christian character and to the Catholic background of his parents in Spain. Many witnesses swore they saw him go to mass and take communion in monasteries and villages near Guayangareo. Pedro de Vargas had known Gómez' father in Spain and in the Indies. He said that Juan Gómez, merchant, was an exemplary Christian. Dr. Manuel Flores, dean of the Metropolitan Cathedral, had been an acquaintance for ten years and he insisted that Gonzalo Gómez treated his slaves very well and required them to be baptized and to be instructed in religion. Diego de Rivera agreed with the testimony of most witnesses who said Corregidor Lope de Sayavedra had jailed Gómez in 1532 out of malice and for economic reasons. He added the information that it had been Hernán Cortés, Marquis of the Valley, who had secured Gómez' release.

Typical of the testimony was that of Francisco de Villegas taken on August 2, 1537. Villegas had known Gonzalo Gómez for seventeen years. He was present during Gómez' controversial discourse on the painting of the Last Judgment and he found nothing heretical in what Gonzalo had to say about it. He documented the hatred between Corregidor Sayavedra and his followers and Gonzalo Gómez. Villegas had actually seen Gómez at mass in Uruápan and other places and he had seen him take communion during the lenten season. Villegas claimed that Gómez was a good Christian and not a blasphemer or a vicious man. Alonso Alvarez de Espinosa testified that Gonzalo Gómez was a faithful Christian: "I have seen Gonzalo Gómez do pious works, fast, give alms and pray." Many of the witnesses gave evidence of Gómez' charity, his generosity to travelers and his gifts to nearby monastic houses.

In answer to this host of friendly testimony, Attorney Cervanes launched a powerful counterattack on August 17, 1537. He informed Zumárraga of two crucial documents which had just come to light. One was a letter from Marcos de Carmona, an employee of Cristóbal de Valderrama, dated July 18, 1537. In the letter Carmona described a broken crucifix which he had "found" in a box under the floor of Gonzalo Gómez' house. Carmona surmised that Gómez had hidden the cross so that he could destroy it and bury it at a later date. The other document was the October 14, 1530 statement given by Alonso de Carrión to the oidores of the first audiencia. Carrión had told Oidor Delgadillo that he had known a reconciled Jew in Sevilla named Juan Gómez Pacholero. This Juan Gómez had been jailed for heresy in Granada, and had been publicly flogged and then reconciled by the Sevillian Inquisition. One of Juan Gómez' sons had entered a friary in Córdoba and it was rumored that the friars later expelled him because he was the son of a reconciliado. Carrión informed Delgadillo there were two sons of Juan Gómez Pacholero living in New Spain. One was called Melchor Gómez and the other was Gonzalo Gómez.

When Cervanes demanded the recall of witnesses presented by Gonzalo Gómez, one of the witnesses, Hernando de Santillana, admitted that it was true that "Juan Gómez and Beatriz Gómez [Gonzalo's parents] were of converso lineage. Everybody knew this to be the case, but they were also known as good Christians." As Marcos de Carmona was called to testify regarding his letter of July 18, 1537, he changed his story. He admitted he wrote the letter out of anger and malice. Actually Gómez had told him the broken crucifix had been left with him for safekeeping by Licenciado Quiroga. Gómez himself substantiated this version of the story. When Zumárraga commanded him to answer charges that he was the son of Juan Gómez Pacholero, on August 17, 1537 Gonzalo denied that his father was ever known as Pacholero.

When Zumárraga queried Gómez as to whether the father had been a tailor, Gonzalo said yes, he had heard that his father was once a tailor, although Juan Gómez never practiced the trade as far as he remembered.

Gómez told Zumárraga that during his imprisonment by the first audiencia, he had never been told the charges except that he was prohibited from being in New Spain, and the judges had failed to provide him with a copy of the testimony against him. He denied having a brother who entered a monastic order. Gonzalo related that he did have relatives in New Spain—Diego Gómez, who lived in the Pearl Islands; Juan Gómez and Francisco Gómez, illegitimate sons of his father, who lived in New Spain. He failed to mention any female relatives in the new world.

By August 31, 1537 Gonzalo Gómez' lawyers were ready to challenge the character of key witnesses against him and to dispute the validity of their testimony. Gómez maintained that none of the witnesses who had denounced him, and no witness for the prosecution, had offered reliable evidence that his father had been a reconciled heretic. Neither had they proven him to be a heretic or a bad Christian. Gómez claimed that Pedro de Sosa was prejudiced against him because of a dispute over a herd of cattle, the same steers which Gómez and Antonio de Godoy both claimed as their own. As for Godoy, Gonzalo Gómez dismissed him as "a vile, blasphemous man," and a cardsharp to boot. He pictured Gregorio Gallego as another of his business rivals, a bitter enemy and a deadbeat who had left a trail of debts throughout the Indies, a man known by everyone in Michoacán as a drunkard and a liar. Martín de Aranda was characterized as a former debtor of Gómez who had tried to default on his legal obligations, and a partisan of Cristóbal de Valderrama in the litigations Gómez had with him over the encomienda. Gómez had had Aranda arrested for his failure to pay up. He said Aranda was "a man who thrived on gossip and lies because he didn't know how to tell the truth." Riobo de Sotomayor had gotten drunk in the city of Michoacán and told Francisco de Castillejo that he intended to get even with Gonzalo Gómez because the latter had refused to support him in his desire to be alcalde of the town. Riobo was denounced as a foulmouthed scoundrel who habitually lied and committed perjury in civil cases in the province of Michoacán.

The bond between Gómez and Villegas, as well as the animosity of Godoy, were apparent in a statement about a business deal when Villegas and Gómez purchased a group of slaves from Godoy, who later reneged on the sale and refused to deliver the slaves until Gómez took the matter to the audiencia. Marcos de Carmona, who worked for Valderrama, also emerged as an enemy whom Gonzalo had to discipline with a club because he was insubordinate to Gómez when the latter was the alcalde. Furthermore, as part of his official duties, Gómez had been responsible for repossessing a ranch which Carmona had taken illegally from its Indian owner. And so the testimony went. Gonzalo Gómez made many enemies in the exercise of his office as alcalde. Almost every person who had contributed to the Gómez denunciation seemed to have had some ulterior motive for giving evidence.

Gómez told Zumárraga that as alcalde he had expelled Martín de Jofre from the Pueblo of Comanja because of his vicious mistreatment of the Indians, and Cortés had upheld Gómez' actions in the matter. Later Jofre was convicted and sentenced to flogging. Gómez' old animosities for Juan Infante also came out in the testimony.[26] He said that he and Infante had not spoken to each other for eight years. Gómez had recruited a henchman to knife Infante, and Juan almost died as a result of the fight and the wound. Special attention was paid by Gómez and his lawyers to the character of Alonso de Carrión, the author of the 1530 accusation that Gómez was the son of a reconciled heretic. Gómez charged that Carrión was a notorious blasphemer whose reputation as a teller of smutty stories was well known. Gonzalo warned:

> If he said anything about me or my parents in this case, he could not possibly have known them, because they died in Sevilla before he was old enough to remember ... and anything he said to prejudice me was done to curry favor with Treasurer Rodrigo de Albornoz and President Nuño de Guzmán.

By mid-September 1537 Vicencio de Riverol had framed yet another interrogatory of fifty-three items to be used in cross-examining Gonzalo's accusers, and to bring out their bad characters through testimony by other witnesses. During the rest of September and the month of October the litigation and the recriminations continued. From time to time both Gómez and Prosecuting Attorney Cervanes interjected interesting bits of testimony. For instance, Gonzalo recounted a scene from the proceso where his opponents had deliberately misinterpreted his behavior. He said one Friday he was riding to Uruápan and he stayed the night at Amatlán on the hacienda of Juan de Godoy, son of Antonio Godoy. Also at the hacienda was Martín Jofre. On Saturday morning when he mounted his horse he found that it had gone lame and he had to delay his journey until Sunday when he could borrow another horse to continue on the way to Uruápan. Gómez said he left after vespers on Sunday and slept down the road from the Godoy ranch. In relating this incident to the Inquisition, those who wished to inculpate Gómez tried to interpret his travel schedule as the Jewish observance of Saturday as the Sabbath.

Gonzalo Gómez informed the Holy Office fully of his various altercations with Cristóbal de Valderrama, the man who denounced him in the first place. Gonzalo charged that Valderrama "is my mortal enemy and he wishes me ill because of a lawsuit over the lands and farms I have and possess in the province of Michoacán." Gómez related for the first time in the trial on October 5, 1537 that it was Cristóbal de Valderrama who was responsible for sending him to jail, the second imprisonment, on trumped-up charges in 1532. Such were the devious ways of Gonzalo Gómez' enemies.

Of course the accused also had his cunning side. He brought in several Indians to testify that they had been responsible for "moving" crosses on the roads near Guayangareo, and one Indian said he did this on orders of Martín Joffre. In regard to his parentage Gómez insisted that witnesses be instructed to differentiate between Juan Gómez, merchant, "my father who was a man of substantial wealth whom everyone knew," and Juan Gómez Pacho-

INQUISITION IN MICHOACAN

lero, who was "a poor tailor with little fortune." Dr. Cervanes also insisted that those who testified be asked, "If Juan Gómez, father of Gonzalo Gómez, had been a new Christian or a convert, and if he had been penanced by the Holy Inquisition." The specificity of the attorney's question left witnesses little room to hedge on their answers. Many of them, however, upheld the Gómez story.

A case in point was the cross-examination of Juan Franco, the jeweler, on October 15, 1537. Franco admitted he knew a Juan Gómez Pacholero, a poor tailor, but he told Zumárraga this Juan Gómez was not the father of the accused. Gonzalo's father, Franco said, was a rich merchant. Perhaps Apostolic Inquisitor Zumárraga had some doubts about the veracity of this testimony, especially since Franco had been tried by the Holy Office as a sorcerer in August 1536.[27] Dr. Cervanes challenged this testimony and that of several other witnesses. He claimed that many witnesses had visited Gonzalo Gómez in his cell during the trial. Alonso de Vargas, the Nuncio of Zumárraga's Holy Office, sustained Dr. Cervanes' views. He said he had "seen many persons enter the room where Gonzalo Gómez was imprisoned, and these people talked to the accused without [official] permission."

V

Climax, November 1537

During late October 1537 Dr. Rafael de Cervanes issued strong protests about the way in which testimony was being taken. For instance, on October 25 Antón de Carmona, who had visited Gómez' cell, tried to help by saying that he knew a Juan Gómez Pacholero in Sevilla, a tailor who had been sentenced by the Inquisition to wear the sanbenito. But Carmona said this man was not the father of Gonzalo Gómez; even so, he said, many people knew that Juan Gómez, merchant, was a convert to Catholicism and Beatriz de Gómez, Gonzalo's mother, was a devout Catholic of old Christian heritage. Because Carmona was one of those seen visiting Gómez, the exasperated Cervanes claimed that "the witnesses I have presented are good and creditable ones without any blot on their characters, while [many of] those whom Gonzalo Gómez has challenged as his enemies are really his friends, and since he converses with them secretly, their animosity is feigned." The attorney demanded a speedy conclusion to the case so that Gómez could be justly punished for his transgressions against the faith.

As a conclusion to the defense of Gonzalo Gómez, his lawyers presented Zumárraga with eight documents designed to strengthen his case. The first was a royal cédula directed to Lope de Sayavedra, corregidor of Michoacán in 1532, demanding that he prove the accusations of guilt against Gonzalo Gómez or set him free and desist from molesting him in the future. There followed a letter from Fray Juan de San Miguel dated in Uruápan October 2, 1537, which recounted the visit of Hernán Cortés to the city during Holy Week of 1535 when the marquis was on his way to Baja California ("La Isla"). The priest said Gonzalo Gómez was also present in Uruápan at that time, fasting, confessing and taking communion. Fray Juan related that Gonzalo Gómez had performed many acts of charity; he gave to the poor and he supported the mission program of the friars.

Another letter from Fray Miguel de Boloña, signed in Uruápan October 2, 1537, stated that he had confessed Gonzalo Gómez during 1536, and "I administered to him the Sacrament of the Holy Eucharist on Candalaria Sunday in the presence of Martín de Aranda and Bartolomé Saucedo . . . in my church in Cinapécuaro." Fray Miguel said Gonzalo had encouraged him to come to Guayangareo to baptize the natives. He considered Gómez "a very good example of Christianity." Fray Francisco de Boloña wrote the Holy Office that he had gone to Guayangareo on October 1, 1535 to confess Gonzalo Gómez when the latter was very ill and about to die. Fray Francisco said his visit heartened Gonzalo and aided in his recovery. He told of other times he had seen Gómez at mass

INQUISITION IN MICHOACAN 67

and at confession and communion during days of religious obligation in 1535 and 1536. Other sworn statements from clergy substantiated that Gómez had gone to confession in Zacatula in 1532, and in the Monastery of San Francisco in Mexico City during 1536.

Fray Jorge de Avila of the mission at Santa Fé near Pátzcuaro gave firm support to Gonzalo Gómez. He said many people had come to him to inquire whether or not Gómez' commentaries on the painting of the Last Judgment were heresy. Fray Jorge told one and all that there was nothing heretical in Gonzalo Gómez' statements. Indeed he affirmed his belief that Gómez was a worthy Christian and that the townspeople in Pátzcuaro and the city of Michoacán were gossips and scandalmongers.

Perhaps these documents swayed Zumárraga to leniency in his sentence of Gonzalo Gómez, but they did not convince him of the prisoner's absolute innocence. Gonzalo Gómez was convicted of blasphemy and uttering "scandalous and evil-sounding things against our Holy Catholic Faith" on November 9, 1537. In his decision Apostolic Inquisitor Zumárraga made no mention of Gómez as a Judaizante.

The sentence was reasonably lenient. Gonzalo Gómez was commanded to appear on Monday, November 12, 1537, at the altar rail of the Cathedral of Mexico City. Kneeling and with a candle in his hand, after the mass, he was to recite five Ave Marías and five Pater Nosters and the Rosary, "so that God would pardon his sins." As a penance he was to be confined in the Uruápan monastery for a period of thirty days to meditate on his sins. Zumárraga also levied the stiff fine of four hundred golden pesos on Gómez and required payment before release from jail.

Then Zumárraga warned him: "From this day forward you are not to say scandalous and evil-sounding things against our Holy Catholic Faith," and "You are to live as an exemplary Christian, observing feast days, and not requiring your servants to violate days of obligation," else the Holy Office of the Inquisition "will prosecute you with the full force of the law, and without mercy." The sentence ended with a statement giving Gonzalo Gómez absolution from the ban of excommunication he had been under during the trial.

The Inquisition trial of Gonzalo Gómez exemplifies the professionalism and apolitical role of the Zumárraga Holy Office. With the administrative stability brought by Antonio de Mendoza as first viceroy of New Spain in 1535, the chaotic political strife of the first decade and a half of the Mexican conquest tended to abate. Partisan views of inquisitors in the 1520's were no longer appropriate as the episcopal sees were erected in the Zumárraga period.

Obviously there were political and economic overtones to the entire Gonzalo Gómez trial, but Zumárraga was careful to sift the religious issues from the partisan ones. Gómez had belonged to the pro-Cortés faction in the early years of the colony and the Cortés rivals were bitter enemies of Gonzalo. As Nuño de Guzmán and the first audiencia assumed power in Mexico City in 1528, Gómez' enemies gained strength in Michoacán, and they caused him considerable trouble. The contest between Gómez and Valderrama over Yztapa dated from this period. Nuño de Guzmán's attempt to preempt control over the northwest country further weakened Gómez' position. His fortunes revived with the appointment of the second audiencia in 1530. Gonzalo Gómez gained the respect of Oidor Vasco de Quiroga, and his appointment as alcalde ordinario of the city of Michoacán after 1533 apparently had Quiroga's approval. Gómez' continued cooperation with Quiroga in Michoacán affairs after Don Vasco became bishop in 1538 is well documented from archival data.

The Gómez trial provides many insights into the society of Michoacán in the 1530's. Gómez' Guayangareo ranch was situated on the major route of travel from Mexico City to central Michoacán. A good cross section of provincial society and commerce passed through his domains. As a rugged individualist with a vicious temper, Gómez made few close friends and many enemies. He was the natural object of criticism in the narrow provincial society where everyone gossiped and spied on everyone else. His position as alcalde engendered jealousy and bitterness among his constituency. Michoacán politics were the politics of economic rivalry in the 1520's and the 1530's. Gómez' industriousness and his success stuck like a thorn in the side of the less wealthy settlers. Was Gonzalo Gómez "framed" in the Inquisition trial of 1536-1537? Certainly Zumárraga must have suspected that he was. But even though there was no real evidence that Gómez carried on Jewish practices, Zumárraga felt there was adequate reason to convict him of blasphemy and indecent language. After Gómez' enemies had made every effort to have him condemned as a Judaizante, they could not make the accusation stick. The evidence was very weak. Of course everything indicated that Gonzalo Gómez was of Jewish ancestry—his family name, his birth in the barrio of Santa Cruz in Sevilla, and his father's life and travels as a merchant. But there was no proof. Even as a blasphemer, one suspects that Gómez' "wisecracks" and his jokes about the painting of the Last Judgment were harshly judged by unctuous individuals and stuffily self-righteous clergy.

Probably what constrained Apostolic Inquisitor Zumárraga to leniency in the Gonzalo Gómez sentence was the dubious nature of major parts of the testimony against him. Cristóbal de Valderrama's obvious plotting to avenge himself for the loss of Yztapa spoke for itself. Everyone agreed that Alonso de Carrión was a liar and an untrustworthy character. The Zumárraga Inquisition had tried Carrión for blasphemy during October 1536,[28] and he had been penanced as a blasphemer by Betanzos in August 1527.[29] The vocal anti-Semitism of Carrión, Juan López and other hostile witnesses in the trial disturbed Zumárraga. Francisco Peñafiel testified on October 22, 1537 that Juan López on many occasions called Gonzalo Gómez "a Jewish dog," because, Peñafiel said, Gonzalo Gómez was rich and López was poor. Many of the other witnesses had police records and some of them had been tried by Zumárraga's Holy Office. Zumárraga used the Gómez trial record to convict Gregorio Gallego and Martín de Aranda for breaking the oath of secrecy required by ecclesiastical law of people who testified before the Holy Office. Their gossip about Gómez in Mexico City and in Michoacán did not go unpunished.[30]

Zumárraga exhibited the same caution in labeling people Jews in Mexico City. While he investigated a Beatriz Gómez, who could well have been a sister of Gonzalo, he found her and her tailor husband Alvaro Mateos innocent of any heresy in 1539.[31] Zumárraga's campaign against the Judaizantes during his 1536-1543 inquisitorial ministry was conducted with restraint, and the many people who were accused received due process and fair treatment.[32] Even when Zumárraga had irrefutable proof against a Judaizante in the trial of Francisco Millán in 1538-1539, he was moved to leniency because he was aware of colonial animosities for merchants and others who had come from Jewish families.[33]

VI

Aftermath, 1572

Gonzalo Gómez died sometime between 1553 and 1564,[34] and his son Amador Gómez succeeded him as encomendero of Yztapa. Memories of their father's Inquisition trial were to haunt Salvador, Juan and Antonio Gómez thirty-five years later. In November 1571 it came to the attention of Licenciado Antonio Bonilla, attorney of the tribunal of the Inquisition, that Juan Suárez de Avila had made it known that he had important Inquisition papers in his possession. Suárez de Avila was willing to sell the papers to relatives of those who had come under the Holy Office's censure in earlier years. Bonilla ordered Suárez de Avila arrested for blackmail, perjury and violation of the secrecy of Inquisition records. On March 1, 1572 Juan Gómez in the name of his family brought suit against Suárez de Avila before Dr. Pedro Moya de Contreras, senior inquisitor of the Mexico City tribunal.[35] Juan Gómez charged Suárez de Avila with having offered for sale to his family "records concerning our father ... for two hundred pesos." In addition the blackmailer's associates wished to be relieved of a debt of over a thousand pesos which they owed Juan Gómez.

Juan Gómez was outraged at this connivance, because his father "was an illustrious man whom Viceroys and Governors honored and entrusted with public office," and his father's sons were people of rectitude and good repute. As Moya de Contreras investigated this accusation, he also looked for missing documents from the Inquisition archive relating to the auto de fé of October 1528. The family of Miguel López de Legazpi were asked to search their personal papers for any stray Inquisition documents which might have been filed there when their illustrious relative was secretary of the Holy Office in the 1530's.[36] It soon became obvious that the Gonzalo Gómez papers had lain for over three decades in the family archive of Zumárraga's Inquisition secretary and Notary Martín de Campos. Campos' son and the son of the Inquisition Constable Pedro de Mendinilla had sold some of the papers to Juan Suárez de Avila.[37] Suárez de Avila bought part of the original proceso of his father, Juan de Avila, who had been tried as a blasphemer in 1541.[38] Among the other papers was an official order written by Zumárraga for the arrest of Gonzalo Gómez on June 1, 1537. Suárez de Avila paid "twenty pesos and a white horse" for the papers.

Juan de Jaso testified that in 1568 he had had an argument with Antonio Gómez over a business matter, and he had told his neighbor Juan Suárez about the controversy one day in the latter's orchards in Chapultepec. Juan Suárez, who also was annoyed with Gómez, "showed" Jaso the Zumárraga document. Jaso had made a copy of the writ for his own use. Apparently there was considerable gossip about the Gómez family as this document made the rounds of Mexican society. Juan Gómez tried to buy it in order to retire it from circulation, but he also counterattacked the Suárez de Avila family by denouncing their father as a man "of suspicious cast, recently converted from Mohammedanism." Juan Gómez offered to name witnesses to substantiate his denunciation, saying that Suárez' ancestry was well known in Mexico. By April 17, 1572 the Gómez family was really annoyed when it became known that Juan Suárez de Avila had sent to Sevilla for the sanbenito which he claimed Gonzalo Gómez had worn as a reconciled heretic. Juan Gómez again protested the defamation of his father's character by the Suárez family. Soon after this last appearance of Juan Gómez before the tribunal the controversy between the two families subsided, probably because Inquisition Notary Pedro de los Ríos tired of the bickering and the tribunal of the Holy Office lost interest in the matter.

Notes

[1] The most scholarly account of the first decade of the Michoacán Province is the soon-to-be-published thesis of F. Benedict Warren, "The Conquest of Michoacán, 1521-1530" (Master of Arts Thesis, Department of History, University of New Mexico, Albuquerque, 1960). Also very valuable are F. Benedict Warren's *Vasco de Quiroga and his Pueblo-Hospitals of Santa Fé* (Washington, 1963) and "The Carvajal Visitation: First Spanish Survey of Michoacán,'" *The Americas: A Quarterly Journal of Inter-American Cultural History* (1963), Vol. XIX, pp. 404-412.

[2] Millares Carlo and Mantecón, Vol. I, *passim*.

[3] See AGN, Inquisición, Tomo 1, exps. 7, 10d, and Chapter One, *supra*, pp. 15-18.

[4] Scholes and Adams, *Proceso contra Tzintzicha Tangaxoan;* Warren, *Vasco de Quiroga*, pp. 78-79.

[5] The trial is found in AGN, Inquisición, Tomo 2, exp. 2, ff. 33-178.

[6] On August 27, 1540 Gómez testified that he was over fifty years old. AGI, Justicia, Leg. 130, ff. 1472-1475.

[7] Icaza, Vol. II, pp. 201.

[8] Lesley B. Simpson, *The Encomienda in New Spain* (Berkeley, 1950), pp. 44-47, sheds some light on Zuazo's activities during this period.

[9] AGN, Inquisición, Tomo 89, exp. 38, f. 4.

[10] AGI, Patronato, Leg. 60, exp. 2, ramo 3. This chronology could well mean that Gómez was Cortés' alcalde mayor in Michoacán before 1528, or that he served in that capacity under a patent from Alonso de Estrada during 1528-1529. Warren, *Vasco de Quiroga*, p. 78, indicates that Antonio de Godoy took authority from December 1528 to May 1529.

[11] AGI, Justicia, Leg. 130, ff. 1494-1495v.

[12] Warren, *Vasco de Quiroga*, pp. 79-81, reviews these events.

[13] AGI, Justicia, Leg. 173, exp. 1, ramo 3.

[14] *Ibid.*, Leg. 130, ff. 1494-1495v.

[15] Scholes and Adams, *Relación de las Encomiendas*, pp. 33-34.

[16] AGI, Justicia, Leg. 130, ff. 1494-1495v. This site (Ytacaro), it was charged, had been occupied by Gómez when it really belonged to the city of Michoacán.

[17] Icaza, Vol. I, p. 132. See also Francisco del Paso y Troncoso, *Papeles de la Nueva España* (México, 1905), Vol. I, p. 132. See also AGI, Justicia, Leg. 130, f. 1495, for Gómez' testimony that Estrada had confirmed his title to Ytacaro four years before, or in 1528.

[18] Warren, *Vasco de Quiroga*, p. 76.

INQUISITION IN MICHOACAN 73

[19] Cf. AGI, Justicia, Leg. 130, f. 969v. and Manuel Toussaint's faulty copy of the 1528 record in his *Pátzcuaro* (México, 1952), p. 223-24.

[20] Blas Brazil, "A History of the Obrajes in New Spain, 1535-1630" (unpublished Master of Arts Thesis, Department of History, University of New Mexico, Albuquerque, 1962), p. 18.

[21] Some of his business activities are alluded to in a ramo of Michoacán letters of 1533-1534 in AGI, Justicia, Leg. 138, ff. 83v.-112v.

[22] The cédula and order to the corregidor are bound into the proceso, AGN, Inquisición, Tomo 2, exp. 2.

[23] *Ibid.*, Tomo 89, exp. 38.

[24] *Ibid.*, Tomo 72. The children of Gómez were being blackmailed by the child of an Inquisition notary who had access to the records in 1537.

[25] For prevailing attitudes on conversion and baptism of the Indian population in New Spain of this era, see Greenleaf, *Zumárraga*, pp. 33-37, 46-50.

[26] See Warren, *Vasco Quiroga*, pp. 60-63, 88-90, *passim*, for the most complete data available on Juan Infante.

[27] AGN, Inquisición, Tomo 38, exp. 1. Franco may have been a Judiazante. The trial recorded that he had Jewish dietary habits and was circumcised.

[28] *Ibid.*, Tomo 14, exp. 3.

[29] *Ibid.*, Tomo 1, exp. 10f.

[30] *Ibid.*, Tomo 40, exp. 6.

[31] *Ibid.*, Tomo 30, exp. 9a.

[32] Greenleaf, *Zumárraga*, pp. 89-99.

[33] Richard E. Greenleaf, "Francisco de Millán Before the Mexican Inquisition, 1538-1539," *The Americas: A Quarterly Review of Inter-American Cultural History* (1964), Vol. XXI, pp. 184-195.

[34] Gómez testified in a lawsuit in Michoacán in 1553, AGI, Patronato, Leg. 60, exp. 2, ramo 3. By 1564 he was listed as deceased: Scholes and Adams, *Relación de las Encomiendas*, pp. 33-34.

[35] AGN, Inquisición, Tomo 72, exp. 29.

[36] *Ibid.*, exp. 32.

[37] Juan Suárez de Peralta, *Noticias Históricas de la Nueva España* (México, 1949), p. xii.

[38] See the fragmented document in AGN, Inquisición, Tomo 14, exp. 39.

Chapter Three

THE EPISCOPAL INQUISITION IN MEXICO
1535-1571

AFTER THE Franciscan bishop of Mexico, Juan de Zumárraga, returned from a trip to Spain (July 1532 to October 1534), where he was formally consecrated in the Franciscan Monastery at Valladolid on April 27, 1533, he began to sign Inquisition trials as ecclesiastical judge ordinary.[1] In order to strengthen his mission as the guardian of orthodoxy, the crown and the Council of the Supreme Inquisition in Spain gave Zumárraga the title of apostolic inquisitor on June 27, 1535, a position which he held until his powers were revoked in 1543. The portfolio as apostolic inquisitor gave Zumárraga no special faculty that was not already inherent in his position as ordinary, and he continued in the capacity of ordinary until his death in June of 1548.

In a previous study, the workings of Zumárraga's Inquisition, 1536 to 1543, have been examined in detail—especially the ways in which the Holy Office of the Inquisition reflected the Mexican intellectual climate of the Renaissance and the Counter Reformation.[2] Perhaps the most important question faced by the Mexican Inquisition was how to treat the Indian in the decades after the conquest. Zumárraga was convinced that his Holy Office needed to discipline Indian idolaters and sorcerers, and he proceeded to try some nineteen Indian heretics during his ministry. The famous trial of the Indian leader and cacique of Texcoco, Don Carlos Chichimecatecuhtli, in 1539 ended with his execution and burning because Zumárraga judged him guilty of undermining the Spanish Church and Spanish political power in Mexico. Because royal officialdom felt that Zumárraga had acted too harshly in remanding Don Carlos to the secular authority for burning, he was reprimanded for his excess zeal and his title of apostolic inquisitor was taken away in 1543.[3]

I

The Indian Inquisition of Tello de Sandoval, 1544-1547

When Charles V and the Council of the Indies determined to submit the viceroyalty of New Spain to a thorough visitation in the era 1544-1547, the decision to make the Visitor Licenciado Francisco Tello de Sandoval apostolic inquisitor of the entire viceregal area was announced. Tello de Sandoval was a member of the Council of the Indies and an experienced ecclesiastical administrator who had served as apostolic inquisitor for the archbishopric of Toledo.[4] Because of the complexity and the burden of the general visitation to the viceregal government, Tello had scant time for the Mexican Inquisition during his stay in the colony. He arrived on February 12, 1544 and departed in early 1547. It is apparent that Tello de Sandoval and his apostolic notary, Luis Guerrero, made use of existing Inquisition machinery in Zumárraga's see and in the provincial episcopates, and it is evident that he proceeded with extreme caution lest he inherit the charges of overzealousness leveled against Bishop Zumárraga. During Tello's inquisitorial ministry there occurred at least fourteen investigations of heresy and proscribed conduct, usually routine matters of bigamy and blasphemy.[5] In the main the apostolic inquisitor reviewed data submitted to him from the various ordinaries, and only rarely did he initiate cases on his own.

Apostolic Inquisitor Tello de Sandoval did inherit from Zumárraga the controversial and perplexing problem of how to deal with Indians who had relapsed into paganism. Overcautiousness led to inarticulate policies, and actions, in Tello's Indian Inquisition. On October 14, 1544, Pedro Gómez de Maraver, dean of the Cathedral of Oaxaca and Bishop Zárate's visitor of the bishopric of Oaxaca, presented Apostolic Inquisitor Tello de Sandoval with a report of his probe into Indian paganism in the Yanhuitlán area. In Tilantongo, Gómez de Maraver had begun to gather testimonies from the caciques and nobles of Tilantongo, Nochistlán, Teposcolula, Etlantongo and others regarding the behavior of three important personages of Yanhuitlán: Don Domingo, the cacique; Don Francisco, the governor; and Don Juan (Xual), a noble of the town. The informants told Maraver that the cacique and nobles of Yanhuitlán regularly performed idolatry and made sacrifices, including human ones. They offered sacrifices of their own blood and hair, and of birds and slaves. Drunkenness during the ceremonies, when they invoked the Devil and while they sacrificed, intensified the cruelties perpetrated on the slaves. Ceremonies connected with the corn harvest and droughts, when they propitiated the rain god, were held in caves in the mountains of the Suchitepeque region, according to Maraver's informants. Maraver told Tello de Sandoval that his evidence showed that human sacrifices of Christianized Indians had been made by the Yanhuitlán nobles. They laughed at the neighboring villagers and ridiculed them for practicing Christianity. Maraver said such circumstances were a bad example for the entire Mixtec region.[6]

In December 1544 Reverend Pedro de Olmos, a priest for the Oaxaca City environs, gave a disturbing report of idolatry and sacrifice among the caciques of Coatlán, a village two days' travel from the capital. He related stories of sacrifices of slaves similar to the Yanhuitlán tales, and he told of a sacrificial site he had visited on the road between Coatlán and Tutupeque. There he found a large stone idol covered with blood, and in the mouth of the idol was a human heart freshly extracted from the body of a child who had been sacrificed just prior to his visit. He also reported that there were some sixteen human heads lying around the shrine, and many sacrificial instruments. Scandalized by this report, Tello de Sandoval ordered a formal investigation of the Coatlán natives and charged Fiscal Cristóbal de Lugo to jail the guilty.[7] Of course such an order was more easily framed than executed.

On December 2, 1544 Pedro Gómez de Maraver appeared before the Tello de Sandoval Inquisition, and Secretary Miguel López de Legazpi took his personal testimony about paganism in the *cacicazgo* of Yanhuitlán. Maraver presented extensive testimonies from natives taken in the course of his tour of the area. As a result of this hearing, Tello de Sandoval ordered the arrest of Don Francisco and Don Domingo of Yanhuitlán on January 30, 1545, and the next day he commissioned Maraver to return to the field and to gather more evidence.[8]

Don Francisco, the governor of Yanhuitlán, was the first Indian tried by the Tello de Sandoval Inquisition. After three admonitions to tell the truth and avoid harsh punishment, Fiscal Cristóbal de Benavente made formal indictment of Don Francisco on April 15, 1545. During the months of April to October 1545 Licenciado Francisco Téllez did his best to defend Don Francisco. In July 1545, in a letter framed for him by Licenciado Téllez, Don Francisco denied the charges against him and pled that his enemies were taking revenge on an old man. He was seventy-five years of age. But during October 1545 the prosecution produced damaging testimony against the governor. Witnesses swore that he had undressed and painted his body like a tiger, saying, "Now I am not a Christian," and that he had proceeded to practice idolatry and to make sacrifices. The witnesses said he drew blood from his own ears for the sacrificial act.

In April 1546 Don Francisco was still in jail in Mexico City and the Inquisition record states that he was ill. During November he pled with the Tello de Sandoval tribunal to bring a speedy termination to his case. Obviously Apostolic Inquisitor Tello de Sandoval was in a delicate position. Not wishing to bear the kind of criticism Zumárraga had gained in the Don Carlos case, Tello de Sandoval submitted the records to a committee, on which Bishop Zumárraga served, on November 20, 1546. The committee recommended, unanimously, an action to be taken. The trial record does not specify what the recommendation was.[9]

One month after Tello de Sandoval began the trial of Don Francisco, he initiated proceedings against Don Domingo, the cacique of Yanhuitlán, in May of 1545. The format of the trial was essentially the same. After three admonitions to tell the truth and thereby avoid possible judicial torture, Don Domingo was formally charged by the fiscal. He disclaimed ever having performed, or having witnessed, sacrifices of the type in the accusation. On November 3, 1545 his attorney, Licenciado Téllez, charged that the prosecution had offered no proof of his client's guilt and that the witnesses from Nochistlán, Etlantongo and Tilantongo had perjured themselves when they accused Don Domingo of idolatry and sacrifices. On November 18, 1545 Tello de Sandoval convoked a committee under his aegis to decide future moves in the prosecution of the cacique of Yanhuitlán. Bishop Zumárraga, Tello de Sandoval, the oidores of the audiencia and a group of prominent Franciscans and Dominicans agreed that Don Domingo as well as Don Francisco and Don Juan should be kept in custody pending further investigations at the alleged sites of the idolatries and sacrifices. On March 16, 1546 the provisor of the Mexican bishopric, Alonso de Aldama, was empowered to proceed with the investigations.[10] The former Inquisition secretary during Zumárraga's ministry, Martín de Campos, was employed to assist the provisor.

By April 1546, Provisor Aldama and Secretary Campos were in Oaxaca gathering additional evidence.[11] They interviewed clergy in the areas where Maraver's witnesses had indicated that idolatry and human sacrifices were made. A long list of witnesses was drawn up. Fray Bernardo de Santa María, vicar of the Monastery of Teposcolula, substantiated evidence that sacrifices had been made —largely, he said, because of the rampant drought and famine. Stories of the human sacrifices of young boys in the Yanhuitlán area were validated.[12] Informants told Aldama and Campos that the Indians, including Don Juan of Yanhuitlán, made human sacrifices and ate the victims on a mountain near Cuaxtepec. Some witnesses sought to place the blame for Yanhuitlán paganism on the encomendero, Francisco de las Casas, for his laxness in instructing the Indians in the tenets of Christianity and his permissive attitude vis-a-vis idolatry and sacrifice.

On December 4, 1546 Inquisitor Tello de Sandoval had a final audience with Don Domingo who was still in jail in Mexico City. The cacique refused to admit guilt or to modify his testimonies. On December 7, 1546 Tello de Sandoval allowed Don Domingo to go free on bail. The bail of two thousand pesos was paid by the Las Casas family with Domingo de las Casas and Licenciado Vicencio de Riverol as guarantors and guardians of the cacique. The Tello de Sandoval inquiries into human sacrifice and cannibalism among the Indians of Cuaxtepec ended in a stalemate in 1546, although the fiscal accused Don Juan of Yanhuitlán of very specific acts of idolatry, sorcery and human sacrifice at Cuaxtepec.[13]

In the Yanhuitlán, Coatlán and Cuaxtepec investigations, the Tello de Sandoval Inquisition never passed sentence. Masses of testimonies certainly substantiated the prevalence of paganism among the Mixtecs.[14] To what extent there was an Indian conspiracy to involve the caciques of Yanhuitlán in a lengthy trial is an interesting speculation but an imponderable aspect of the investigation. Apparently the de las Casas family was able to influence the inquisitorial proceedings. They may have exerted influence to have the charges against Don Domingo of Yanhuitlán dismissed, after he was released on bail. Tello de Sandoval's natural caution, and perhaps the advice of Bishop Zumárraga, kept him from taking any categorical action in the case. Since the Tello visitation of New Spain was drawing to a close in December 1546 and Tello was scheduled to leave within a matter of weeks in early 1547, he probably felt disposed to allow the bishop of Oaxaca to take jurisdiction as ordinary. Perhaps the Oaxaca bishop was unwilling to punish the caciques if there was any possibility that the furor over Indians before the Holy Office would result in criticism similar to that of the Carlos of Texcoco case.

After the investigations of idolatry and sacrifice in the Mixteca, Inquisitor Tello de Sandoval became interested in paganism and religious syncretism in the wider context. He read a report directed to him on October 12, 1545 by Gerónimo Flores, the corregidor of Izucar (de Matamoros). The corregidor informed that he had arrested an Indian for sorcery and idolatry and had subjected him to judicial torture. The culprit, Tomás Tunalt, had been an itinerant sorcerer and *curandero* (healer). He sacrificed food, plumes and animals in caves of the region and carried his paraphernalia in a small bundle which he stored in chapels of ranches in the Izucar area.[15] There is no record that Tello de Sandoval ordered Corregidor Flores to continue the prosecution of Tunalt.

In the accusation against Don Juan, cacique of Teutalco, Inquisitor Tello conducted the proceedings personally. On December 10, 1546 Tello heard evidence from Indian informants that Don Juan had ordered sacrificial ceremonies to the rain god in order to alleviate the drought in his cacicazgo. The ceremonies took place on a mountain called Tonaltepeque. Several witnesses testified that Don Juan kept an idol called Ometochtli (the god of wine) in his home and he regularly offered sacrifices to the god, getting drunk and dancing as part of the ceremonies. Servants of Don Juan's household confirmed these things and more. It appeared as though the cacique went out of his way to offer a bad example of conduct to his subjects. He refused to go to confession and he ate meat on Fridays and during Lent. He made his servants work on Sundays. When Miguel López de Legazpi, Fray Pedro de Molina and Tello de Sandoval questioned Don Juan in Mexico City, his knowledge of basic Catholicism was very fuzzy. However, Don Juan denied the charges of idolatry and sacrifice and challenged the judges to offer more proof.

The trial of the cacique of Teutalco was concluded on March 11, 1547 without any judgment as to his guilt or innocence. From the fiscal's accusations and recommended punishments, one assumes that Don Juan paid a stiff fine, but the record does not specify the amount.[16] It is noteworthy that the cacique's trial was the last action of Licenciado Francisco Tello de Sandoval as apostolic inquisitor.

After March 1547 the inquisitorial function in New Spain reverted to the bishops as ordinaries or, in the absence of bishops,

THE EPISCOPAL INQUISITION 81

to monastic prelates in the provinces. A proceso of May 26, 1547 seems to indicate that the apostolic inquisitor had left Mexico. On that day the vicar of the mines of Zumpango, Reverend Rodrigo de Gallegos, tried Don Pablo Tecatecle, a noble of Zumpango, for practicing idolatry and making sacrifices to the Devil "according to the ancient rites." Testimony from Indians of the area showed that Tecatecle was the leader of a group of elderly sorcerers who had given advice to nobles of the community on how to unseat the incumbent cacique. Apparently they had invoked the demons and had proceeded to cast spells. It was not until November 1547 that Don Pablo Tecatecle was released from jail after he had paid a fine of fifty gold pesos and had received a stern warning about his future conduct.[17] The only other Inquisition trial involving Indians during the next decade came in 1557 when the Holy Office tried Tomás and María of Tecoaloya for concubinage.[18]

II

The Holy Office and Protestantism, 1543-1569

During the decades after the departure of Tello de Sandoval, and before the establishment of a formal tribunal of the Holy Office in Mexico in 1571, the ordinaries turned attention away from problems of Indian orthodoxy and focused attention on colonists and foreigners who appeared to echo Protestant ideas. The prevalence of nonpeninsular subjects of Charles V in Mexico during 1526 to 1549 led the apostolic inquisitors Zumárraga and Tello de Sandoval to examine orthodoxy in the colony within a Counter Reformation framework.[19] It is probable that many pseudo-Protestants lived in Mexico during the first fifty years of the colony, just as there were also many crypto-Jews. Zumárraga tried five people for Protestantism during his ministry, and Tello de Sandoval found it necessary to discipline Juan de Bezos and Alonso Pérez Tamayo, a bailiff, for blasphemy verging on heresy.[20] Apostolic Inquisitor Tello began to punish eroding orthodoxy among the clergy when he investigated the sermons of a French friar in Zapotlán, Fray Arnoldo de Basancio, who had criticized the sale of bulls of the holy crusade in a manner similar to Martin Luther's objections to the sale of indulgences.[21]

The bishops of the viceroyalty of New Spain and the monastic prelates had a difficult time combatting new religious ideas which came to be lumped under the generic term *luterano* (Lutheran). The word "Lutheran" came to have a very broad meaning in the vocabulary of the clergy and often was applied to actions and beliefs which had nothing to do with Lutheranism or Protestantism. It seemed as though the word foreigner *(extranjero)* became a synonym for Protestant, and Catholic foreigners in Mexico were usually suspect. Mystics, liberal clergy and many orthodox dissenters fell prey to the Counter Reformation mentality of the hierarchy clergy in New Spain. The raids of corsairs in the islands of the Caribbean and along the coasts of Veracruz and Yucatán intensified the zeal of the ordinaries to stamp out Protestantism. In the early 1560's before the bishopric of Yucatán was established, the Franciscan prelates had a busy time investigating the orthodoxy of French corsairs who were captured there.[22]

Alonso de Montúfar had succeeded Zumárraga in 1554 as the second archbishop of Mexico after the latter's death in 1548. Montúfar exercised the office of inquisitor ordinary without any specific delegation of authority from the crown or the Council of the Supreme Inquisition. Montúfar, as archbishop and in his portfolio as ordinary, undertook to prevent the incursion of Protestant ideas in his see as well as throughout the viceroyalty of New Spain.[23] He encouraged his subordinate bishops to refer foreign heretics to the Mexican capital if it was at all feasible to do so. As archepiscopal mentor of the entire hierarchy in Mexico, Montúfar was able to extend his influence in Inquisition matters far beyond his own jurisdiction as ordinary of Mexico, and he assumed supervision of the Counter Reformation prosecutions from Zacatecas to Honduras during the years 1558 to 1569. In the area of his direct jurisdiction Montúfar and his provisors set the example for the provincial bishops to follow.

THE EPISCOPAL INQUISITION 83

In September 1558 Cristóbal de Toledo, attorney of the archepiscopal see, started a formal denunciation of a heretic before Montúfar's ordinary Inquisition. The accused, a Portuguese merchant named Simón Falcón, was already in the Inquisition jail.[24] Toledo demanded severe penalties for Falcón whom he characterized as a blasphemer and a heretic. According to testimony gathered by the Montúfar court, Simón Falcón had a dangerous relativistic view of comparative religion and he had maintained that Judaism and Mosaic law or Mohammedanism and Allah presented the individual with just as valid a route to salvation as Roman Catholicism. Falcón's theories about Judgment Day made Montúfar brand him a heretic. Falcón said that when the Last Judgment came, animals, birds and fish would be resurrected and corporally restored.

On September 20, 1558 Montúfar called Simón from his cell to testify. The merchant affirmed that he was thirty-seven years old and that he had been born in Braga, Portugal, of parents who were old Christians. They were dead, but they had been buried with the last rites of the Church and in hallowed ground. Falcón was married to Ana Méndez, a native of the Madeira Islands, but his wife had remained in Spain while he came to the New World to make his fortune. He told the inquisitors he had hopes of returning to Spain to be reunited with her, and only recently he had sold his store in Mexico City for some three thousand and three hundred pesos so that he could make the trip. He professed to be a practicing Catholic who had gone to confession as often as required. His last communion was taken in Ixmiquilpan. He gave a statement of his properties and accounts receivable as well as due. He denied any knowledge of personal wrongdoing or that he had blasphemed or committed heresy.

Fiscal Cristóbal de Toledo then made specific accusation of Simón Falcón as a heretic. Toledo began with an incident some five years previously when Falcón disputed a sermon given in the Monastery of Santo Domingo on a feast day of obligation. At that time witnesses heard him expound his views of the validity of Mohammedanism and the Law of Moses as a path to salvation.

It was during this same conversation that Simón Falcón had made his controversial statements about the Last Judgment. Other witnesses substantiated that Falcón had not altered his views from that day to the present.

Immediately, Falcón hired a defense lawyer and answered Fiscal Toledo's brief at length. Falcón charged that no reliable evidence pointed to his being a heretic or a blasphemer, and that investigation would confirm his character as an orthodox Catholic. He accused the fiscal of having gathered testimonies from hostile witnesses, from men who were his enemies in the business world. Falcón singled out the persons who had given Toledo his data—one Jorge Mendoza, a teacher who was one of Falcón's debtors; a merchant named Juan de Toro who had assumed Mendoza's debt to Simón Falcón and bore him animosity because he had been unable to collect; and a youngster named Antonio, said to be Falcón's nephew. Falcón said Antonio hated him because he threw Antonio's concubine out of his house and because he had told Antonio that he was not a nephew at all but the son of a prostitute. Antonio had threatened his "uncle," swearing vengeance against him. Falcón and his lawyer, Licenciado Pereira, demanded that these witnesses be challenged with a set of questions which would show their biases and their hate of the accused.

The fiscal proceeded with an interrogatory which tried to establish whether Simón Falcón had committed the heresy of which he was charged, and whether he came from Jewish or Moorish lineage. Jorge de Mendoza testified that on September 27, 1558 he had made the denunciation against Simón Falcón and that he would repeat it if the Inquisition so required. Antonio Gómez Falcón, the nephew, reaffirmed charges against his uncle and agreed to reiterate his uncle's blasphemies and heresies. The defense attorney sought to establish his client's good character and to uncover the hatred borne him by the nephew and Jorge de Mendoza. Pereira also used his questions to point to the illness of Simón Falcón—he was chronically asthmatic and was using his money to effect a cure for his condition. Alonso Pérez and Domingo Hernández, merchants of substance in the Mexico City community, testified on Simón Falcón's behalf. Both men supported Simón Falcón as an honest, upright, Christian citizen. They were both aware of the nephew's hatred and Jorge de Mendoza's animosity toward Simón Falcón. They confirmed that Falcón and Mendoza were not speaking to one another and that Mendoza was a very emotional person. As Falcón insisted in his second brief before Montúfar, neither Antonio Falcón nor Jorge de Mendoza were reliable witnesses. Falcón said that it was obvious that his nephew hoped to inherit his property by denouncing him to the Inquisition.

Apparently Montúfar was faced with a difficult decision. He neither trusted Antonio Falcón and Mendoza nor did he believe completely in Simón Falcón's innocence. The accused pled for a speedy end to the case, because of the delicate state of his health and the unhealthy conditions in the jail. He begged Montúfar for mercy and a suitable penance if the case went against him. The archbishop was lenient. He commanded Simón Falcón to walk on three successive Fridays to the Church of Our Lady of Guadalupe and to pay for mass to be said, each time, for all the souls in purgatory. Falcón himself was to repeat the seven penitential psalms and to pay a fine of six pesos de oro to be used for charity and the costs of the trial. Montúfar required Simón Falcón to make public abjuration of the things he was accused of saying, and he was warned not to stray from the teachings of the Church lest he be punished severely.

The most famous trial of an Englishman by the Mexican Inquisition was Montúfar's prosecution of Robert Tomson who had come to Mexico in 1555. Tomson became an aide to Gonzalo de Cerezo, the alcalde mayor de Corte in the viceregal government, whom he had met through the introduction of a Scotsman, Thomas Blake, a resident of Mexico City. On September 9, 1559 Robert Tomson was arrested by the Holy Office of the Inquisition because he was not a practicing Catholic. At the end of the trial in March 1560, Tomson was reconciled by the Montúfar Inquisition as a Lutheran heretic.[25] G. R. G. Conway has published the proceedings along with Tomson's own reminiscences of his life in Mexico which he entitled "The Voyage of Robert Thomson Marchant, into Nova Hispania in the yeere 1555."[26] A page in Cerezo's household denounced Tomson to the Holy Office for spreading English views on the mediation of saints, the veneration of images and the Anglican Church's reforms of the clergy. When Montúfar's provisor interrogated Tomson he admitted some of the things which Cerezo's servants reported he had said, but he maintained he had partaken of the sacraments of the Roman Catholic Church—confession, the Eucharist, mass—as a loyal Catholic should. At any rate Montúfar's Inquisition convicted him and he was punished in the auto de fé of March 17, 1560.

In later years Robert Tomson described the ceremony in the Cathedral of Mexico. He and a companion, Agustín Boacio, wore penitential garb (the sanbenito and the *coroza*) and they went through the formal procedures of abjuration and reconciliation while thousands of people watched, folk who had no idea of what Lutheranism was. Tomson was sentenced to exile in Spain where he was to be incarcerated by the Holy Office in Sevilla for one year, and he was to wear the sanbenito for three years. When he fulfilled the sentence, he was set free. He later married a Spanish heiress, whose money had come from the mines of Mexico, and they lived in Málaga.

The trial of Agustín Boacio during the years 1558 to 1560 for Lutheranism has been obscured owing to the amount of notoriety given the Tomson prosecution. But from the point of view of Mexican intellectual *ambiente* and Inquisition procedure the Boacio trial merits more attention, for from the proceso one can study the operation of the Holy Office on the northern frontier of the viceroyalty.[27] On May 7, 1558 in the city of Zacatecas, Juan Bautista de Lomas, curate and vicar of the mines of the area, began the trial of Agustín Boacio, a merchant and shopkeeper from Genoa, Italy, who was pictured as a proselytizer of Lutheran heresies. The denunciation began with a report of remarks Boacio had made in the orchards of Diego de Ibarra. He had claimed that there was no scriptural basis for the concept of Purgatory, especially since Christ had already died to redeem mankind from sin.

Boacio claimed that no two souls were identical and that it was impossible for a soul to inherit blemishes or to be dirtied by the sins of others. Obviously these statements not only denied the existence of Purgatory and its function in helping man on the road to salvation, but they also called into question the doctrine of original sin.

By August 11, 1558 Curate Juan de Lomas was gathering testimony from acquaintances of the accused. On that same day, Alonso de Ayala deepened the suspicions of Boacio's Lutheranism. Ayala had known Agustín Boacio and his younger brother in business and from friendly conversations. The younger brother never discussed religion, but Agustín had definite views on the Roman Catholic Church and its sacramental system. He had urged Ayala to read a book in Tuscan which the latter perused in a cursory manner. Ayala informed him that it contained heresy. Boacio had told Ayala that it seemed wrong to him for the Church to spend money on buildings and ornaments if God loved apostolic poverty, and he felt that priests ought to marry. Ayala reported to Juan de Lomas that Boacio had not gone to confession and had not obeyed the precept of abstinence on Fridays while he lived in Zacatecas. Boacio had ridiculed the practice of making pilgrimages to shrines in and around the mines. When it came to his personal views about confession, Ayala told the curate that Agustín Boacio said it was never necessary to tell one's sins to another man. One should confess only to God.

Prefatory to any action in the Boacio case, Curate Lomas called additional witnesses on August 12, 1558. Gaspar Pinto gave damaging evidence. Although he had known the brothers Boacio for over six months, he had never heard the younger brother say anything about religion. But Pinto and Agustín Boacio had talked at length. One day in the doorway of Pinto's home Boacio had said that the Roman papacy was a corrupt, sinful, scornful place. He laughed at the ridiculousness of the sale of indulgences and he questioned the power of the Pope to command obedience from men or to pardon their sins. Boacio had said there was no religious value to the mass and that one ought to confess his sins only to

God rather than to intermediaries. He characterized expenditures for Church ornaments as wasteful.

Pinto, scandalized by these statements, told Agustín Boacio, "I believe in God and the Holy Mother Church." Boacio replied that he was also "a believer." Although Pinto had seen Boacio take communion during the Jubilate, he told the Zacatecas curate that he did not believe that Agustín was "a Christian." Instead he branded him as "a Lutheran." To document his accusation, Pinto related that Boacio kept his shop open for business on Sundays and feast days, saying that he must put his family before God. Boacio told Pinto, "You ought to be converted to my faith."

After Juan de Lomas consulted the Alcalde Mayor of Zacatecas, Juan de Villagómez, about the evidence against Agustín Boacio on August 12, 1558, they both went to Boacio's home to place him under arrest and to embargo his property. He was placed, shackled, in the Zacatecas *juzgado*. On that same day Curate Lomas put Boacio under oath and began the first of many Inquisition interrogations that were to last for over two years. Boacio affirmed that he was twenty-eight years old, and that he had been born in Genoa of Christian parents. He had left Genoa for Spain some fourteen years before, and in Cádiz he had wed Gerónima Enríquez. He had come to New Spain and north to Zacatecas one year previously, on the same fleet with a Sr. Mariaca who lived in Zacatecas and Juan Serrano, a Mexico City cobbler. The questioning revealed that the heretical book to which Ayala had referred was a work dealing with Savonarola. Boacio claimed to have purchased the book from a Moorish sailor since the text was in Tuscan, the native dialect of Genoa. The defendant had read the book and he told Lomas he saw nothing evil in it. He hastened to add that if there was anything wrong in what he had done, he would gladly repent and ask for mercy.

When Lomas asked Agustín Boacio whether he had discussed this book, or other things having to do with religion, with anyone in Zacatecas or elsewhere, Boacio related that two years ago in Cádiz he had met a gentleman from Mantua who had resided in England. The Mantuan told him about Lutheranism in Great

Britain, how they had justly removed images from the churches, and how friaries had been suppressed. He had learned about mental confession as opposed to Catholic confession and many other Lutheran doctrines from his Italian friend. Boacio said the Mantuan spoke so elegantly, and so saintly, that what he said had the ring of truth about it. These conversations took place long before he acquired the Savonarola book.

Agustín Boacio admitted that he had discussed the ideas of the gentleman from Mantua with his friends in Zacatecas—Alonso de Ayala, Gaspar Pinto, Manuel Carvallo and others. Among the items they talked about were the following: confession should be a personal, mental contact between the individual and his God; denial of the existence of Purgatory; the Pope has no power to excommunicate or to absolve persons who have sinned; the invocation of saints is an untenable theological proposition. Boacio reassured the curate that he was willing to do penance for having discussed any of these matters. He claimed to be a devout Catholic who had received communion and who was known as a practicing Catholic by the clergy of the Zacatecas region. It was assumed that even though Boacio agreed with the ideas of the Italian Protestant, he partook of the sacraments of the Roman Catholic Church because of public pressure and fear of censure if he had failed to do so. Boacio had spoken too freely to substantiate his view that he was nothing more than a man who liked to argue about religion. For instance he had said to several witnesses that people who lived and died within the Lutheran faith would achieve salvation.

On the day of Boacio's testimony the curate allowed Alonso de Ayala, the chief witness against Boacio, to deposit two thousand pesos de oro in escrow to guarantee the property of Boacio—his store and his dwelling place which Ayala hoped to sequester. Since Agustín's brother was silent and never heard from in the Inquisition trials, and since all witnesses made a point to absolve him of any heresy, one wonders if Ayala and Boacio the younger were not in some kind of collusion. Certainly there is no evidence to warrant such a conclusion, but it is an interesting speculation.

On August 13, 1558 Nicolás Lozano, Agustín Boacio's attorney, tried to save the day by way of a cleverly worded plea. Lozano pictured his client as an honest but argumentative man who liked to talk about religion—a latter-day Socrates who actually strengthened people's beliefs by asking questions. Lozano said no reliable evidence had been presented that proved Boacio to be a heretic. He requested Lomas to set his client free because of lack of proof and he informed the judge that if any doubt remained regarding Boacio's sincerity, his client would gladly do any penance prescribed. Attorney Lozano failed to convince the court that Boacio was a sincere man, and on August 13, 1558 in a final session of his court, Curate Juan de Lomas indicted Agustín Boacio as a heretic. It was ordered that Boacio be sent to Guadalajara where the dean of the Cathedral, who was acting as ordinary since the Guadalajara See was vacant, would engage in the formal prosecution of Boacio as a Lutheran heretic.

During the fall of 1558 to March of 1559, Agustín Boacio languished in the jail of the bishopric of Guadalajara while the dean, Don Bartolomé de Rivera, reexamined the evidence. Finally, in March of 1559, Boacio was sentenced.[28] Royal Scribe Francisco de Robertanillo described the trial procedures in Guadalajara. After repetitive testimonies, the dean decided to reconcile Boacio if, "with a clean heart and without any deception," he agreed to abjure point by point the Lutheran heresies of which he had been accused. After so many months in jail, Agustín Boacio was more than willing to submit to the abjuration ceremony, and he freely accepted the dean's warning that any future relapse into error would mean death by burning at the stake. After the abjuration the dean sentenced Boacio to a fine of sixty pesos de oro and to banishment from New Spain. He was to be incarcerated in the archepiscopal jail in Mexico City until Montúfar could arrange his passage to Spain. There he was warned to lead an exemplary life, reunited with his wife, if he wished to avoid further punishment.

Agustín Boacio was conducted to Mexico City sometime before October 1559. Presumably, since the prisoner had to pay for his

THE EPISCOPAL INQUISITION 91

room and board in the Montúfar jail (this was a part of the dean's sentence), the provisorate in Mexico City saw no need to rush matters. From October 1559 until March 1560, Boacio was imprisoned in the same jail with Robert Tomson. During this time Montúfar's provisor, Dr. Luis Fernández de Anguis, decided to review the Boacio case and to take additional testimony from the prisoner. It appeared as though Boacio was able to retain a lawyer and that he hoped to be allowed to remain in Mexico. During the seven months of prison and litigation in Mexico City, Agustín Boacio and Robert Tomson became friends and confidants.

On October 6, 1559 Dr. Anguis required Boacio to testify. In skillful questioning the provisor reviewed the Zacatecas and Guadalajara proceedings. Boacio denied that he came from heretic ancestry. Much the same data about Boacio's views on the sacraments and the power of the Pope emerged from Anguis' examination, but the provisor went into considerably more detail on matters which were diagnostic of Lutheranism, especially the question of transubstantiation versus consubstantiation in the Eucharist. In each case he read Boacio the questions put to him by Vicar Juan Bautista de Lomas in Zacatecas and Dean Bartolomé de Rivera in Guadalajara, and he compared the defendant's answers on each point of theology. Then Dr. Anguis gave the prisoner a searching investigation of his knowledge of formal Catholicism. Agustín Boacio could repeat only the Ave María and the Pater Noster. He told the provisor that he knew much more about the articles of the faith, the *Salve* and other things but he could not remember them because he was so perturbed owing to his long incarceration. Boacio further testified that he no longer had any property—that all of his estate had gone for his defense and fines in Zacatecas and Guadalajara, as well as for his living expenses during his imprisonment.

On March 15, 1560 Dr. Anguis and Fiscal Cristóbal de Toledo issued a review sentence in the case of Agustín Boacio. The sentence verified that Boacio had been found guilty of Lutheran heresies and as a result had been deprived of all of his properties as a fine. On the following Sunday, March 16, 1560, Agustín

Boacio was paraded in sanbenito and coroza in the same auto de fé as Robert Tomson. Once again both abjured their heresies in the formal ceremonies in the Cathedral of Mexico. Anguis sentenced Boacio to life imprisonment in Spain with the proviso that he was to wear the sanbenito for the rest of his life. He and Tomson were conducted in chains to San Juan de Ulúa to await shipment to Spain. Fifty pesos de oro were appropriated for Boacio's travel expenses and food during the journey to Spain.

We know from a document in the Inquisition archive that Boacio and Tomson were deported from Veracruz on April 2, 1560.[29] Robert Tomson, in his famous travel account, informed that Agustín Boacio was able to jump ship in the Azores. He was desperately afraid that the Sevillian inquisitors would burn him if he had to disembark in Spain. The Tomson account indicated that Boacio went by caravel to Lisbon and France, and that he finally settled in London where he lived the rest of his life, presumably as a Protestant.

Eleanor B. Adams suspects that the bays and coastal cities of sixteenth-century Central America were the homes and business headquarters of many non-Spanish intruders.[30] Besides French corsairs and English traders, who violated Spain's closed-port system, there were many other Europeans in Guatemala and Honduras. Just as Simón Falcón, Robert Tomson and Agustín Boacio settled in Mexico City and on the northern frontier of New Spain and fell prey to the Holy Inquisition, their compatriots settled on the southern periphery of the viceroyalty, in the general area called the kingdom of Guatemala.

A representative case among the French Protestants before the Central American bishops was that of Nicolás Santour, a young sailor, who was tried between January 1560 and May 1562.[31] It is plain that Santour might never have come before the Holy Office had he not made enemies among the cadre of Frenchmen living in the Trujillo, Honduras, area. It was their denunciations to the episcopal offices, and Santour's own lack of discretion in conversing with others, which led to the Inquisition trial.

On January 10, 1560 Nicolás Santour had his first encounter with the inquisitors, and it appeared as though he had convinced them of his orthodoxy. On that day, after several weeks of secret investigations, the Trujillo Inquisition Fiscal Juan Sánchez interrogated Santour about remarks he had made in the presence of Diego Hernández de Mesa and Francisco de Hoyos. Santour had given his views on the power of the Devil, whose existence he doubted, and his feelings about burying people in hallowed ground *(campo santo)*. Nicolás denied that it was necessary to bury people in any specific cemetery designated by the Church, and he shocked his listeners when he proclaimed that the Cross had no power to counteract the presence of the Devil. The ecclesiastical judge was lenient with Santour since he was able to present evidence of his good family background and he was able to secure proof that he regularly took the sacraments. On January 13, 1560 owing to his statement of contrition about his views, the Holy Office sentenced the prisoner to hear mass while he stood in church with his hands bound and with a gag in his mouth. He was charged to wear a large wooden cross around his neck until his penance was deemed complete.

Fiscal Juan Sánchez continued to amass data on Nicolás Santour during the next year, and Santour moved rather freely around the Honduras area during the interim. Finally in 1561, the attorney ordered the Frenchman to be arrested a second time, and he presented an indictment which pictured Santour as a probable corsair and a Lutheran. Sánchez said that evidence pointed to the fact that Santour had denied the sacraments, especially mass and the priest's power to invoke transubstantiation, and he had attacked the spiritual and temporal power of the Pope. He had said other heretical things about the veneration of saints and their position as mediators between man and God, and he ridiculed prayers for the dead and for souls in purgatory.

Santour was fortunate to have a diocesan priest as a witness on his behalf. Father Francisco de Viezma proclaimed that Nicolás was a good Christian of a noble French family. He said Nicolás had come to him to partake of the sacraments and that he was his confessor. He informed the Holy Office that charges against Santour were based on evidence given by other Frenchmen who bore Santour hatred and ill will. He then related that his parishioner had fulfilled the penance of January 1560 by wearing the wooden cross for over two weeks, and then Nicolás Santour had placed the cross over his bed as a remembrance of the penance.

Despite the intervention of Father Viezma in the Santour case, the fiscal was determined to carry through his prosecution. It should have been obvious to all parties that Fiscal Sánchez had irrefutable proof. During the first of three major interrogations of Santour, much new data on his background emerged. He testified that he was twenty-two years of age, a native of the town of Santour in the duchy of Burgundy, where his father owned the major castle. He denied that he or any member of the family were Lutherans, but he did admit hearing from other French sailors many Lutheran ideas on the sacraments. He claimed that his reading habits were confined to his only book, an edition of Boccaccio's *Decameron,* and he was steadfast in his position that he had never read any suspicious literature of Lutheran taint. Santour explained that in Burgundy all books printed in Geneva had been prohibited since the Lutheran activity there.

Nicolás Santour's imprisonment and trial dragged on through the entire year of 1561, until on December 4 the Holy Office decided to use harsh measures to get at the truth. On that day the provisor and Inquisition judge of the Trujillo Cathedral, Don Alonso Mexía, took his notary and other members of his staff to Santour's cell in the Inquisition jail. At length they reasoned with the young man and gave him the three required admonitions to confess and ask for reconciliation with the Holy Mother Church. Inquisitor Mexía reviewed items of the denunciation against Santour and urged him to clarify or to explain his views. The prisoner refused.

It was then that Mexía and his staff decided to subject Nicolás Santour to judicial torture. He was taken to the torture chamber and ordered to strip himself naked. In order to obtain the confession, Mexía had Santour sit down on the rack and he reasoned with him again. After three admonitions went unheeded, the staff stretched Santour on the rack and began to twist the cords on his arms and legs. Very soon he agreed to confess. While he was still bound on the torture table, Mexía's notary read sections of the denunciations of several people who had given testimony against Santour. The proceso includes depositions by Guillermo Carpintero (Charpantier?) and other compatriots of Santour named Bebandiole "Francés," Juan Gascon and another Guillermo "Francés." The original denunciations of Francisco de Hoyos and Diego Hernández de Mesa were read to the defendant.

Nicolás Santour confessed that he was a French corsair who had participated in raids on Puerto de Caballos and the city of Trujillo, and he admitted the truth of the denunciations against him. He even agreed that the ideas he expounded were Lutheran and heretical. As this testimony was taken down by the scribe, Santour was removed from the rack so that he could affix his signature to the confession.

When Inquisitor Mexía wrote his decision in the Santour case, prefatory to passing sentence, he summarized the Lutheran heresies of the accused. They included his belief that the celebration of mass had no significance; that the Host was nothing more than bread and the priest had no power to change bread and wine into the body and blood of Christ; that the clergy say mass for the purpose of making money; the sacrament of confession was untenable because men ought to confess only to God; pardons, indulgences and dispensations had no validity because they were only clerical devices to gain revenue; the power of the Pope was unfounded; the veneration of images and the mediation of saints were ridiculous concepts.

In addition, Judge Mexía pronounced Santour's views on the Devil and his thoughts on hallowed ground in cemeteries to have been heresy. Before he passed final sentence the inquisitor asked the opinions of the president and the judges of the audiencia de los *confines* (Guatemala) on the culpability of Santour. There was every possibility that Mexía intended to relax him to the secular arm for burning. However, owing to the confession and petition for mercy on the part of Nicolás Santour the inquisitor felt that a less harsh sentence was in order.

In his definitive judgment of May 20, 1562 Provisor Alonso Mexía pronounced Nicolás Santour guilty of Lutheranism. He condemned him to be taken through the streets of Trujillo bound and gagged, and while a town crier proclaimed his guilt he was to be given two hundred lashes. For one year thereafter Santour was to be required to wear penitential garb during the hours when he was not asleep. He was forced to participate in a public ceremony of abjuration of his heresies with the admonition that any relapse into error would mean death at the stake. In addition there were other caveats on Santour's behavior. He went to jail for another forty days; he and his descendants were forbidden to bear arms or to wear silken clothing, jewels or silver; all of his properties were confiscated.

Individual entries in the final pages of the trial record describe the abjuration ceremonies and the punishment and incarceration of the young heretic as well as his formal act of reconciliation with the Holy Church. An interesting postscript to the trial was a document executed in Valladolid, Honduras, by Inquisitor Alonso Mexía on June 25, 1563. On that day it was proclaimed that Nicolás Santour had fulfilled his sentence and that he was free to go wherever he liked and whenever he chose. Apparently the young sailor had convinced his religious superiors of his spiritual regeneration.

Although the Mexican Inquisition records for the first decades of the institution often show leniency toward the foreign heretic, the Santour case was probably the exception rather than the rule. The number of foreigners remanded to Spain for prosecution and their fate at the hands of the Holy Office there and in Mexico show that the Counter Reformation mentality of Philip II was becoming very strong by 1570.

A case in point was the 1569 prosecution of Guillermo de Orlando in Mexico City and in Sevilla.[32] On February 23, 1569 Orlando was interrogated by Fray Bartolomé de Ledesma, one of the ecclesiastical judges of the archepiscopal see. Testimony by Pedro de Colmenares pointed to the suspicion that Orlando was an English Lutheran. William had arrived in Veracruz with the Hawkins raiders in 1568, but owing to his charm and social abilities he had become a page in the viceregal court of Martín Enríquez; indeed he claimed to have come to Mexico "with the same fleet" as the viceroy. As the Hawkins expedition stopped in Veracruz to trade and take on supplies, the Mexican viceroy arrived at the same time and Martín Enríquez blockaded the Englishmen in the harbor and later destroyed their fleet. One of the hostages sent by Hawkins during the various truce negotiations was William Orlando. He remained with the other Englishmen in a stockade after the prisoners were sent to Mexico City. There he inveigled his way into the good grace of the clergy, and into a job in the Enríquez household.

Pedro de Colmenares and soldiers in the viceregal guard heard Guillermo Orlando utter heresy. Colmenares told the judge that they were conversing in the guardroom of the palace when he said in a joking way to the Englishman, "If you had gone to Spain, they would have burned you as a Lutheran." Colmenares related that Guillermo got angry and replied, "If they burned him he would say that God was the Devil and the Devil was God." The others present cautioned him to watch his language; and prodded by them, Guillermo said he would die for his queen even if she were a Lutheran. Then he left the room, running and acting as though he were drunk. The nature of Colmenares' denunciation led to a deeper investigation of the affair by Dr. Estéban de Portillo, provisor of the archbishopric on February 25, 1569.

William Orlando told the provisor he was a native of London, some twenty years old, and that his family were members of the English nobility. He said he had resided in the queen's palace before he came to Mexico "on the fleet that entered Veracruz at the same time that the Viceroy arrived." After his trip to Mexico City he had been housed in the viceregal residence. Orlando swore he was a loyal, practicing Catholic—and he told how in London he had sneaked away to the privacy of his father's home to hear mass and to partake of the other Roman Catholic sacraments forbidden in Elizabethan England. After he left the British Isles, Orlando went to the Canaries, British Guiana and the mainland coast of South America. During the year and a half of his journey he always heard mass, went to confession and took communion. He knew what the substance of the denunciation against him was, and he denied it.

They had been talking "man's talk" about women, young Orlando said, and whether it was permitted for a man to take a woman during a period of fasting. Orlando said he had defended the right of a man to do so. Then Colmenares and another soldier named Francisco Hurtado had made the remarks about Lutheranism. The accused claimed one could not be burnt for taking his pleasure with women, but saying something like "God is the Devil and the Devil is God" was grounds for execution. He did not remember stating he would die for his queen even if she were a Lutheran.

Apparently William Orlando had friends in the city and in the viceregal court, because he was able to post bond through a guarantor, Luis Ortíz. Fulgencio de Vigue, a well-known attorney, was appointed his defender before the Inquisition court. During the next week, Dr. Portillo took additional evidence from Pedro de Colmenares and Francisco Hurtado. Both men substantiated their denunciations against Orlando. Finally on March 1, 1569 attorney Vigue offered his defense. Vigue pointed to the heat of the argument between the men and the fact that one witness said the defendant acted as though he were drunk. He excused his client on these grounds. The attorney tried to convince the Holy Office that Orlando's loyalty to his queen and his avowal that he would die for her was a thing to be commended. His loyalty to the Roman Catholic Church was equally commendable. Vigue presented testimony by two Mexico City friars who had known William while he was still in the stockade with the other corsairs.

A deposition by Fray Juan de Arias of the Dominican Convent said he had met young Orlando in the prison camp and that he had become convinced of William's knowledge of Catholicism. For instance they had conversed in Latin, and the boy had shown sophisticated understanding of articles of the faith. He had been to hear mass and Fray Juan had confessed him, and he had taken communion. Another Dominican friar, Andrés Ovilla, testified that William Orlando came to mass and took the sacraments. Both friars claimed that the accused acted as an orthodox Catholic should act.

Whether William Orlando's involvement with the viceregal household was an embarrassment to Martín Enríquez is a moot point. At any rate it was the viceroy who instructed the Holy Office of the Inquisition to grant Guillermo Orlando a change of venue. On March 8, 1569 the Inquisition scribe incorporated into the proceso an order by the viceroy that the prisoner was to be remanded to Sevilla for further questioning. He was to leave on the next fleet. Whether the viceroy wished to rid himself of a vexing problem in the Orlando case or whether he hoped to get the young man off easily is difficult to determine.

The trial had a tragic ending nevertheless—because Sevillian records indicate that Guillermo Orlando died in the jail at Sevilla soon after he arrived on the fleet in 1569. The cause of death was not specified.[33] Perhaps the arduous sea voyage in unhealthy circumstances led to some disease which saved the Spanish Holy Office the trouble of continuing the trial of the twenty-year old Hawkins raider. Many other Hawkins men met harsh fates in Mexico during the 1570's and others were tried in Spain and executed. It would appear that Robert Tomson's cellmate Agustín Boacio was entirely correct when he told Tomson that risking one's fate with the Sevillian Inquisition was a foolhardy thing to do.

III

Faith and Morals in the Colony

The general tenor of the Inquisition trials during the Montúfar archepiscopacy suggests more a fear of heretics who might contaminate others than a concern for doctrinal error in itself.[34] Certainly the trials of foreign heretics by the bishops of New Spain suggests this, and routine investigations of the conduct of colonial citizens and the native populations indicate that punishment of bad examples of Christianity was the main goal of the Holy Office. Over the entire viceroyalty of Mexico there were only forty-two investigations of orthodoxy in the ten years between 1550 and 1560. Most of these cases were blasphemy and bigamy matters handled by the ordinary or his delegates in specific areas. During the decade of the 1560's the tempo of Inquisition business accelerated, and papers in the Holy Office archive show at least three hundred prosecutions in the bishoprics of Mexico, Oaxaca, Guadalajara, Yucatán and Guatemala.[35]

The nature of the colonization of Mexico frequently excluded the migration of entire families, and often husbands came without their wives, hoping to send for their families at a later date. Bigamy and concubinage were natural results of such a circumstance. Many legajos of trial records before the Mexican Inquisition deal with the Church's attempts to preserve and protect holy matrimony.[36] Both men and women were tried by the ordinaries when there was evidence of bigamy or polyandry. Sentences were harsh, and without exception the Inquisition required the defendant to return to the legitimate spouse unless it could be proven that the husband or the wife was deceased.

Many investigations exposed the seamier side of sixteenth-century Mexican society. The 1569 trial of the mulatto woman Francisca López and her lover Juan Pérez, a clerk of the audiencia of Mexico, was illustrative of the administrative problems facing the ordinary.[37] Francisca and Juan claimed to have been man and wife before they had a violent quarrel in the city streets, and Juan knifed her pretty badly. As a result, and seemingly motivated by vengeance, she sued Juan for a divorce before the ordinary court. His relatives swore he was out of town at the time and they accused Francisca of being a bigamist. Both partners were jailed and Juan eventually agreed to marry Francisca after she finally convinced the ordinary that her first husband had died in the Mexican provinces.

Another case of a picayune administrative nature shed light on Inquisition procedures when Hernando Pacheco, a merchant and minor municipal official of Temascaltepec, was tried for blasphemy and violation of the right of sanctuary during February and March of 1569.[38] Pacheco had pursued a debtor, Amador de Soto, into the parish church of Santa Catalina. When de Soto refused to come with Pacheco and claimed the right of sanctuary, his adversary used intemperate language saying, among other things, "the Church of Santa Catalina and everything in it were of no value" in protecting Amador de Soto from arrest.

There were witnesses to the controversy and later on de Soto denounced Pacheco to the Holy Office for blasphemy. The case was appealed to the ordinary in Mexico City who fined Hernando Pacheco six pesos and four pounds of white wax for the church he had insulted. Many similar documents show the day-to-day workings of the less spectacular side of the Mexican Inquisition.

Indians continued to be subject to the jurisdiction of the ordinary Inquisition until 1571, and even after that time the Holy Office continued investigations of native idolatries, superstitions and other proscribed conduct. During May and June of 1557 a curious trial of Indians was carried on in the bishopric of Oaxaca. It came to light that Domingo Hernández had secured a burial plot for his father in the cemetery of the Church of Chacavastepec, despite the fact that the deceased had never been baptized as a Catholic.[39] The old Mixtec, called Xiqhy in his own language, had been bedridden and deaf for many years according to the son. His inability to hear or to walk had obviated his conversion to Catholicism and his baptism. In league with an Indian woman, Catalina García, whose husband had been the mayor-domo of the village, Domingo had the old man buried in the churchyard.

When the Oaxaca provisor examined the cacique of the village and the Indian governor of the province, it became clear that Xiqhy had never been taken into the body of the Church and that he had never wished to be baptized. After Catalina García testified, the provisor judged her and Xiqhy's son to have been faithful Christians who tried to do the right thing for the old man. Catalina was required to do penance for her part in the burial.

Indians rarely blasphemed. The only recorded investigation of native blasphemy came from Guatemala City in 1560.[40] Melchor Martín had argued over a debt he owed Alonso Martín de Chemenal. Melchor became so angry he said that the Devil had created the world rather than God and that God hated the world. The ordinary fined Melchor ten pesos de oro and required him to fast and to perform other spiritual penances. While blasphemy was not a trait of the Indians of New Spain, there were many evidences of Indian thievery.

A case in point was the 1571 trial of the Tarascan, Antón, who had become the sacristan of the church in Zacatecas.[41] Antón had taken from the church three boxes of books which had been confiscated from the citizenry of the mines. The books had been marked as heretical literature and the church authorities were waiting for the opportunity to send them to the dean and cabildo of the bishopric of Guadalajara. Antón had sold the books in and around the Zacatecas mines, probably to some of their original owners. Since Antón and his Indian cohorts were judged to be innocent of any heresy in the act of thievery, the Inquisition case was dismissed and a civil trial was begun. Whether the books were recovered by the Holy Office in Zacatecas was not recorded in the trial.

A controversy over the trials of Mayan Indians for idolatry and sacrifice by the Franciscan Provincial Diego de Landa in Yucatán in the early 1560's was still raging in 1571 when the tribunal of the Holy Office of the Inquisition was finally established in New Spain.[42] But after the erection of a bishopric in Yucatán in 1562 there was no question about the authority of the ordinary over Indian orthodoxy. All over the viceroyalty of New Spain there continued to be conflict of jurisdiction in Indian cases. As the sixteenth century ended and the seventeenth century began, the question was not really resolved.[43]

IV

The Inquisition and the Medical Profession, 1551-1570

One group of prominent leaders in the viceroyalty were medical men and they often found themselves at odds with the religious establishment. Their ideas, their activities and their intemperate language confirm that the doctors had a penchant for getting into controversies when science and theology seemed to disagree, and when the issues were focused on specific medical problems. While the Holy Office of the Inquisition performed a service to the profession by taking firm action against medical quacks, it also antagonized doctors who wished to be free of clerical meddling in the art of healing.[44] Often the physicians reacted against clerical control with blasphemous invective. When they did this in public, the Holy Office moved against them as heretics and prosecuted them to defend public morality and to uphold the dignity and status of the Church and its hierarchy.

The most celebrated trial of a doctor during the decade of the 1550's was conducted in Puebla de Los Angeles during the fall of 1551. Dr. Pedro de la Torre was taken to task for saying that God and nature were the same thing.[45] Testimony had been gathered in Veracruz as early as September 14, 1551, when Reverend Bartolomé Romero heard Pedro de la Torre affirm that he was not only a medical doctor but also a theologian and that God and nature were the same phenomena. The priest said that de la Torre cited St. Thomas as his source. Subsequent testimonies revealed that de la Torre's medical view of natural law was an adaptation of Thomistic teaching on natural law and divine law.

Reverend Romero denounced the doctor to the Puebla provisor because he felt that de la Torre's views were eroding the faith of the orthodox. Another surgeon of the city of Veracruz, Licenciado Francisco de Toro, substantiated the views of Reverend Romero. After a lengthy probe the attorney of the bishopric of Puebla, Miguel Blanco, made formal accusations against Dr. de la Torre in the court of the ordinary. He insisted that the defendant's views on God and nature were heresy and blasphemy, and that the doctor's utterances were dangerous thoughts for the less sophisticated colonist. The fiscal accused Dr. Pedro de la Torre of being a Lutheran.

Other items in the indictment charged the doctor with blaspheming during card games and using scandalous language. He was also suspected of using black magic *(nigromante)* in curing the sick, and the attorney claimed that Dr. de la Torre had encouraged married women to have illicit relations with unmarried men. The wording of the accusation makes the doctor appear as some kind of procurer or pimp. Apparently he used some kind of magic incantations, probably autosuggestion, to cure toothaches and arthritic aches and pains. Blanco was able to get Dr. de la Torre arrested and jailed pending the outcome of the trial.

During November and December of 1551, Dr. Pedro de la Torre attempted to use the Mexico City archbishopric as a lever against the Puebla authorities and to secure a change of venue for his trial. He also transferred title to his properties to others by declaring that they were his creditors and by using a power of attorney to his lawyer-friend, Diego de Agundes. Doctor de la Torre insisted that he was a resident of the viceregal capital and that he only temporarily exercised his profession in Veracruz. Lawyer Agundes compiled data on de la Torre's background and his lineage of Christian nobility in Spain. But by December 9, 1551 the attempt to change the location of the trial had failed and the Puebla ordinary passed sentence. Dr. Pedro de la Torre was forced to publicly abjure his heretical views on God and nature, and after he paid a stiff fine of one hundred golden pesos, he was exiled from New Spain.

Other doctors had similar altercations with the Holy Office in the decade of the 1560's. Perhaps the most notorious trial was that of Dr. Pedro de Santander in May 1561.[46] As early as 1545, Santander was an official of the *Protomedicato* in New Spain, and he had served as health officer for the Spanish fleets when they put into the Veracruz area.[47] He had a blasphemous nature, and a violent temper, as well as a healthy disrespect for established forms. Once again the Inquisition felt that the activities of this doctor smacked of Lutheranism.

In Mexico City several witnesses gave evidence about the scandalous remarks of Dr. Santander. He had ridiculed the procedure of the provisor in giving permission for mass to be said in private residences despite a papal pronouncement that allowed such a ceremony when it was necessary. Dr. Santander had become so angry during the argument over the papal dispensations to say mass in private homes that he attacked papal bulls in general, saying, among other obscene things, that the bulls of the Pope should be used for toilet paper. Even the witnesses to the argument accused Santander of Lutheranism. Perhaps provisor Luis Fernández de Anguis took personal offense at the doctor's remarks since Anguis had given the specific permission which had started the controversy. At any rate Provisor Anguis called many witnesses during the month of May 1561, and he imprisoned Dr. Santander in the archepiscopal jail during the interim. He was denied bail.

Apparently the need for doctors in the viceregal capital and the notorious irascible nature of Dr. Santander led Provisor Anguis to a more moderate sentence than the one given Dr. Pedro de la Torre. Santander was required to make a retreat in the Monastery of San Francisco for two weeks after he was released from jail. At the end of that time he was fined fifty pesos de oro, the fine to be used by the Hospital of Amador de Dios and for the dowry of an orphan girl who wished to marry. The physician was given a stern warning that any recurrence of his prior behavior would result in prosecution "with the full force of the law."

The closing year of the episcopal Inquisition in Mexico saw the trial of the viceroyalty's most famous doctor who was also a leading philanthropist. Licenciado Pedro López, medical doctor, resident of the area of the Villa of Dueñas in Spain, made a formal request in Valladolid in October 1548 to migrate to Mexico so that he could take up residence with two of his sisters who lived in Mexico City.[48] After he arrived in Mexico he continued his studies and the practice of medicine, and he received the title of doctor of medicine in 1553. He founded the Hospital of San Lázaro and the Hospital of Los Desamparados in the 1570's; and when he died in 1596, he left a large portion of his estate for their upkeep.[49] During May 1570 Dr. Estebán de Portillo, ecclesiastical judge of the archepiscopal see, began a proceso against Dr. Pedro López, when the attorney of the ordinary, Pedro Díaz de Aguero, presented a formal denunciation.[50] The denunciation contained information about Dr. López from a friend who had known him for twenty years. Juan Gutiérrez de Aguilar, a merchant with whom López had many business transactions, related to the court that he had been into a room in the doctor's house on Calle Tacuba where there was a huge religious statue which resembled Christ crucified. The image had one arm broken off and Dr. López had affixed it high on the wall, horizontally, near the ceiling. Gutiérrez de Aguilar told the court that he was scandalized by the sight of the image, extremely dirty and placed as it was. He denied any knowledge of Dr. Pedro Lopez' lineage when the interrogator asked him if López was of Moorish or Jewish descent. It became obvious that Fiscal Díaz de Aguero was attempting to establish the Jewish ancestry of Dr. López, since many Judaizantes used crucifixes in a similar manner. Pedro Martínez, another business associate of Dr. López, gave credence to the Gutiérrez de Aguilar story. Martínez had seen the large image in the Doctor's house and he declared it to be a broken crucifix.

The fiscal called a secret witness from Coyoacán whom he hoped would uphold the suspicion of López' Judaism. Catarina Quiñones, wife of Pedro de Lara, had grown up as a ward in Dr. López' household before she married. She testified that the servants and other people in the house were always given specific instructions by the doctor when it came to cleaning the room where he had an altar "... and if on it by mistake they placed any vessel of silver or other thing, the Doctor reprimanded them for it."[51] The young matron denied any knowledge of Dr. López' ancestry.

Testimony against Dr. Pedro López was still being taken during the months of July and August 1570. On August 1, Eugenio Fernández Castellano, who had known Dr. López twelve years, told the inquisitors about common gossip among professional people that López was a heretic and that the Holy Office ought to burn him. He repeated the crucifix story as it had been discussed by Licenciado Contreras, Licenciado Martel, Dr. de la Fuente, Gutiérrez de Aguilar and Pedro Martínez. Apparently one of the gossip sessions had taken place in the presence of Dr. Francisco Hernández, royal protomedicato. When Dr. Hernández was called to testify he was unable to add anything to the data already assembled by the fiscal.[52]

It is interesting that Dr. Pedro López was never interrogated, and that the ordinary refused to have him arrested despite Fiscal Díaz de Aguero's writ. Certainly the evidence was highly circumstantial and there were overtones of conspiracy on the part of the doctor's associates to frame him for being a Judaizante. Perhaps Dr. Hernández' refusal to be drawn into the web of circumstantial evidence determined the ecclesiastical judge to discontinue the investigation. There can be no doubt that Dr. Pedro López heard through gossip or from official sources the charges leveled against him. The devout and pious wording of his last will and testament in 1596 and his conspicuous good works and philanthropy in founding hospitals in the 1570's were all evidence of his Christian character and conduct.[53] It is to the credit of the Holy Office of the Inquisition that it recognized his actions as those of a Christian gentleman.

V

Judaizantes, 1558-1564

While the ordinaries of New Spain concentrated on Reformation heresies in the years 1550 to 1570, they all but ignored the Judaizantes in the colony. It is unusual for Inquisition records to contain the biographies of heretics through four separate trials and over a period of four decades. But in June 1558 the ordinary Inquisition of the bishopric of Guatemala gathered information from three previous trials of a notorious Judaizante in Mexico City and Oaxaca, and the ordinary began a fourth proceso against Diego de Morales, who had avoided burning at the stake for forty years. After Morales was penanced in the auto de fé of 1528 in Mexico City, the same auto in which his brother Gonzalo Morales had been remanded to the secular arm for burning, he migrated to Oaxaca where the Holy Office again penanced him for heretical blasphemy bordering on Jewish practices in 1538.[54]

Sometime during 1540 Diego de Morales took up residence in Guatemala and he resumed his career as a merchant.[55] By 1558 he had amassed a considerable fortune and his daughter had married a rich encomendero. Apparently Morales already had family in Guatemala City and other members of the clan had migrated there from Mexico. The proceso informs that he was the paternal grandfather of Licenciado Bernabé de Sosa, the holder of the encomienda of Mazatenango, and that Sosa was an applicant for a position as commissary of the Holy Office of the the Inquisition.

During his episcopacy, Bishop Francisco Marroquín conferred the title of ordinary inquisitor on the Dominican procurator of Guatemala, Fray Tomás de Cárdenas, who conducted the 1558 trial of Diego de Morales. On June 3, 1558 Fray Diego Ruíz presented a formal denunciation of Morales to the ordinary. He claimed that Diego de Morales was a bad Christian who had blasphemed and committed heresy. He told the court of records in the bishop's office which pointed to the fact that Morales had been tried by the Holy Office as a Judaizante both in Mexico City and in Oaxaca. That same day Fray Tomás de Cárdenas took testimony about an incident when Morales had used irreverent language while collecting debts in public places. He remarked sarcastically to his servants that he would feed them as Christ had fed the disciples at the Last Supper, and he was reported as having raised a tortilla and consecrated it as a priest consecrates the Host during celebration of the mass.

Other testimonies showed that Morales' brother had been burned at the stake in Mexico and one witness Juan Copete de Figueroa told the Holy Office that he had witnessed the burning of Gonzalo de Morales in Mexico some thirty years before. Copete de Figueroa said he had seen Diego de Morales penanced in the same auto de fé. He pronounced Diego to be a weak Christian; and although he had seen him at mass, he felt that Diego did not go to confession nor partake of communion. A large number of other witnesses substantiated this testimony.

When the Holy Office called Diego de Morales to testify in the first instance, he admitted that his brother Gonzalo had been burned at the stake in Mexico and that he himself had been penanced in the same auto. He also owned up to the Oaxaca prosecution for blasphemy, but he claimed that he was a baptized, practicing Catholic who had spent forty years as a merchant in the Indies. He told Fray Tomás de Cárdenas that he had behaved badly and had used irreverent language before the oidores of the audiencia of Guatemala when he became involved in a lawsuit calling one of his opponents "a usurious old Christian." When they put him in jail, Morales told them to bring a barber to cut his hair so that the barber could tell by the way his hair cut whether he was a Moor or a Jew. Morales claimed that he said this in presence of the Alcalde Juan Vásquez de Coronado.

The Guatemalan inquisitors visited Diego de Morales on four additional occasions to take more testimony. Each session brought out more of Morales' Jewish background. From the signed interrogatories one gathers that Diego was obscene in his speech and exhibited a loathing for the Christian Church and its dogma. He went out of his way to ridicule the sacraments. His private life, especially his carnal relations with his slaves, scandalized the inquisitors. From the collective testimonies a picture of a cantankerous, argumentative, indecent old man emerged. In his business relations he combined a Jewish shrewdness with frequent wisecracks about believers. When he bargained for merchandise, he tried to talk the price down to three pesos in honor of the Trinity. He made the usual remarks about Christ not being the Son of God, as orthodox Jews were wont to do. He scoffed at the story of the Nativity and made cynical remarks on Christmas Eve. Witnesses accused him of having a crucifix under the chair where he usually sat. Although he sold images in his store, he made fun of people who purchased them. When he forced himself on one of his servants with carnal intent he blasphemed against the Virgin, and he likened his wife's reactions to sex to the "Fifth Agony."

It was public knowledge that Diego de Morales was a blasphemer. He often cursed, using the words "God Damn," "I renounce God," "May it spite God" and many other phrases considered irreverent. When he counted his money, he often raised his hands toward Heaven and muttered what some people thought was a Hebrew prayer. He often told people, to "Go to Hell." During his final testimony before Fray Tomás de Cárdenas on July 27, 1558, Morales admitted most of the charges against him involving blasphemy, but he continued to deny that he had relapsed into Judaism. He expressed his contrition for doing wrong and asked Cárdenas for a merciful penance.

By August 1558 Inquisitor Cárdenas had made his decision in the heresy trial of Diego de Morales. He pronounced a reasonably harsh sentence. Morales was forced to make formal retraction of all of his blasphemies in a public auto de fé. He had to attend mass shirtless and barefoot, gagged and with a penitential candle in his hands. The Holy Office composed for him the formal speech of abjuration he was required to make. Before he could be released from the episcopal jail, Diego de Morales was to pay the rather stiff fine of fifteen hundred pesos de oro. Cárdenas further decreed that Morales should pay the entire costs of the trial, including the necessary referrals to Mexico City for information. As it turned out the ordinary's treasurer totaled these expenses as some eighty-eight pesos de oro, not including stenographic help and the time expended by the Inquisition staff.

Morales was released from jail upon guarantee that he would pay the fine and costs of the trial, and he participated in the abjuration ceremony in the church of the Dominican Monastery in Guatemala City on August 4, 1558. The entire ecclesiastical establishment and the judges of the audiencia of Guatemala witnessed the proceedings. The financial documents appended to the trial record show that Diego de Morales engaged in a complicated series of litigations before the Holy Office was able to collect the fifteen-hundred-peso fine. What is abundantly clear is that Morales had friends in high places who protected him from more stringent punishment. The encomenderos and the lawyers in the immediate family acted as powerful levers on Diego Morales' behalf.

The failure of the bishops of New Spain to initiate trials against Judaizantes from 1543 to 1571 may have stemmed from the growing suspicion on the part of the clergy and the crown that the colonists of Mexico often denounced their economic competitors as Jews.[56] Perhaps the Zumárraga prosecutions of Gonzalo Gómez in 1536-1537 and of Francisco de Millán in 1539 conditioned this attitude. At any rate Inquisitor Tello de Sandoval left the Jews alone and the episcopal Inquisition of Alonso de Montúfar failed to make any Judaizante investigations up to 1570. Many cases of blasphemy during this period appear to border on Judaizante prosecutions and the Diego de Morales trial in Guatemala had its counterpart in other provinces of the viceroyalty.

The 1564 investigation of Juan Bautista Corvera in Guadalajara for blasphemy and composing heretical verses looks suspiciously like a Jewish probe.[57] Francisco de Tijera was labeled a Portuguese Jew by the civil authorities and the clergy in Toluca in 1564 when he was tried for blasphemy, but the prosecution stayed within the confines of blasphemy and did not investigate Jewish practices of the accused.[58]

VI

Usury

Counter Reformation views on faith and morals in the Mexican colony led to an attack on sharp trading in violation of established ecclesiastical norms. The Council of Trent had reviewed some Church economic theory, especially regarding usury, and the Spanish Church had given instructions to the colonial bishops on how to proceed against usurers. On November 30, 1565 Archbishop

Alonso de Montúfar informed the Spanish King of the ruinous usury practiced by the merchants and moneylenders of the viceroyalty of New Spain. He especially singled out usury and illegal business contracts negotiated by the merchants of Puebla de Los Angeles. The archbishop explained that usury had been a topic of discussion by the bishops in the Second Mexican Church Council (1565), and that they had decided to investigate immoral economic practices within the various episcopates. The council had decided to threaten usurers with excommunication if they persisted in charging excess interest.[59]

Between 1564 and 1568 a celebrated usury case came before the ordinary Inquisition of Michoacán and the archepiscopal provisor in Mexico City. Gonzalo Robledo of Guanajuato was a sharp trader, moneylender and merchant with far-flung economic interests. He had lent to two business associates, one at a time, the combined sum of one thousand pesos de oro. When they could not make repayment of the principal he charged exorbitant rates of interest and required his debtors to pay interest in barrels of wine pegged at wholesale prices rather than retail value. At the same time he compounded their interest to inflate the total indebtedness to one thousand six hundred pesos. Soon thereafter he gave his power of attorney to collectors with instructions to foreclose on the properties of his debtors. Since part of the business of the debtors was in Mexico City and part in Guanajuato, the civil and religious authorities of both jurisdictions became involved in the debtors' suit against Robledo for usury.[60]

The ecclesiastical visitor of the bishopric of Michoacán, Alonso de Pasillas, was drawn into the case as inquisitor ordinary because he happened to be in the Guanajuato area discharging his responsibilities when the usury charges were made before ecclesiastical authorities in 1568. When he commanded Gonzalo Robledo to testify, the defendant manipulated his accounts in order to explain away the charges. When his ruse became known, the visitor referred the matter to the audiencia of Michoacán and finally to the Inquisition court of Archbishop Alonso de Montúfar in the viceregal capital.

THE EPISCOPAL INQUISITION 113

While Gonzalo Robledo was specifically charged with having made illicit and usurious contracts prohibited by civil and canon law, there were other evidences of unorthodox conduct and immorality in the testimony against him. Robledo showed defiance of the authority of the Church to direct his behavior in business enterprise and he made indiscreet references to the bishop. By July 1568, Robledo's personal life was under investigation by the Holy Office and it was ascertained that he kept concubines. Presumably the episcopal ordinary in Michoacán was unable to determine whether some of the evidence against Robledo was fabricated by his business associates, and he decided to refer the entire matter to the Montúfar Holy Office in the capital. There the dossier rested, probably because the Montúfar Inquisition was preoccupied with other matters—a conflict between the hierarchy and the regulars, and the Avila-Cortés conspiracy.[61]

Notes

[1] Zumárraga's first signature as ordinary is recorded in AGN, Inquisición, Tomo 36, exp. 1.

[2] Greenleaf, *Zumárraga*.

[3] AGN, Inquisición, Tomo 2, exp. 10. The printed version of the trial is *Proceso Inquisitorial del Cacique de Tetzcoco* (México, 1910). The most detailed analysis of the Don Carlos case can be found in Greenleaf, *Zumárraga*, pp. 67-75. More light on the genealogy of Don Carlos is given in Howard F. Cline, "The Oztoticpac Lands Map of Texcoco, 1540," *The Quarterly Journal of the Library of Congress* (1966), Vol. 23, pp. 77-116. Cline used the map and a document provided by Greenleaf from AGN, Inquisición, Tomo 139, exp. 11, for his primary analysis. Cline appears to disagree with Robert Ricard, *The Spiritual Conquest of Mexico*, trans. Lesley B. Simpson (Berkeley, 1966), p. 272, and Greenleaf, *Zumárraga*, p. 68, on Carlos' possible education at the Franciscan Missionary College of Santa Cruz de Tlaltelolco.

[4] Vasco de Puga, *Provisiones, Cédulas, Instrucciones de Su Magestad, Ordenancas de Difuntos y Audiencia Para la Buena Expedición de los Negocios y Administración de Justicia y Gobernación de esta Nueva España y Para el Buen Tratamiento y Conservación de los Indios Desde el Año de 1525 Hasta este Presente de 1563* (México, 1878), Vol. I, pp. 452-453; Medina, *Primitiva Inquisición*, Vol. II, p. 33; Mariano Cuevas, *Historia de la Iglesia en México* (México, 1946), Vol. I, p. 381.

[5] AGN, Inquisición, Tomos 144, 42, 212, *passim*.

[6] *Ibid.*, Tomo 37, exp. 5.

[7] *Ibid.*, exp. 6.

[8] *Ibid.*, exp. 7.
[9] *Ibid.*, exp. 8.
[10] *Ibid.*, exp. 9.
[11] *Ibid.*, exp. 10.
[12] *Ibid.*, f. 19.
[13] *Ibid.*, exp. 11.
[14] *Ibid.*, exps. 5-9 have been extracted for ethnological data by Wigberto Jiménez Moreno and Salvador Mateos Higuera, *Códice de Yanhuitlán* (México, 1940), pp. 37-47. The recent ethnohistorical study of Ronald M. Spores, *The Mixtec Kings and Their People* (Norman, 1967), places the trials in proper historical perspective, especially pp. 25-27, 179.
[15] AGN, Inquisición, Tomo 42, exp. 20.
[16] *Ibid.*, Tomo 37, exp. 12.
[17] *Ibid.*, Tomo 40, exp. 9.
[18] *Ibid.*, Tomo 34, exp. 6.
[19] Greenleaf, *Zumárraga*, pp. 76-88.
[20] AGN, Inquisición, Tomo 14, exp. 35, 44.
[21] *Ibid.*, exp. 37-bis.
[22] Much work remains to be done on corsairs and the Inquisition. Scholars are awaiting the book of Eleanor B. Adams, "Before the Buccaneers: Non-Spanish Intruders in the Caribbean 1492-1610," which promises to be the definitive study. Of more limited scope is her "The Franciscan Inquisition in Yucatán: French Seamen, 1560", soon to appear. See corsair cases in AGN, Inquisición, Tomo 33, exp. 2, beginning with the year 1560. See also AGI, Justicia 1029, exp. 9, for 1565 data on Yucatán pirates. G. Baez Carmargo, *Protestantes Enjuiciados por la Inquisición en Iberoamérica* (México, 1960), includes alphabetical lists by century of Protestants tried in the hemisphere. Valuable background studies are Antonio Rumeu de Armas, *Los Viajes de John Hawkins a América (1562-1595)* (Sevilla, 1947) and Héctor Pérez Martínez, *Piraterías en Campeche (Siglos XVI, XVII, XVIII)* (México, 1937).
[23] Cuevas, *Historia de la Iglesia*, Vol. 2, pp. 274-280.
[24] AGN, Inquisición, Tomo 15, exp. 15.
[25] *Ibid.*, Tomo 32, exp. 8.
[26] G. R. G. Conway, *An Englishman and the Mexican Inquisition* (México, 1927).
[27] Because Agustín Boacio is given prominent mention in Robert Tomson's *relación*, many writers mention the trial in passing. Until this present study there has not been an examination of the actual proceso which is found in AGN, Inquisición, Tomo 31, exp. 3.
[28] Because the trial record from three different places was torn apart and put together again without replacing some pages in proper order, the actual date of the Guadalajara sentence is unknown.
[29] AGN, Inquisición, Tomo 43, exp. 7.
[30] See note 22.
[31] AGN, Inquisición, Tomo 3, exp. 1.
[32] *Ibid.*, Tomo 9, exp. 6.
[33] Baez Camargo, pp. 48-49.

THE EPISCOPAL INQUISITION 115

[34] AGN, Inquisición, Tomos 2, 18, 30, 31, 32.
[35] Greenleaf, *Zumárraga*, pp. 15-19; AGN, Inquisición, Tomos 3-10; J. Ignacio Rubio Mañé, *Archivo de la Historia de Yucatán*, Vol. III (México, 1942).
[36] AGN, Inquisición, Tomos 14, 23, 24, 25, 34.
[37] *Ibid.*, Tomo 29, exp. 1.
[38] *Ibid.*, Tomo 21, exp. 1.
[39] *Ibid.*, Tomo 43, exp. 1.
[40] *Ibid.*, Tomo 16, exp. 11.
[41] *Ibid.*, Tomo 72, exp. 18.
[42] France V. Scholes and Ralph L. Roys, *Fray Diego de Landa and the Problem of Idolatry in Yucatán* (Washington, D.C., 1938); and France V. Scholes and Eleanor B. Adams, eds., *Don Diego de Quijada Alcalde Mayor de Yucatán 1561-1565* (2 vols., México, 1938).
[43] Richard E. Greenleaf, "The Inquisition and the Indians of New Spain: A Study in Jurisdictional Confusion," *The Americas: A Quarterly Review of Inter-American Cultural History*, Vol. 22 (1965), pp. 138-166.
[44] See Greenleaf, *Zumárraga*, p. 117, for the 1538 trial of Dr. Cristóbal Méndez who applied astrology to medical science.
[45] AGN, Inquisición, Tomo 2, exp. 13.
[46] *Ibid.*, Tomo 17, exp. 6.
[47] Francisco del Paso y Troncoso, *Epistolario de la Nueva España* (16 vols., México, 1939-1942), Vol. IV, doc. 242.
[48] AGI, Indiferente General, Leg. 1208, exp. 2. This unpublished document was provided the author by France V. Scholes.
[49] France V. Scholes and Eleanor B. Adams, eds., *Ordenanzas del Hospital de San Lázaro de México: Año de 1582* (México, 1956), pp. 7-10. See also Joaquín García Icazbalceta, "Los Médicos de México en el Siglo XVI," *Obras* (México, 1896), Vol. I, pp. 86-89.
[50] AGN, Inquisición, Tomo 72, exp. 11.
[51] *Ibid.*, f. 101.
[52] For a life of Dr. Francisco Hernández, see Germán Somolinos d'Ardois, *Vida y Obra de Francisco Hernández* (México, 1960). The title of royal protomedicato is found in AGI, Audiencia de Méjico, Leg. 18.
[53] The will of Dr. Pedro López was discovered by Professor France V. Scholes in AGN, Tierras, Tomo 3556.
[54] See Chapter One for an analysis of the early prosecutions of Diego de Morales.
[55] AGN, Inquisición, Tomo 31, exp. 2.
[56] Seymour B. Liebman, *A Guide to Jewish References in the Mexican Colonial Era* (Philadelphia, 1964), p. 14, finds only two suspects who were investigated but not tried from 1540 to 1570.
[57] AGN, Inquisición, Tomo 4, exps. 10, 10-bis. See also Julio Jiménez Rueda, *Herejías y Supersticiones en la Nueva España* (México, 1946), pp. 44-45.
[58] AGN, Inquisición, Tomo 18, exp. 64.
[59] Del Paso y Troncoso, *Espistolario*, Vol. X, doc. 566.
[60] AGN, Inquisición, Tomo 44, exp. 5.
[61] See Chapter Four.

Chapter Four

THE MONTÚFAR INQUISITION AND THE MEXICAN CLERGY
1555-1571

THE FIRST DECADES of the spiritual conquest of Mexico were years of ideological ferment within European Catholicism and in the Spanish Empire. The Church in New Spain was far from a unified institution either in theological orientation or in patterns of action. Conflicting opinion among the clergy of Mexico over how to apply Renaissance Humanist beliefs to colonization policies created a viable intellectual atmosphere within the religious establishment. The similarity of some Christian Humanist ideas with doctrines of the Reformation made for a confused ideological milieu. The conflict between the regular and secular clergy in New Spain provoked differing interpretations of the mission of the Mexican church. Arguments over orthodoxy ensued, and those entrusted with the enforcement of theological orthodoxy stiffened their intellectual posture and became very zealous in investigating those who were suspect.

As the reverberations of the Protestant revolt reached New Spain, and as the Council of Trent (1545-1563) began to revamp and to clarify religious dogma and practice in Europe, the episcopal Inquisition of the second Mexican archbishop, Alonso de Montúfar, O.P. (1554-1571), attempted to fulfill its ministry to preserve and defend the faith in the colony. Since the Protestant revolt originated partially from within the ranks of the regular clergy, special attention was given by the Montúfar Inquisition to clerical orthodoxy, lest the same pattern be repeated in the viceroyalty of New Spain. Unfortunately, those who decided what was orthodox as opposed to heretical were often intemperate diocesan administrators whose commitment to the prerogatives of the secular clergy led them to look upon their mendicant colleagues as heretics or dangerous liberals.

This essay is a case study of the inner-directed processes of inquisitorial activity among the Mexican clergy at a critical juncture when the Trentine doctrines were being applied in Mexico, and when there was great internal dissension within the Church.

The conflict between the missionary orders and the secular clergy was intense and the issues were hotly contested. Administration of the sacraments under the quasi-episcopal faculties granted the regulars in the 1520's (taken away by the Council of Trent, and reaffirmed temporarily by the King and the Pope in 1567); competition for the loyalty and affection of the Indian population; the question of secularization of the *doctrinas* (essentially a quasi-parish administered by a missionary priest); the collection and administration of tithes—all of these were burning issues in the two decades of 1550-1570.[1] When the Council of Trent pronounced its famous dictum that only hierarchy clergy subject to the episcopal powers of the bishops could serve as parish priests and could administer the sacraments, the Mexican order clergy were able, with the help of Philip II, to get the order suspended in New Spain and to have the faculties of regulars reaffirmed in the papal bull *Exponi nobis nuper* of 1567.[2]

Bishops and archbishops were resentful that they had diocesan responsibilities but lacked authority over friars and their prelates within the same episcopal boundaries. The authority of the bishop as ecclesiastical judge ordinary, and his provisor (vicar general), was ignored by the friars since they were responsible only to their prelates who held quasi-episcopal authority from the papacy and the Spanish king. Endless lawsuits over benefices, faculties, tithes, enforcement of discipline and privileges of the missionary clergy vis-a-vis the hierarchy deepened the bitterness and animosity between the two groups of clergy. The conflict had not been resolved when the Church celebrated its golden anniversary in 1570, and the victory of the seculars did not come until 1574.[3] In some areas the seculars had to wait until the seventeenth century or later for full exercise of their powers.

The first bishop and archbishop of Mexico, the Franciscan Juan de Zumárraga (1527-1548), was able to maintain good relations with the missionary orders because of his own character and personality, and because of the fact that his own episcopacy was not confronted with enforcement of Trentine doctrines or combating serious Reformation heresies. The primitive nature of the Church and the relative simplicity of administrative organization of the spiritual conquest spared Zumárraga for the most part from internal conflict within the Church, although the clash of religious and economic motives of empire caused him grave problems with civil authority and the materialistic colonist.[4]

Zumárraga's successor and the second archbishop, the Dominican Alonso de Montúfar (1554-1571), was unable to preserve the earlier rapport between the orders and the hierarchy even though Montúfar rose from the order clergy to become archbishop.[5] Alonso de Montúfar had the difficult task of strengthening the doctrinal authority, the jurisdiction and the economic position of the seculars during his episcopacy. Perhaps Montúfar was too old and inflexible for the job. His critics seem to think so.[6] Certainly he lacked the diplomacy of Zumárraga and the administrative creativity to harmonize conflicting interests. While attempting to advance the position of the episcopacy, Montúfar encountered vested interests. His somewhat abrasive personality led him into conflict not only with the regulars, but with his own cathedral chapter, subordinates, and civil authority as well. Montúfar often lacked the necessary patience needed in his tasks, and frequently he exhibited traits of pettiness when it came to reinforcing his authority in matters of dignity and position. His inability to govern the diocese himself was manifested by delegation of episcopal authority to other administrators in the hierarchy who were understandably

THE INQUISITION AND THE CLERGY 119

partisan in the conflict between the seculars and the religious. In 1560, Montúfar brought to Mexico a vigorous young Dominican, Fray Bartolomé de Ledesma, whose role as administrator of the diocese, provisor and censor of printed matter was paramount in the Montúfar operation. Ledesma's thirty-eight years stood out in sharp contrast to Montúfar's seventy-one years in 1560, and as the decade advanced the archbishop left more of the running of the diocese to Ledesma.[7]

Dr. Rodrigo Barbosa and Dr. Estéban del Portillo also acted as provisors during the Montúfar incumbency, and Dr. Luis Fernández de Anguis became general counsellor to the archbishop and acted as his agent in special circumstances. Anguis was a major force in the anti-Protestant campaign of the Mexican Inquisition, and the nature of his letters to Philip II cause some authorities to conclude that he was a secret agent of the King and the Council of the Indies.[8] Anguis certainly exhibited hostility to the three orders in almost everything he wrote.

During the Montúfar period the friars continued to deal with the moral conduct of individual colonists and the Indians. However, the procedures for the enforcement of orthodoxy had been established clearly during the Zumárraga era, especially during his inquisitorial ministry (1536-1543). The Holy Office of the Inquisition had been vested in the bishop's portfolio as ecclesiastical judge ordinary.[9] Montúfar assumed the function of ordinary when he became archbishop in 1554. But the areas of jurisdiction over Indian orthodox conduct remained confused; and the friars, especially in places where there were no bishops or where the episcopal see was two days distant, retained inquisitorial functions. Montúfar was annoyed by this circumstance, and his letters to Philip II made no bones about his feelings concerning the activities of the Franciscans and others in punishing Indians for idolatry, sorcery and other proscribed practices.

Particularly valuable insights into the conflict between regulars and seculars are gained from a letter Montúfar wrote to the King on February 4, 1561.[10] The archbishop began by stating that no one could deny the great contribution of the Franciscans, Dominicans and Augustinians in the evangelization of the Indians, and he called attention to the friars' courageous defense of the natives in the face of the rapacious conquerors. But Montúfar informed the King that the religious were exercising spiritual and temporal powers and they were governing the natives as their own vassals, excluding the secular clergy and civil authorities from the process. Montúfar complained that some friars had made themselves bishops, and they encouraged the Indians to resist their pastors, thereby causing great dissension in the colony. Such a circumstance, Montúfar maintained, prevented the proper administration of the sacraments and violated the royal patronage. He particularly resented that the friars obstructed the collection of tithes by the diocesan clergy, and the fact that everywhere in New Spain the regulars seemed to have the confidence and support of the King and viceroy. The archbishop singled out the Augustinians in Michoacán for particular criticism. He informed that they built "royal edifices" for the use of a few friars and staffed the establishments with a raft of Indian servants.

Montúfar proceeded to a discussion of the friars' invasion of his own inquisitorial functions. He said that the orders had contrived an entire judiciary to discipline the Indians, and that they had established their own Inquisition to punish unorthodox conduct among the friars and the natives alike. He related how the Franciscans and the Augustinians punished friars for saying mass without faculties to do so, and how they used the Holy Office to enforce clerical discipline when they felt like doing so. Montúfar lamented the fact that the friars refused to recognize him or his provisor as ordinary. They staged their own autos de fé and meted out harsh punishments to the natives, particularly to prominent Indian leaders. He told the King that when he first came to Mexico the friars asked his permission to punish the natives. "Now they no longer ask, because they claim faculties superior to the bishop."

Montúfar gave Philip II a suitably anonymous description of the monastic Inquisition in action. He maintained that his description was standard practice on the part of the friars. Some three months ago, Montúfar wrote that a friar had put on an inquisi-

THE INQUISITION AND THE CLERGY 121

torial display, hoping to frighten some Indian heretics. He had four Indians tied to four poles in the plaza and had placed a great deal of firewood around the poles. A fire was lighted and the wind blew it out of control so that two of the Indians were burned alive and the other two were seriously injured before they could be released from the stakes. Another friar had subjected an Indian to torture and had told him the torture would be repeated the next day if he failed to confess. When the jailer came to the cell the following day, it was found that the Indian had hanged himself in order to escape further torture.

Dr. Luis Fernández de Anguis in a letter of February 20, 1561, informed the monarch about the same incidents.[11] There are documented accounts of excesses in Inquisition-like punishments of the Indians in Yucatán at the time Montúfar was criticizing the friars in his letter to the King.[12] What is interesting in light of Montúfar's obvious bias is that he did not go into any details about the Dominican excesses in 1560, where the friars tortured the natives and staged an auto de fé in Teitipac.[13]

As the bishoprics were established in the Mexican provinces and as the ordinaries began to assume control, as Bishop Francisco de Toral did in Yucatán in 1562, many friars lost their authority under their quasi-episcopal faculties. However, Archbishop Montúfar did little to change the friars' activities in the remote areas. For one thing the shortage of hierarchy personnel militated against change; for another the question of faculties was not resolved until after Archbishop Montúfar had passed from the scene.

Montúfar as ordinary might not have had power to discipline friars within the episcopacy, but as inquisitor (a function of the ordinary) he had broad, relatively unrestricted residual authority for the enforcement of orthodoxy. He used this authority to launch investigations of clerical orthodoxy. With considerable zeal Montúfar and his delegates haled monastic prelates and individual friars before the Inquisition, questioning their sermons, investigating their publications. It is difficult to question Archbishop Montúfar's correctness in prosecuting clerical personnel during his reign, and he did try hierarchy clergy as well as friars, but the nature of some investigations leads to speculation whether diocesan politics was a motivating factor in trials of regular clergy.

One of Montúfar's most important concerns was the proper supervision and control of books printed and used in the episcopacy. His predecessor, the Franciscan Juan de Zumárraga, had assumed the licensing function until his death in 1548. Zumárraga's career as bookman, censor and patron of publishing in New Spain is well known. Conflicting interpretations of the first archbishop's editorial procedures and his use of Erasmian ideas still appear.[14] His publication of Constantino Ponce de la Fuente's *Doctrina Christiana* in 1546 without giving credit to the author has been interpreted to mean that Zumárraga remained an Erasmist until he died in 1548.[15] The almost universal identification of Erasmist thought with Lutheranism by the Spanish Inquisition was echoed in New Spain during the Montúfar inquisitorial ministry.[16] The problem of Zumárraga's Erasmism, and whether it was heretical when he expounded it, is difficult to resolve because of the rapid change of posture of the Spanish Inquisition on Erasmism versus Lutheranism in the two decades between 1530 and 1550.

An important policy adopted by Archbishop Montúfar during the meeting of the First Mexican Church Council in 1555 was the decision to have examined all printed manuals used in religious instruction of the Indians, to ascertain if they were theologically orthodox and accurately translated into the native dialects.[17] The resultant inquiries terminated in the censure and prohibition of two treatises by the eminent Franciscans Juan de Zumárraga and Maturino Gilberti. Whether or not Montúfar intended to do so at the time, he injected the inquisitorial function of his office into the conflict between the regular and the secular clergy in Mexico. The Franciscan order strongly resented the Dominican archbishop's attack on two of its most distinguished colleagues, and they felt constrained to take the matter to the crown and the papacy as the quarrel developed.

While the Montúfar Inquisition might have questioned Zumárraga's affinity for Erasmus and his publication of Constantino Ponce de la Fuente, confessor to Charles V and a Spanish Erasmist mistakenly convicted by the Sevilla Inquisition as a Lutheran, in 1560 the archbishop concentrated on a section of Zumárraga's 1544 tract *La Doctrina Breve Muy Provechosa* and had it examined for heresy.[18] Particular attention was focused on a section of the Doctrina Breve which dealt with the resurrection of Christ. Zumárraga had explained that the blood of Christ which had been spilled was gathered up by the divine person and reunited with the body when the resurrection occurred.[19] Montúfar claimed that many people had grave reservations about this statement. He presented the passage to a group of experts who were charged to decide whether to suppress the tract "in order to avoid scandal" and to protect the beliefs of the faithful.

Three of the examiners were Dominican friars; the other two were diocesan administrators. Fray Diego de Osorio, prior of the Dominican Monastery in Mexico City, pronounced the passage scandalous and "bad sounding." Fray Domingo de la Cruz felt that it was dangerous reading for persons who were not licensed theologians. Fray Bartolomé de Ledesma, Montúfar's censor, said Zumárraga's view of the resurrection and the spilled blood of Christ was heresy. Dr. Luis Fernández de Anguis and Licenciado Orbaneja, Montúfar's legal aides, recommended that the book be suppressed pending its examination by the Holy See. Consequently, on November 3, 1559, the Montúfar Inquisition withdrew the Zumárraga tract from public use. The Doctrina Breve was proscribed until 1573 when a papal pronouncement reinstituted its use in modified form.[20]

Montúfar's foremost ally in his struggle to assert episcopal authority over the friars was the bishop of Michoacán, Vasco de Quiroga. As a result of the First Mexican Church Council meeting in 1555, in which sermons in Indian languages were examined for their orthodoxy and accuracy of translation, Montúfar carried on investigations of sermons and books in the native dialects. A decade later, the Second Mexican Church Council ordered that all such sermons and books have the bishop's imprimatur. Of course there was good reason to subject works in the indigenous tongues to close scrutiny. There were many problems in translation of abstruse theological dogma into languages where the words and concepts had only approximate meanings. Improper translation often aided the process of recurrent idolatry and religious syncretism in the mind of the Indian.[21]

The second controversy between Montúfar and the Franciscans came about as the result of the Montúfar-Quiroga probe into the writings of the great Franciscan linguist Fray Maturino Gilberti in 1559.[22] Already the author of a Tarascan grammar and dictionary, Gilberti in 1559 published, under the seals of the viceroy and the archbishop, his *Diálogo de la doctrina cristiana en legua Tarasca* for religious instruction of the natives. In order to discourage idolatry among the Tarascans, Fray Maturino explained in the Diálogo the veneration of images and crucifixes, teaching that one does not adore a wooden object, but "one prays to or adores the Lord our God who is in heaven."

Many complaints reached Bishop Quiroga that Gilberti was spreading dangerous Protestant ideas among the natives on the veneration of images. Quiroga made a preliminary investigation of the matter, and he ordered a Spanish translation of the Diálogo before he submitted the case to Archbishop Montúfar who on April 6, 1560 prohibited its sale and use.[23] The supreme Inquisition in Spain confirmed the prohibition of the Gilberti tract until 1576,[24] but the Franciscans used the work despite the caveat of the suprema, and Gilberti was reported as telling his flock not to pay any attention to the diocesan administrators. Robert Ricard was quite correct in interpreting the Gilberti controversy in the context of the struggle between the regular and the secular clergy.[25] Certainly Montúfar and the Franciscans had very chilly relations for the next decade.

In the bishopric of Michoacán there had been considerable friction between Vasco de Quiroga and the Augustinian order.[26] The Augustinians were further estranged from the episcopacy when Archbishop Montúfar accused their foremost scholar-administrator, Fray Alonso de la Vera Cruz, of heresy in 1558. Montúfar's accusation came as a direct result of the argument between the regular and the secular clergy over the question of whether the Indian should pay the tithe.

Vera Cruz's treatise *De Decimis* (1555)[27] argued that the Indian ought not to pay the tithe because there was no need for bishops in the new world. Furthermore his view of the Royal Vicariate of the Indies, in which he proclaimed that the King had become in theory and in fact vicar and prelate of all of the regulars in the Indies, obviated the establishment of episcopal power in the new world, and negated the collection of tithes.[28] Vera Cruz argued that the special faculties of the religious granted them by the papacy made secular clergy unnecessary in New Spain.

These devastating views of the leading Augustinian in Mexico could not go unchallenged by the archbishop. On January 31, 1558 Montúfar and Ledesma sent a lengthy denunciation of Vera Cruz and his writings to the Council of the Supreme Inquisition in Spain.[29] The Augustinian, Fr. Arthur Ennis, feels that Fray Alonso did defend unorthodox views in *De Decimis*, and he judged that "carried to their logical extremes his arguments would deny the nature of the episcopate as established in divine and common law."[30]

Montúfar's attack on Vera Cruz before the Spanish Inquisition had powerful repercussions in Mexico. In many ways Fray Alonso had assumed the leadership of the three orders in fighting to retain their faculties; and owing to his efforts in Spain, Pope Pius V supported the regulars in the bull *Exponi nobis nuper* of March 24, 1567.[31] Before this victory Vera Cruz had been recalled to Spain by Philip II on August 4, 1561.[32]

Ennis feels that Montúfar's recurrent letters to the Spanish Inquisition accusing Alonso de la Vera Cruz of heresy prompted Philip's action.[33] However, in Spain Vera Cruz won the major battle for the regulars in their struggle to maintain status in face of Montúfar's determination to institute episcopal supremacy under the dictates of the Council of Trent. Ennis argues that Vera Cruz's defense of his own orthodoxy was strengthened by his "unqualified defense of royal authority in the New World" and

"Philip II not only dismissed the charges against him, but also gained a high respect for him, recognizing his ability and value to the Crown."[34] Obviously Archbishop Montúfar's attempt to discredit Vera Cruz backfired. Surely the regulars were heartened and felt that the King was on their side in the controversy.

The Montúfar Inquisition spent considerable time investigating the moral conduct of the clergy of New Spain. The archbishop apparently felt that minor breaches of deportment among the clergy might create a milieu in which major heresy could thrive. The order clergy were not permitted to forget that Martin Luther had been a friar. From sixteenth-century accounts written by the seculars in the Inquisition papers, one gets the impression that the regulars were the clerical party of treason. Of course prelates and bishops alike demanded impeccable personal behavior on the part of their subordinates so that the colonists and the Indians might have good examples of Christian conduct. But it does seem as though, given the slightest provocation, Montúfar and his provisors launched "security investigations" of friars who were accused of unfortunate public utterances, playing prohibited games or gambling, violating precepts of clerical celibacy, or who otherwise demonstrated their unworthiness. While Bishop Zumárraga had reprimanded clergy who broke the rules and then let them off lightly, Montúfar made a major issue of any unseemly conduct. Archbishop Montúfar set the pattern for other bishops in the viceroyalty because the Inquisition records are filled with cases of provincial clerical discipline.

Of particular note were Montúfar's investigations of the pattern of monastery and school life. Inmates of friaries and seminary students often wished that they had spoken more discreetly to their fellows because the Inquisition had informants everywhere.[35] Dr. Barbosa's investigation of student discussions in 1564 provoked the trial of a young priest in minor orders, Bartolomé Díaz de Piza, for arguing that in the Eucharist there appeared in transubstantiation no more than the person of the Son.[36]

In Oaxaca, where the Dominicans had entrenched privileges, there was a series of clashes between the order and the hierarchy.

THE INQUISITION AND THE CLERGY 127

As early as 1556 the Dominicans had ignored ecclesiastical censures of the cathedral cabildo of Oaxaca City, and were administering sacraments to those under censure.[37] Dominican priests Fray Andrés de Moguer, Fray Pedro de Farías and Fray Juan de Olmedo were hauled before the ordinary for ridiculing the ecclesiatical cabildo of Antequera (Oaxaca) which was acting in lieu of the bishop because the see was vacant in 1556.[38] It looked as though the cabildo in Oaxaca was glad to retaliate against the friars and to examine a charge that one of their number was a Lutheran in 1564.[39] But the Oaxaca ordinary was far from one-sided in his inquisitorial ministrations. He traveled far to supervise the secular clergy as well as the Dominican friars. In 1567 he asked the fiscal to arrest and to prosecute a diocesan priest, Pedro Pablo de Acevedo, for making heretical statements in a sermon delivered in the Villa de los Zapatecos.[40]

The ordinaries in Michoacán were equally industrious in following Montúfar's lead to discipline friars in an inquisitorial capacity. In 1560 Quiroga's delegate began a proceso against an Augustinian, Fray Francisco de Acosta, for saying that if he was in a state of contemplation and he became hungry and wanted to eat, contemplation could go to the Devil![41] In 1568 Alonso de Pazillas, cantor of the Valladolid Cathedral, acted as delegate of the ordinary in the trial of the vicar of San Miguel (de Allende?) who had scandalized his flock by an unorthodox sermon.[42] In this case and others it appeared as though the regular and secular clergy were tattling on one another in order to induce inquisitorial investigations. Among such reports was the charge that a Michoacán vicar lunched before he said mass,[43] and a Franciscan friar in Zacatecas had committed heresy in contending that his order was more perfect than the Augustinian order.[44] So the ordinaries whiled away their days investigating tedious and gossipy charges of one group against the other.

The pattern of pettiness in "security matters" was by no means confined to one or two bishoprics. In Yucatán and Guatemala much the same thing happened. For example in 1563 the priest of the Villa of San Francisco de Campeche was tried for setting a bad example and using intemperate language with his parishioners.[45] In 1568 the curate of the Villa of Tabasco was investigated because he uttered heresy in a sermon.[46] A Guatemala case of 1565 led to the punishment of Reverend Bartolomé de Valdespino of the Villa of Trinidad for having preached a sermon in which he stated that "the Saints are more worthy than Our Lady the Virgin Mary and even some of us are more worthy than she is."[47]

With such proceedings as these it is not surprising that the Montúfar Inquisition and the ordinaries in the provincial bishoprics were also delving into the private lives and moral conduct of the clergy. Many volumes of investigatory documents deal with the *solicitantes* (priests who solicited women in the confessional),[48] and with those clergy who had unorthodox views on concubinage.[49] Certainly from trial records in the Inquisition archives, neither the Montúfar Holy Office nor the ordinaries in the outlying areas could be accused of maliciously prosecuting the regulars in matters of clerical discipline while the seculars were allowed to go free. Probably, however, the Bishop's invasion of the province of the order prelates in prosecuting the friars for moral offenses added fuel to the fires of conflict between the regular clergy and the hierarchy.

Inquisitorial jurisdiction over public utterances of the friars was much easier for Montúfar to enforce than any control over their private activities. The archbishop was meticulous in his investigations of sermons preached since he could subpoena witnesses and present verifiable testimonies. By the opening years of the decade of the 1560's it became apparent that Montúfar had problems with liberal friars within his own Dominican order. While the Order of Preachers usually represented theological conservatism in the sixteenth-century colony, there were many liberal Bartolomé Las Casas–like figures among its ranks.

Montúfar as archbishop, and as a conservative Dominican, spent many hours bolstering the orthodoxy of his own group. It is not known whether Montúfar's enemies among the regulars and his foremost adversary in the hierarchy, Dr. Alonso Chico de Molina, called into question a sermon given by the Dominican Prelate

Fray Pedro de la Peña in July 1561.[50] The provincial was required to submit to Montúfar's judgment whether the context and interpretation of four statements he made in his sermon verged on heresy. Peña had preached that God grew the soul of man in Heaven and when man died the soul returned from whence it had come. The padre had contended that the mind of man was of angelic nature and that the true Church had existed in heathen times, even before the Christian era. He had gone so far as to contend that "man without the light of God was not technically a man but a brute animal likened to a donkey."

As religious ferment increased in Europe and in Mexico, the view that the immortality of the soul was a pagan concept rather than a new one emanating from Christianity was considered as particularly dangerous; and it appeared as though someone had accused the Dominican provincial of preaching heresy on the one hand and attesting to the animalism of the Indian on the other hand. If for no better reason than to protect the order, Montúfar required Peña to give written discourses on the meaning of these potentially dangerous theses.

On December 10, 1561 Dr. Luis Fernández de Anguis, Montúfar's vicar general and delegate inquisitor, informed the archbishop that another friar had preached in the Santo Domingo Church a sermon which had caused great scandal because of its daring contents. Thus began a long investigation of a well-known Dominican friar of liberal views, Fray Tomás de Chávez.[51] Chávez appears in the testimonies as a kind of latter-day Antonio de Montesinos who took the Spanish State and Church to task for its Indian policies, and as a critic of clerical pomp and circumstance in New Spain. He had decided views on the practice of selling indulgences as well. When he spoke of ecclesiastical processions he ridiculed the use of exaggeratedly large crosses in the parades (referring to them as *crucifijagos*) and pointed to the more modest and tasteful crosses carried in similar processions in Spain. His statements that Christ had to do penance for mankind because men would not do it for themselves shocked some of his listeners.

Montúfar called in two friars from the Dominican convent to

get more details on the sermon. Friars Tomás de Mercado and Martín de Zárate were ordered to appear before Montúfar within four hours of their notification. They produced written versions of the Chávez sermons, one of which appeared to have been corrected and emended by Fray Pedro de Pravia. In Fray Tomás de Chávez' remarks on Indian policy he had criticized the viceroy and the archbishop for their failure to protect the natives.

On January 29, 1561 Archbishop Montúfar called a meeting of dignitaries to examine Fray Tomás de Chávez' conduct. Present were Bishop of Michoacán Vasco de Quiroga; oidores of the audiencia of Mexico Villalobos and Vasco de Puga; the attorney of the audiencia, Mateo Arévalo Sedeño; and Dr. Luis Fernández de Anguis. After perusing the evidence, the group decided that there was not enough evidence to warrant the arrest of Chávez. Since he was so well known and liked in New Spain, it was recommended that, in order to avoid notoriety, Fray Tomás should be sent to Castilla where the Dominican provincial could deal with the matter.

Bishop Quiroga took exception to the recommendation, saying that he could see no justification for such an action. Quiroga did feel, however, that Fray Tomás should be watched closely when he preached in the future. Apparently Quiroga's views guided the decision of Archbishop Montúfar because Fray Chávez stayed in Mexico until he had a second altercation with Montúfar's Inquisition in February 1564. This controvery reached all the way into the halls of the Council of the Supreme Inquisition in Madrid.[52]

Details of the second incident are lacking, but Dr. Rodrigo Barbosa composed an account of Fray Chávez' entry into the archepiscopal offices on February 4, 1564 to say some extremely harsh things to Montúfar. Many witnesses were present, including the Notary Juan de Ibarreta, Montúfar's Secretary Fray Diego de Maldonado, Fray Bartolomé de Ledesma and others. Apparently by this time Montúfar had determined to exile Chávez to Castilla, and Chávez was waging a noisy protest. Visitador Licenciado Jerónimo de Valderrama filled in the details of the Chávez episode when he

THE INQUISITION AND THE CLERGY 131

wrote a letter to the King on February 24, 1564.[53] Valderrama recounts the sermon Chávez gave in which he called the monarchy a thief for taking so much from the Indians. Valderrama noted that the audiencia of Mexico was sending a complete report on Fray Chávez' sermon to Spain. It seems that many Dominicans shared Chávez' view because Valderrama quoted to the King a statement made by Fray Pedro de Pravia:

> His Majesty has no more authority here than what the Pope gave him; and the Pope could not give dominion except for the spiritual welfare of the natives, and the day that they have their own government and are instructed in the Faith, the King has the obligation to return the land to its natives.[54]

Obviously Montúfar had to contend with some very modernistic friars among the Dominicans.

The Montúfar rift with the Augustinians and Franciscans continued to develop in 1563 as the inquisitor investigated the orthodoxy of Fray Antonio de Velásquez, O.S.A., and Fray Gregorio Mejía, guardian of the San Francisco Monastery, for questionable tenets in sermons they had delivered. The Velásquez case was probably the less serious of the two but far more technical from the theological point of view. On March 14, 1564 Fr. Velásquez had delivered a sermon in the Mexico City Cathedral which led to Montúfar's investigation of March 16, 1564. Montúfar and Ledesma had attended the sermon and Ledesma made the opening statement in the Inquisition testimony. He related that Velásquez in discoursing on Christ and the Scribes and Pharisees claimed that Christ expelled devils not by power of Beelzebub but by his *own* strength and power.[55] Dr. Barbosa gave like testimony.

When Montúfar commanded Fray Antonio Velásquez to appear before the court of the ordinary Inquisition, Velásquez admitted that these were his own ideas and that he could not document them in scripture or the writings of the Church Fathers. Montúfar aired the entire theological matter before selected judges of the audiencia and theologians from the secular and religious houses of the city. One wonders if such technicalities and specificities were called for on the part of Montúfar in the Velásquez case. Perhaps he was subtly assuming power in such matters, and this was his way of securing recognition of authority among the regulars.

The case against the Franciscan guardian promised to assume more serious proportions. The lawyer of the audiencia, Francisco de Carriago, came before Montúfar on May 12, 1564 to tell of a suspicious sermon he had heard Fray Gregorio Mejía preach about a year before.[56] It seemed strange that the attorney had not come forward earlier with the information. It seemed that a concerted effort was made to compile faults of the regulars in their preaching. Carriago claimed that Fray Mejía made evil-sounding remarks about the Mother of God and the Trinity, more especially that Mary had ceased to be the Mother of God in the three days that the body of Christ was in the sepulcher. He reported Mejía had claimed that after Christ died the disciples lost their faith which had to be restored to them later. Carriago said that Viceroy Luis de Velasco and several oidores of the audiencia had heard the sermon as well as Pedro de Ahumada Sámano, the governor of the Cortés estate.

The governor of the Marquesado del Valle was required to testify on the same day as Carriaga's denunciation, and Fray Gregorio was asked to defend his statements. He claimed to have used a text from the Apostle Paul as a basis for the sermon. The fragmentary proceso does not inform us of the disposition of Montúfar's investigation. Maybe at this juncture, owing to turmoil in the hierarchy caused by Dr. Alonso Chico de Molina, the archbishop needed allies and he decided not to make any criticism of the Franciscan guardian.

One of the particular concerns of the sixteenth-century Inquisition in Mexico was to see that individuals who attacked the theory of the Church on sexual morality were punished. From the earliest times of the conquest it became a common failing of the orthodox to claim that simple fornication was not a mortal sin. By this they meant that intercourse between two unmarried individuals was

THE INQUISITION AND THE CLERGY 133

not as sinful as adultery. Given the rapid growth of a mestizo population in New Spain by the 1560's, it is apparent that the clergy, while not condoning simple fornication, were permissive in their views.

Montúfar took the Augustinian Friar Andrés de Aguirre to task for making a public statement that simple fornication was not a sin.[57] On July 3, 1568 Fray Bartolomé de Ledesma informed Archbishop Montúfar that Fray Aguirre had given absolution to a person who claimed that simple fornication was not a mortal sin. Ledesma had received his information from Presbyter Luis de Olid Biedma, vicar of the Villa de los Valles, who knew of the incident which took place in the Augustinian Convent of Atotonilco.

An agent of the Inquisition had arrived at the convent escorting a prisoner. When the agent was asked about the prisoner's crime, he told the friars that the man had said simple fornication was not a mortal sin. Aguirre told them of an incident some years before when he had met a truly contrite man in the Villa of Guadalupe who was doing penance for saying the same thing, and he had absolved him of any error. Nothing came of the investigation. Whether Montúfar felt that the substance of the denunciation was too flimsy or whether he was compiling denuncias for future confrontation with the Augustinians, and kept the Aguirre matter in his file, we can only speculate.

In his capacity as ecclesiastical judge ordinary, Archbishop Montúfar initiated the first heresy trials of nuns in New Spain. The two inquisitorial investigations in convents during the 1560's exemplify the episcopate's determination to assert authority in this realm of the life of the regular clergy. In the case of the Nun Elena de la Cruz there are discernible political overtones, since the sister's family were implicated in the Avila-Cortés conspiracy. Montúfar's first proceso of a nun began on December 5, 1562 when Fray Bartolomé de Ledesma investigated the views of Francisca de la Anunciación, an inmate of the Monastery of the Immaculate Concepción in Mexico City.[58] The mother superior and five nuns of the convent, all of whom had known Sister Francisca for over a decade, gave testimony about her views on suicide and the laws of the Church. When one of the nuns hanged herself, Francisca de la Anunciación declared quite forcefully that the unfortunate one should not be condemned by the group and that God would not send her soul to Hell. When the body was found, Francisca said it appeared to her that the soul was still in the body and the face was in repose.

As the inquisitorial investigation proceeded, Ledesma and the nuns painted a picture of Sister Francisca as an unstable woman who often appeared on the verge of insanity. Whether the six nuns testified as they did out of charity, and in order to excuse Francisca of any theological error, seemed to be Ledesma's major preoccupation. When the accused was questioned, she appeared to be a rational witness who had been severely shocked by the suicide. She had dreamed that the spirit of the deceased had appeared to her on several occasions. Apparently, very rashly, she had told her coreligious about the dreams, and they were scandalized by her statements. When Ledesma questioned her, she denied any family history of Jewish or Moorish lineage and she denied that her family, the Francisco Chávezes, had ever been involved with the Holy Office of the Inquisition. Montúfar and Ledesma were disposed to let the matter rest after they charged the nuns to be on the alert in the future for heretical statements among their group.

It is not clear whether the same person who brought the Francisca de la Anunciación matter to Montúfar's attention also denounced Elena de la Cruz on July 16, 1568.[59] It is interesting that many of the same nuns gave testimony, including Francisca de la Anunciación who appeared twice before the ordinary. Elena de la Cruz was a daughter of Licenciado Juan Gutiérrez Altamirano, Cortés' attorney and one-time governor of the Cortés estate. She was probably a second cousin of Martín Cortés.[60] Elena's kinship to the Cortés family and the fact that the conspiracy had aborted and the second marquis was being tried in Spain, obviously had some bearing on Montúfar's decision to act harshly in this instance. It was upsetting to the hierarchy clergy that such an articulate theo-

THE INQUISITION AND THE CLERGY

logian as Elena de la Cruz existed in a Mexican nunnery. Sister Elena could very well be considered as the sixteenth-century precursor of Sor Juana Inéz de la Cruz, if not in orthodoxy then certainly in intellect.

It had come to Montúfar's attention in July 1568, that Elena de la Cruz of the Monastery of the Immaculate Conception had discoursed at length, before many witnesses, on the powers of the papacy, the binding nature of the decrees of the Council of Trent and the nature of sin. Elena had questioned the coercive power of the Pope and of Archbishop Montúfar to oblige obedience to Church mandates outside of the realm of the seven mortal sins. She contended that Montúfar had no real power to concede pardons or indulgences for violation of divine law.

When questioned by Ledesma and Montúfar, Elena de la Cruz answered in a forthright and intelligent fashion. She confirmed that she was the daughter of Licenciado Altamirano and that she had lived all her forty-three years in Mexico City, although family tradition had it that she was born in Cuba. She told Montúfar she knew precisely why she was in the halls of the Inquisition. She reiterated her belief that not even the Pope could increase the number of the seven mortal sins. She had told some companions that the Holy Father was interested more in the saving of souls than in condemning believers. Her own reading and reflections led her to believe that if one obeyed the Ten Commandments and did not commit a mortal sin, he would be assured salvation. It developed that Elena had read books of Fray Luis de Granada which were prohibited by the Inquisition, and a treatise by "a Carthusian" which contended that man achieves perfection by a simple observance of the Ten Commandments. Many of Elena de la Cruz's ideas seemed to be a reworked type of Erasmian thought, although the name of Erasmus never emerged in the testimonies.

On August 14, 1568 the Montúfar Inquisition ordered Elena de la Cruz imprisoned, pending the outcome of her trial. Fray Bartolomé de Ledesma required the abbess of the monastery to see to it that the prisoner communicate with no one in the establishment and be allowed to see no one from the outside. The only exception to the rule of isolation was that the abbess was to be allowed to visit Elena "and to console her" as she deemed necessary.

Because it was virtually impossible to keep the trial from public notoriety, the Altamirano relatives found out about Elena's predicament. By August 27, 1568 Elena de la Cruz had a lawyer defending her. Certainly Juan Vellerino was appointed her defender by the family and not by the court, because appointed defenders invariably were indicated in the procesos. Licenciado Vellerino contrived a clever and intelligent defense of his client, playing up her unworldly feminine side rather than her intellect, and excusing her actions on the basis of her sincere desire to repent. He related that she had already humbled herself before the assembled sisters of the convent and "on her knees with tears streaming down her cheeks" she begged forgiveness for her conduct.

Vellerino blamed many of Elena de la Cruz's misguided statements on her reading of Fray Luis de Granada, and other ideas which she had picked up decades ago before she entered the order. He ended a powerful brief in her behalf by pointing to her laudable Christian life and her position as daughter of a hildalgo, Licenciado Altamirano, who now deceased, had set a good example for a whole generation of colonists. By September 17, 1568 the defendant had yet another lawyer, Licenciado Fulgencio de Vigue, laboring to extricate her from inquisitorial punishment. By this time Elena de la Cruz was incarcerated in the jail of the archepiscopal see, because it was there that she heard the sentence pronounced.

Bartolomé de Ledesma's sentence was very light, considering the length of the trial and the admission of error on Elena's part. On a feast day she was required to stand in the chorus of her convent with a penitential candle in her hand and to hear mass. She was to repeat the penitential psalms and make a public abjuration of error. She was commanded to fast on three successive Fridays and to repeat the psalms again. The sentence concluded with a strong admonition "that from this day forward Elena de la Cruz was not to hold, to utter or to affirm any of these heretical propositions or

THE INQUISITION AND THE CLERGY 137

to say any other thing contrary to the teachings of the Holy Mother Church of Rome." If she should violate this order, Ledesma promised that the Holy Office would proceed against her with the "full force of the law."[61]

As the decade of the 1560's came to an end, it was evident that each year the regular clergy were losing ground to the hierarchy in the general struggle to retain faculties and in their attempt to remain free of the ordinary in doctrinal matters. By January 1569 Archbishop Montúfar had appointed Fray Bartolomé de Ledesma as administrator of the diocese and he had also created a special portfolio for Dr. Estéban de Portillo, calling him "inquisitor delegate in matters relating to the regulars." Montúfar and Portillo maintained that this office had been established pursuant to the dictates of the Council of Trent. It was against this background that the climactic fracas over inquisitorial authority began between Montúfar and the orders.

Fray Alonso Urbano, a distinguished Franciscan preacher who had been guardian of the Franciscan monasteries in Tacuba and Toluca, preached a very controversial sermon on the day of the Feast of the Circumcision in January 1569. Montúfar was so disturbed over the reports he had received about the sermon that he instructed Dr. Portillo to arrange for the arrest of the Franciscan.[62]

Citing his commission from Montúfar and the authority of the Council of Trent, Dr. Portillo ordered the provincial of the Franciscan order and the guardian of the convent to escort Fray Alonso Urbano to the archepiscopal offices to explain the sermon. The mandamus placed Urbano, the provincial, and the guardian under the pain of excommunication if they failed to comply, and Portillo warned the two functionaries they would be liable to prosecution by the Holy Office if they obstructed its functions. These rather strong words evoked a similar reply. The secretary of the Holy Office, Damaso de Leyva, told Portillo he had taken the writ to the Monastery of San Francisco on January 21, 1569. He had read the proclamation aloud to reverend fathers Fray Miguel Navarro, provincial of the O.F.M. and Fray Diego de Mendoza, guardian of the convent. They gave the secretary a disconcerting reply. As much as they revered the Archbishop and his delegates, they did not feel obliged to obey in this instance because Pope Pius V had exempted regulars from episcopal authority in the *Exponi nobis nuper* of 1567. As for the penalty of excommunication mentioned in Portillo's letter, the friars stated categorically that they could not accept the archbishop's faculty as judge, and therefore the order was null and void.

Archbishop Montúfar sent three additional commands to the Franciscans using the most explicit language. On January 22, 1569 he said, "For the present we require and command the Father Provincial of the Franciscan Order . . . to bring before us Father Fray Alonso Urbano." Damaso de Leyva again had the task of delivering the summons. Friars Navarro and Mendoza made it clear in their reply that if Montúfar was "ordering as pastor and seignior" they would be glad to answer him, but if he was "commanding [them] as a judge," they had to refuse his jurisdiction. Montúfar became so annoyed at the second reply that he issued a third mandamus, expecting compliance within three hours. No doubt he intended to have it out once and for all with the regulars. He told Navarro and Mendoza he would excommunicate them and begin inquisitorial proceedings against them immediately.

After four days elapsed, the Franciscans began to file their legal briefs. The secretary of the Holy Office was told by the Franciscan provincial that the responsible officer to deal with the archbishop's request was Guardian Mendoza, because he was not only the provincial's delegate but also Fray Alonso Urbano's immediate superior. On January 26, 1569 Mendoza talked to the secretary and indicated that he would be glad to respond to the first summons from the archbishop but the episcopacy had failed to send him a certified copy of the document requested days before. Apparently a "war of procedure" was being waged by the Franciscans, and of course they wanted signed evidence of Montúfar's actions should it become necessary to appeal to the audiencia and to Spain. In the meantime, Guardian Mendoza agreed to discusss the matter with Leyva on the second-echelon level. He questioned the archbishop's authority to investigate the orthodoxy of Franciscans in an Inquisition court under the power of the Council of Trent. Mendoza then went on to recapitulate papal bulls from 1522 to 1567 which confirmed the privileges of the religious and exempted them from the inquisitorial jurisdiction of the bishops.

On that same day, Guardian Diego de Mendoza began a formal legal answer to the archbishop. In the name of his provincial, Mendoza reviewed the history of the present controversy and stated firmly that the Franciscans

> were not obligated to obey his command, because their Order and the friars within it are exempt and free of all subjection to ordinary prelates, and are immediately suffragan to the Holy See; these privileges have been confirmed by many pontiffs, and more recently by concession of the Holy Father Pius Fifth, after the "Sacred Tridentine Council."[63]

Fray Domingo then went on to relate it was public knowledge all over the city that His Reverence had compiled an *información* regarding what Fray Alonso Urbano had said in the pulpit. The guardian requested that Montúfar make this document available to the Franciscans so that they could punish Urbano if they deemed him culpable. Mendoza stated that he would take the matter to the audiencia and to the King if necessary in order to resolve the dispute. The Franciscan guardian challenged Montúfar to present any specific papal brief post-dating the 1567 *Exponi nobis nuper* which subjected the religious to episcopal jurisdiction. He assured Montúfar that if such a bull were presented, the Franciscans would obey it.

Montúfar answered the Mendoza brief by explaining that the archepiscopal office did not have spelled out for it special areas of residual authority under the revised procedural laws of the Council of Trent. However, the archbishop claimed the Trentine dictum which said that only clergy subject to the episcopal powers of the bishops could serve as priests and administer sacraments was ample to substantiate his jurisdiction. Montúfar contended that the power delegated to him in Mexico by the Council of Trent included the inquisitor ordinary, and that he in turn was entitled to delegate the authority throughout his episcopal hierarchy. It appears as though the Franciscans and other order clergy were aware that the days of autonomy were numbered. This could be the only reason for the provincial's decision to order Urbano to appear before Montúfar to answer charges. Certainly the provincial did not wish notoriety for his order before the audiencia of Mexico and the Council of the Indies in the Urbano case, because there was adequate theological ground to question the orthodoxy of parts of the controversial sermon. In any event Fray Alonso Urbano appeared before the Montúfar Inquisition on February 8, 1569 to stand trial.

The investigation was unusually long and tedious. Full questioning on Urbano's family history revealed he was of ancient Catholic lineage and no member of his family had been punished by the Inquisition. When queried on the reasons for his appearance before the Montúfar Inquisition, Fray Alonso quoted three of the major objections raised against his sermon on the day of the Feast of the Circumcision. These were that Christ was made to be a sinner, that Christ was made to be foolish and that God his Father had detested Him. Fray Urbano explained his meaning in each case and quoted scriptural foundation for his text from Jeremiah, Saint John and Saint Peter. Montúfar and his counsellors found Fray Urbano unorthodox in his interpretations of scripture. There ensued long theological questioning by analogy. Urbano's use of the word *necio* (foolish) was given close scrutiny, and it was deemed to be "an injurious word according to the common use and understanding of it."

Dr. Estéban de Portillo meted out a harsh punishment to Fray Alonso Urbano. Obviously the Montúfar Inquisition wished to use the sentence as an example of what the other orders might expect if they got too daring with their preaching, and if they fell under the censure of the Holy Office. On March 13, 1569 Fray Alonso was required to present himself at the pulpit of the cathedral after the offertory of the major mass of the day, and he publicly retracted the questionable propositions in his sermon. Portillo and Montúfar wrote the retraction, and Urbano was charged to read it ver-

THE INQUISITION AND THE CLERGY 141

batim "without adding or deleting one single word," or he would be branded a heretic and guilty of contempt. Furthermore, the Holy Office forbade Fray Alonso Urbano from preaching "any sermon, anywhere, and in any language" for a period of four years. The sentence was handed down by Portillo on March 8, 1569. The celebrated confrontation between Montúfar and the Franciscans thus ended with an episcopal victory. When Philip II wrote the cédulas founding a formal tribunal of the Inquisition in Mexico in 1569, he made it clear that the court did have jurisdiction in enforcing orthodoxy among the friars.[64] It is apparent that this action of the crown somewhat mollified the episcopacy; because Fray Bartolomé de Ledesma commuted the Urbano sentence on May 1, 1572 after Archbishop Montúfar had died.

Alonso de Montúfar's decision to enforce clerical orthodoxy extended beyond the regular clergy. A series of controversies between the archbishop and Dr. Alonso Chico de Molina, archdeacon of the Cathedral of Mexico and dean of the cathedral chapter, illuminates the shifting concepts of orthodoxy among hierarchy clergy in the Trentine epoch. Against the background of Montúfar's struggles with the orders, Chico de Molina's activities took on important meaning. As a young, studious, intellectually combative diocesan administrator and theology professor, Chico de Molina caused intellectual ferment in the hierarchy, and he divided the cathedral chapter into liberal and conservative camps. He also focused attention on hierarchy politics during a crucial six-year interval, 1560-1566, when the Dominican archbishop and his fellow religious allied against the Franciscans and Augustinians in the conflict over competencies. As a matter of practical politics Dr. Chico de Molina aligned himself with the regulars and the restive conquering families who were losing their power in New Spain in the 1560's.

The Inquisition procesos against Chico de Molina show how he counterattacked Montúfar's cohorts, accusing them of heresy, and the records also reveal how episcopal biases influenced the definition of orthodoxy. Perhaps in using the techniques that he did, Chico de Molina exhibited the traits of pettiness he so abhorred in others. Montúfar and the diocesan administrators embroiled the archdeacon in complicated ecclesiastical litigation over his conduct, and while the Council of the Supreme Inquisition in Spain exonerated Chico de Molina of heresy, his superiors succeeded in disciplining him for insubordination. In 1560 Archbishop Montúfar had to abide the arrogant autonomy of a regular clergy, but he did not permit the archdeacon's obstreperous conduct within the hierarchy. Chico's alliance with the friars could not be tolerated by the episcopacy.

Alonso Chico de Molina had been in Mexico six months when his first altercation with the Montúfar Inquisition developed. It all began on September 5, 1560 at a dinner party in the archbishop's quarters. Montúfar, Fray Bartolomé de Ledesma, the Dominican Prior Diego de Osorio and Chico de Molina were sitting at the table after the meal when a heated theological argument occurred. Montúfar left the room before the discussion got out of hand but his Dominican companions remained to dispute with Chico de Molina. The issue at point concerned the sacraments, and Montúfar and Ledesma had maintained that the sacraments in and of themselves conferred grace on the individual believer. Dr. Chico de Molina argued that adult believers *already* in a state of grace were not given grace by the sacraments of the Church. When the archbishop and Ledesma said their view was the one determined by the Council of Trent, Chico "perversely ignored the Archbishop" and was reprimanded by Montúfar before he retired for the night, leaving the discussion to his subordinates. When Ledesma reported to the archbishop how the discussion developed, Montúfar on September 6, 1560 decided to prosecute the archdeacon for heresy.[65] The diocesan administrators Ledesma, Anguis, Barbosa and Portillo, along with the Dominican prior, were the chief witnesses for the prosecution.

In subsequent testimony by Fray Bartolomé de Ledesma, it was revealed that after Montúfar left the theological discussion, Dr. Chico de Molina lost his temper. When Ledesma quoted to him a commentary by Soto Irano which held that the sacraments *ex opere operato* (in and of themselves) confer grace, and when Ledesma cited the authority of the councils of Trent and Florence for the commentary, Chico de Molina contended that the dicta of the Council of Trent were not binding because the papacy had not given approval to the Trentine deliberations. When the Dominican prior, Diego de Osorio, contradicted Chico and substantiated Ledesma's argument, the archdeacon said very impolite things to them. Chico became so enraged that he grabbed Osorio by the cape and contended neither he nor his entire "Black Order" would force him to accept their theological interpretations. It was then that Chico de Molina left the house in anger after the two Dominicans threatened to denounce him to the Inquisition for his views. Both Ledesma and Osorio entered their testimony into the trial record the morning after the incident.

Montúfar's provisor, Dr. Luis Fernández de Anguis, called on Chico de Molina on three separate occasions between September 6 and September 9, 1560. He tried to induce the archdeacon to apologize to Montúfar and Osorio before it was too late. Each time he found Chico de Molina surly and combative. Anguis testified that he urged the archdeacon to humble himself before his superior and accept the fact that he was mistaken in his views, but each time Chico replied he was a learned man whose data and opinions were correct. He showed Anguis a book by Fray Domingo de Soto which said the sacraments in and of themselves did not confer grace. Anguis told Chico de Molina his interpretations of Fray Domingo de Soto were incorrect, and later he implied to the Inquisition court that Chico was engaging in dangerous individual interpretation of scripture, something akin to Protestantism. As the result of the provisor's third visit to Chico de Molina's quarters, the latter agreed to put his views in writing. Anguis looked over his shoulder as Chico composed the letter to Montúfar, and Anguis testified he cautioned moderation in the phrasing. Then Anguis delivered the epistle to the archbishop who entered it *in toto* in the Inquisition proceso.

After Provisor Anguis failed to get Chico de Molina to retract his controversial statements, Montúfar as inquisitor ordinary interrogated him on September 9, 1560. The archdeacon found ways to include important ideas in his testimony. For instance, he told Montúfar that as an orthodox Catholic and doctor of theology he felt the obligation to defend orthodoxy as he understood it. Chico de Molina said he had acquired his view of the sacraments as a student in the class in Thomistic theology at the University of Salamanca, and what he had said at Montúfar's dinner was the accepted and public view of professors at Salamanca. When Prior Osorio had argued with him at Montúfar's house, Chico claimed that the prior would not even discuss the Salamanca theory, and the archdeacon added with a certain guile that even the archbishop had told him to "shut up." Then in the course of the testimony, Chico de Molina apologized to Montúfar for being impertinent and kissed his ring as a sign of obedience.

What really annoyed Montúfar in this first testimony was Chico de Molina's contention that he had discussed his views with theologians of the three orders and that they had listened to his statements and affirmed he was correct. Chico de Molina had arranged a consultation in the San Francisco Monastery to get advice and support for his position. Fray Juan Focher, O.F.M. and other Franciscans had been present, as well as the Augustinian friars Antonio Isidro, Joseph de Herrera and Francisco de Solís. Fray Antonio Isidro was the incumbent prior of the Augustinian house in Mexico City, and was a licensed theologian. On September 10, 1560 Inquisitor Montúfar commanded the Augustinians to testify. They told the archbishop-inquisitor that in their view Chico de Molina's statements were not censurable but his views on the Council of Trent were rash. Obviously Montúfar was interested to find out what Franciscans and members of his own Dominican order had told Chico de Molina, and he was disconcerted to learn that the friars had given written *pareceres* to the archdeacon.

Because the Chico de Molina affair threatened to become a theological *cause célèbre* in the struggle between the hierarchy and the religious, Montúfar proceeded cautiously for the next two weeks. He needed to verify information on the extent of the involvement of the orders in the case. On September 26, 1560 he found it advisable to call in expert legal assistance. His consultants from the audiencia and Dr. Anguis felt that a great scandal was in the making, and since the friars apparently had filed views which conflicted with those of the archbishop, they recommended the entire case be referred to the Council of the Supreme Inquisition in Spain. Meanwhile they advised Montúfar to give stern warnings to the archdeacon and to the friars who had submitted pareceres, informing them they were liable to excommunication if they made their views public. As a result of this meeting, Chico de Molina's license to preach was suspended pending resolution of the case. Because of considerable behind-the-scenes gossip about Chico de Molina and his quarrel with the archbishop, Dr. Anguis recommended that Montúfar continue his own inquisitorial investigations lest it appear that the Holy Office had been intimidated.

As a result of his discussions with the lawyers, Montúfar as ordinary issued several commands to Archdeacon Chico de Molina. On the afternoon of September 26, 1560 he instructed Chico that he was not "to mention or to talk about publicly or privately" any matter connected with his trial. In a separate order he commanded the archdeacon to submit to the Holy Office all of the pareceres given him by the friars. On the same afternoon Chico de Molina answered his archbishop—and with a certain amount of humor. Unfortunately, he had entrusted all the pareceres to the Augustinian Fray Alonso de la Vera Cruz, who had taken them with him on a tour of the provinces. Dr. Chico de Molina's tone seemed to project that he was perplexed by Montúfar's attitude. He reminded his superior it was common knowledge that he encouraged theological disputation at his dinners.[66] When the companions of Montúfar called him a heretic, Chico de Molina said he consulted "with the most important theologians of *all three* orders" to validate his own position, and they had done so with signed statements.

In his letter to Montúfar of September 26, 1560 Chico de Molina went on to say that none of the friars felt that there was theological error in his statements at the dinner table. However he told

Montúfar that if in the heat of the moment, and by a slip of the tongue, he said anything wrong, it was without any intent to offend. He begged Archbishop Montúfar to determine "if I *really* committed heresy in anything I said about the Council of Trent or the Holy Church." Montúfar's anger was apparent when he summoned Dr. Chico de Molina for his second audience before the Holy Office on September 30, but it was matched by the archdeacon's cold and calculating venom in the testimony. In this session Chico de Molina brought the issue of Dominican politics in the episcopacy out into the open. He attacked the good faith and conduct of Fray Bartolomé de Ledesma, pointing out the obvious fact that both the archbishop and his witnesses were Dominicans and were neither objective nor honest in their appraisal of Chico's views. He complained that both Ledesma and Osorio had "said publicly and in many places that I . . . was a heretic" and that "Your Reverence and the Prior of Santo Domingo were right and I was wrong."

At this point Dr. Chico de Molina unleashed his attack on Montúfar. He accused the archbishop, by proceeding as he had, of casting doubt "on my honor, fame and the good name I have in this community as a licensed theologian and a person of quality." He said Montúfar had proceeded "maliciously," using the Holy Office as a weapon to stifle honest disagreement, and he protested Montúfar's competence as a judge in this particular case since there was abundant proof of his prejudice. Dr. Chico de Molina ended his second audience before Montúfar by hinting that it might be necessary for him to appeal the matter to Rome.

Perhaps Dr. Chico de Molina did in some measure intimidate the archbishop. During October and November of 1560 Montúfar took voluminous testimony to help substantiate his own position. On October 21, 1560 he called as witness Bachiller Alvaro Pérez Marañón, who was acting as provisor of Indians at this time. Pérez Marañón informed the Holy Office there was considerable scandal in the community engendered by the archdeacon's view that the sacraments did not confer grace. The provisor of Indians said he considered such statements very evil "at a time when

THE INQUISITION AND THE CLERGY 147

the Church was beset by Lutherans and heretics." He told Montúfar he had said this very thing to Dr. Chico de Molina several days ago, and Dr. Chico had assured him that the matter had been cleared up. He told Pérez Marañón he had the opinions of many lawyers, Dominicans as well as Franciscans and Augustinians, who proclaimed his views as orthodox. Chico had shown Pérez Marañón some of the documents when they stopped to chat outside the archdeacon's dwelling. Among the letters was a special one written to Chico de Molina by Fray Alonso de la Vera Cruz, and Chico had read its contents aloud. Fray Alonso, as a licensed theologian, had shared the archdeacon's view of the sacraments.

Montúfar continued to gather interesting testimony. On October 21 Fray Bartolomé de Ledesma appeared once again in the Inquisition Court. Provisor Anguis had told him of Pérez Marañón's conversation with Chico de Molina and the Alonso de la Vera Cruz letter. Ledesma also gave a critique of a conversation he had with Dr. Chico de Molina the week before. In that meeting, in Chico de Molina's rooms, the archdeacon had made two strong statements. He informed Ledesma he would burn before he would retract his views, and he would pack up and leave Mexico if need be.

On October 21, 1560 the Montúfar Inquisition secretary, Juan de Ibarreta, recorded some new developments in the Chico de Molina case. Fray Diego de Osorio revealed for the first time in the trial record that it was the Franciscan guardian, Fray Diego de Olarte, who got Dr. Chico de Molina to make the half-hearted apology to Montúfar on September 9, 1560. Osorio prefaced his remarks with a description of an encounter he had with Chico de Molina on September 7 in the yard of the Dominican monastery. At that time he had counselled the archdeacon that the theological dispute was not for the general public to know about, but rather a matter for experts. He told the archdeacon he could only harm himself by talking about the case indiscriminately. Osorio then proceeded to relate Chico de Molina's decision to apologize. According to the prior, Dr. Chico de Molina had prevailed upon the guardian of San Francisco to mend his fences, and the guardian had approached the Dominican prior for advice on how to proceed. Chico wanted to find a way to reestablish relations with the hierarchy without recanting, and Osorio said he repeated to both of them again that he would burn before he would retract his views. Later, when Montúfar quizzed Olarte on this point the Franciscan demurred, saying that he did not remember any statement about burning. Olarte told Montúfar he had seen the pareceres of the friars who supported Chico de Molina's side of the argument.

On November 5, 1560 the Chico de Molina case entered another crisis when reports reached Montúfar that the archdeacon had preached a sermon in spite of the prohibitions to the contrary. Ledesma had heard part of the sermon and he told Montúfar that it smacked of Lutheranism. On November 5, 1560 the archbishop called a top-level meeting to discuss Dr. Chico de Molina. Oidores from the audiencia of Mexico Villalobos and Vasco de Puga attended, as well as the fiscal of the audiencia, Dr. Maldonado. It was agreed to refer the whole matter of Chico de Molina's orthodoxy to the Sevilla tribunal of the Holy Office and in the meantime to warn Chico de Molina not to preach or express theological opinions. Montúfar wrote the priors of the Dominicans, Franciscans and Augustinians ordering them to stop discussion of the Chico de Molina case in their monasteries. Anyone who violated Montúfar's instructions in this matter was to be excommunicated forthwith.

Archbishop Montúfar suffered a severe defeat when the Council of the Supreme Inquisition in Madrid found Dr. Chico de Molina innocent of heresy sometime in 1561. The decree of the suprema was lost at sea but somehow Chico de Molina learned its contents for he wrote to Philip II on February 17, 1564 asking for a copy of the sentence of exoneration.[67]

After the decision to send the Chico de Molina información and pareceres to the suprema, Archbishop Montúfar's relations with the dean of the cathedral chapter steadily deteriorated. Evidence of the continuing struggle between Chico and the archbishop is contained in administrative records of the archdiocese for the years 1561 and 1562.[68] On October 26, 1562 Montúfar in-

THE INQUISITION AND THE CLERGY 149

corporated testimonies from members of the metropolitan cathedral chapter into a document critical of Dr. Alonso Chico de Molina's behavior. Montúfar began the written statements with one of his own. He informed that his dean had insulted him without any provocation in the archepiscopal offices, saying things that were very injurious, disrespectful and irreverent. Montúfar added that it was Chico de Molina's habit to behave in this way. Dr. Rodrigo Barbosa gave testimony about Chico de Molina's rudeness and disrespect to Montúfar in the chapter meetings and in public. Other functionaries bore witness to Chico's ill will for his archbishop. Dr. Luis de Anguis, as Montúfar's provisor, placed Chico under house arrest pending further investigation. Chico de Molina, through offices of his lawyer Vincencio de Riverol, filed briefs against the archbishop charging him with malicious prosecution because he dared to disagree with Montúfar. Maestro Francisco Cervantes de Salazar was one of the illustrious witnesses for Montúfar, and the famous author upheld the charge that Chico de Molina had exhibited hatred and disrespect for his superior. It is apparent from comments in his own correspondence that Chico de Molina had many allies in the cathedral chapter, and the chapter was divided into pro-Montúfar and pro-Chico camps. The diocesan records, however, contain only the pro-Montúfar, anti-Chico data.[69]

After all the testimonies were gathered in this particular case, Montúfar delayed taking any action. Most likely he was awaiting the decision of the suprema in Chico de Molina's heresy prosecution. When that decision finally arrived in 1564, Chico de Molina again resumed full duties in the cathedral and the chapter. From that time forward Chico became more obstreperous than ever.[70] He accused his enemies of heresy in two famous incidents during 1564 before he joined the Martín Cortés conspirators.

It had been a pattern for the hierarchy clergy to cast doubt on the orthodoxy of the religious by attending sermons preached by the friars. They then informed the Inquisition of dubious theology in the preaching. Chico de Molina decided to use this same stratagem in dealing with Montúfar's two chief assistants—his provisor,

Dr. Rodrigo Barbosa, and his censor and administrative assistant, the Dominican Bartolomé de Ledesma. In Chico's struggles with the episcopacy, 1564 was a climactic year. After that time he enlisted in the Cortés faction to overthrow the political power of the King and the Dominicans in Mexico. In April of 1564 Dr. Barbosa felt impelled to ask Montúfar for a full airing of charges of heresy made against him by the dean. He complained that Chico de Molina had made public statements in many places that Barbosa had uttered heresy in a sermon. Dr. Barbosa appealed to Montúfar to compel the dean to appear before the Inquisition court to substantiate his gossip. On April 9, Montúfar subpoenaed the dean to appear and to give testimony upon pain of excommunication if he failed to do so.[71]

Apparently Barbosa had made a rash and joking statement during a sermon in which he had stated that if husbands were not faithful to their wives, was it not just that wives should also play the field? Chico de Molina claimed Barbosa had scandalized the populace by giving married women license to commit adultery. Obviously the dean was giving Barbosa a hard time by coloring his interpretations of the incident. Just as obviously the dean was teaching the administrators of the diocese that he would employ the techniques against them which they had used to cast aspersions on his own orthodoxy. In order to protect Barbosa, Montúfar called in many people to testify, including mature women who had heard the provisor preach. The testimonies confirmed that Barbosa had made such a statement, but he had used it as a teaching device and in a humorous way. As one might expect, many members of the cathedral chapter who had testified against Chico de Molina now testified to the orthodoxy of Dr. Barbosa's sermon. Many witnesses, including Doña Magdalena de Nava, wife of one of Mexico City's alcaldes, remembered Barbosa had provoked laughter with his statement, but all declared that the incident had no element of reprehensibility.

The investigation ran on through the month of May until Dr. Barbosa lodged formal charges against Dean Chico de Molina on May 18, 1564. Barbosa demanded that his good name and Christian character be vindicated. No doubt a great deal of surreptitious gossip and secret smiling was being indulged in by the friars and the pro-Molina seculars. A complicated interrogatory was framed and many people were called to testify on behalf of Dr. Barbosa. Perhaps the most illustrious witness was Licenciado Jerónimo Valderrama, the visitor general who was engaged in his searching visita of the viceroyalty at this time. On May 30, 1564 Valderrama informed that he had talked to Chico de Molina on occasions and was aware of the unpleasantness going on in the cathedral chapter as well as the disputes among the dean and Barbosa and Ledesma. Valderrama said he could see no point in allowing the arguments between the Chico de Molina faction and the archbishop to go any further. Valderrama echoed the same sentiments in his letters to Spain deploring the episcopal politics which he found in Mexico.[72]

Chico de Molina's quarrels with Montúfar and Barbosa were bound to extend to Montúfar's second in command, Fray Bartolomé de Ledesma. Since the archbishop and Ledesma were co-religionists, the animosity was intensified. Chico de Molina also took Ledesma to task for specific ideas in Ledesma's public sermons.[73] For the most part Dr. Luis de Anguis stayed out of the feud, but his letters to Spain, while openly partisan to the episcopacy, definitely deplored the inner conflicts in Montúfar's archepiscopal see.[74]

Archbishop Montúfar, in order to defend his authority, actually began a second abortive trial of Alonso Chico de Molina on April 10, 1564.[75] Much the same data was included in the proceso as in the Montúfar administrative documents of 1561 and 1562. Chico de Molina's behavior and his utterances in the chapter and in his sermons were given close scrutiny. It appeared as though the Barbosa and Chico de Molina squabble had turned the cathedral chapter into a theological debating society, and charges of heresy and indecorum were hurled back and forth. Each issue and each function of the chapter came to be a case study in the application of disputed theology. The debates in the cathedral chapter and the personal attacks of Chico de Molina and Barbosa were leaving no time for routine business. If petty politics of this sort characterized the inner workings of the episcopacy, one can well imagine the intensity of the friction between the seculars and regulars outside of the hierarchy proceedings.

Little is known of the secret liaison between Dean Chico de Molina and the Avila-Cortés conspirators while the Montúfar quarrels with the dean were taking form. As the conspiracy developed between 1564 and 1568, Chico de Molina became extremely close to the second Marqués del valle. He officiated at the christening of Cortés' twins in 1566, and he assumed a major role in the proposed coup. He agreed to act as diplomat for the marquis and to go to Rome to secure the papacy's support of the new kingdom after Cortés was proclaimed king. He was to make similar representations before the King of France. Of course, Dean Chico de Molina went to jail when the conspiracy was quelled, and he accompanied the marquis to Spain where he was subjected to judicial torture in the ensuing investigations.[76]

No doubt the Montúfar Inquisition felt that its treatment of Dr. Alonso Chico de Molina was completely justified when the dean became a leader in the Avila-Cortés conspiracy. One of the lawyers who worked for the episcopacy, Licenciado Alonso Núñez, wrote to Philip II in January 1568 and referred to Alonso Chico de Molina as "a companion of the Marqués, a heretic traitor and a *'simoniático'* " (practitioner of simony).[77]

This essay raises the fundamental question of whether the sixteenth-century Mexican colony had a Renaissance or a Counter Reformation intellectual milieu. While survivals of medievalism are evident in the colony and Renaissance Humanist social attitudes and Erasmian ideals pervade the thinking of many of the early Mexican clergy, it is apparent from a study of the Inquisition papers that the Mexican Renaissance was quickly overtaken by the Mexican Counter Reformation. From the conquest to 1571, more often than not, the regular clergy exemplified the Renaissance, and the secular clergy came to assume a Counter Reformation posture. The conflict between the religious and the episcopacy was far more than a struggle over privileges and faculties. It also became an ideological struggle between a Renaissance view of the

THE INQUISITION AND THE CLERGY 153

mission of the Mexican Church and a Counter Reformation view. As Erasmist thought and reformist ideas became identified with Protestantism in the minds of many, Mexico's Renaissance clergy were subject to accusations of heresy. Obviously much that was considered orthodox in 1530 was suspicious in 1560.

Alonso de Montúfar, the second archbishop, was a Dominican—and his order had a proud tradition as defenders of orthodoxy in Europe and in Mexico. In New Spain the Dominicans tended to be the most conservative of the regular clergy when it came to ideological matters. They used Thomistic theology as an effective weapon against the erosion of philosophical and theological orthodoxy in the sixteenth century. The Dominican struggle with the Augustinians in Europe (Johann Eck versus Martin Luther) was paralleled by a similar dialogue in Mexico (Montúfar versus the regulars). Alfonso de Valdés' view that the beginning of the Reformation was a monkish quarrel had some relevance for the Mexican quarrel between the regular clergy and the Dominican archbishop. The diocesan administrators, particularly the Dominican Friar Bartolomé de Ledesma and Dr. Luis Fernández de Anguis, often counselled Montúfar that the ideas and the actions of the regulars smacked of Lutheranism.

The Montúfar Inquisition succeeded in asserting the power of the episcopacy to define orthodoxy among the regulars. Montúfar called the First and Second Mexican Church councils (1555, 1565) to devise ways to apply the legislation of the Council of Trent to Mexico. Assumption of doctrinal authority by the archbishop over the religious was the crucial problem. The letters of Montúfar and Dr. Anguis, and the commentaries of Licenciado Valderrama, did much to influence Philip II to shift his support from the regulars to the hierarchy by the end of Montúfar's ministry. The secular position was reinforced with the arrival of the Jesuits in 1571; their frank Counter Reformation orientation supported the hierarchy. By 1574 the King had made the fundamental decision to give full authority to the bishops of New Spain. Certainly the struggle between Montúfar and the regulars over inquisitorial jurisdiction influenced Philip II to establish a tribunal of the Holy Office of the Inquisition in Mexico in 1569. Controlled by neither the episcopacy nor the orders, the court was impartial in clerical controversies, and after the tribunal of the Holy Office began to function in 1571, the question of doctrinal jurisdiction over the order clergy ceased to be a burning issue.

Notes

[1] Two equally sophisticated treatments of the struggle between the regular and the secular clergy are the works of Ricard, *The Spiritual Conquest of Mexico*, pp. 39-263, and Arthur Ennis, *Fray Alonso de la Vera Cruz O.S.A. (1507-1584)* (Louvain, 1957), pp. 100-137.

[2] Perhaps the best survey of Trentine doctrines is Enrique Denzinger, *El Magisterio de la Iglesia. Manual de los Símbolos, Definiciones y Declaraciones de la Iglesia en Materia de Fé y Costumbres* (Barcelona, 1959). For the *Exponi nobis nuper*, see Ricard, *The Spiritual Conquest of Mexico*, p. 245; and Ennis, *Fray Alonso*, p. 124.

[3] Robert C Padden, "The Ordenanza de Patronazgo 1574: An Interpretative Essay," *The Americas: A Quarterly Review of Inter-American Cultural History* (1956), Vol. XII, pp. 333-354.

[4] Greenleaf, *Zumárraga*, pp. 33-37.

[5] Robert Ricard, "Notes sur la biographie de Fr. Alonso de Montúfar, second archeveque de México," *Bulletin Hispanique* (July-September, 1925), pp. 242-246; Ernest J. Burrus, ed., *Ordenanzas para el Coro de la Catedral Mexicana* (Madrid, 1964), pp. 10-15.

[6] Ennis, pp. 116, *passim*.

[7] García Icazbalceta, *Bibliografía Mexicana*, pp. 201-202. See also Ennis, pp. 116, 157, *passim*; and AGN, Inquisición, Tomos 3-29.

[8] Cuevas, *Historia de la Iglesia*, Vol. II, p. 262; Cuevas, *Documentos Inéditos del Siglo XVI para la Historia de México* (México, 1914), pp. 250-267.

[9] Consult Greenleaf, *Zumárraga*, pp. 13-17, *passim*, for the function of ordinary.

[10] "Carta a Su Magestad del Arzobispo de México, de cuatro de febrero de 1561", AGI, Indiferente General, Leg. 2978, ff. 650-656.

[11] "Carta del Dr. Anguis a Felipe II, México, 20 de febrero de 1561," Cuevas, *Documentos*, pp. 250-267.

[12] See Scholes and Roys, and Scholes and Adams, *Don Diego de Quijada*, for the documents. See also Greenleaf, "The Inquisition and the Indians," pp. 138-166.

[13] The 1560 Oaxaca trials are documented by the chronicler Burgoa; see José Antonio Gay, *Historia de Oaxaca* (4 vols., México, 1950), Vol. I, pp. 629-634.

[14] See Greenleaf, *Zumárraga*, pp. 33-40, for pertinent bibliography and modern interpretations of Zumárraga's intellectual milieu. Román Zulaica Garate, *Los Franciscanos y La Imprenta en México en el Siglo XVI* (México, 1939), and

THE INQUISITION AND THE CLERGY 155

Alberto María Carreño, "The Books of Fray Juan de Zumárraga," *The Americas: A Quarterly Review of Inter-American Cultural History* (1949), Vol. V, pp. 311-330, offer valuable insights into Zumárraga's career as an editor.

[15] William B. Jones, "Evangelical Catholicism in Early Colonial Mexico: An Analysis of Bishop Juan de Zumárraga's Doctrina Cristiana," *The Americas: A Quarterly Review of Inter-American Cultural History* (1967), Vol. XXIII, pp. 423-432.

[16] Two excellent monographs by John E. Longhurst exemplify the confusion of Erasmian with Lutheran ideas in Spain, *Erasmus and the Spanish Inquisition: The Case of Juan de Valdés* (Albuquerque, 1950), and *Luther and the Spanish Inquisition: The Case of Diego de Uceda* (Albuquerque, 1953).

[17] Francisco Fernández del Castillo, *Libros y Libreros en el Siglo XVI* (México, 1914), pp. 81-85.

[18] AGN, Inquisición, Tomo 43, exp. 4. "Censura y prohibición de la Doctrina del Ilustrísimo Don Fray Juan de Zumárraga Obispo de México, 1559." The investigation is printed in Fernández del Castillo's work, pp. 1-3.

[19] ". . . que dice (Zumárraga) hablando de las uniones que se hicieron en la Santa Resurrección de Nuetro Redentor Jesucristo, que la sangre derramada, fué recogida por la Potencia Divinal, á lo menos la que era necesaria para el cuerpo, y fue unida á la Divinidad."

[20] See Fernández del Castillo's work and José Toribio Medina, *Primitiva Inquisición*, Vol. II, pp. 50-53, for an interesting document from Archivo General de Simancas, Inquisición, Leg. 760-764, f. 279, which commented, "no hay que prohibir el libro del Arzobispo."

[21] Fernández del Castillo, pp. 570, 81-85.

[22] The Gilberti investigations are contained in AGN, Inquisición, Tomo 43, exps. 6, 20; Tomo 72, exp. 35; Tomo 117, exp. 8. Fernández del Castillo, pp. 6-18, 33, 455, publishes extracts of the trial records.

[23] Fernández del Castillo, p. 7.

[24] AGN, Inquisición, Tomo 117, exp. 8.

[25] Ricard, *The Spiritual Conquest of Mexico*, p. 60.

[26] Ennis, pp. 118-124, reviews the Augustinian conflict with Bishop Quiroga.

[27] See the analysis of the *De Decimis*, an unpublished manuscript housed in the Escorial, Ennis, pp. 140-144, 157-160.

[28] *Ibid.*, pp. 145-150.

[29] Archivo Histórico Nacional, Madrid (hereafter cited as AHN), Inquisición de Méjico, Tomo 4427, exp. 5. Ennis examines the document, pp. 157-160.

[30] *Ibid.*, p. 161.

[31] *Ibid.*, pp. 166-167.

[32] *Ibid.*, pp. 162-163.

[33] The Montúfar Inquisition continued to inform the Spanish authorities about Alonso de la Vera Cruz's heresies. On June 20, 1558 the Archbishop wrote Philip II, charging Vera Cruz with heresy, and on August 15 he sent the King further denunciations. Ennis used these letters from MS4349 AHN. In a letter to the suprema, undated, but probably in 1560, Montúfar informed that he had withdrawn Vera Cruz's published works from circulation in Mexico because he questioned their orthodoxy, AHN, Inquisición de Méjico, Tomo 4442, exp. 41; Burrus, pp. 85-90, reproduces this letter. See also Robert Ricard, *Études et*

documents pour l'historie missionaire de l'Espagne et du Portugal (Louvain, 1930), pp. 92-111.
[34] Ennis, p. 165.
[35] AGN, Inquisición, Tomo 4, exp. 1.
[36] Ibid., Tomo 5, exp. 2.
[37] Ibid., Tomo 2, exp. 14.
[38] Ibid., Tomo 42, exp. 28.
[39] Ibid., Tomo 3, exps. 5b, 5c. The denunciation was malicious; and the witness, Mateo de Monjarrás, was tried for bearing false witness.
[40] Ibid., Tomo 7, exp. 3.
[41] Ibid., Tomo 29, exp. 9, f. 81.
[42] Ibid., Tomo 8, exp. 4.
[43] Ibid., Tomo 44, exp. 4.
[44] Ibid., Tomo 29, exp. 10.
[45] Ibid., Tomo 4, exp. 3.
[46] Ibid., Tomo 7, exp. 13.
[47] Ibid., Tomo 5, exp. 13.
[48] Ibid., Tomos 68, 69, 70, passim. See Greenleaf, Zumárraga, pp. 108-110, for a discussion of the Holy Office and the problems of clerical morality.
[49] AGN, Inquisición, Tomo 34, exp. 8; and Tomo 68, exp. 2.
[50] Ibid., Tomo 3, exp. 3.
[51] Ibid., Tomo 17, exp. 9.
[52] AGI, Indiferente General, Leg. 1217, ff. 1-5v.
[53] France V. Scholes and Eleanor B. Adams, eds., *Cartas del Licenciado Jerónimo Valderrama y otros Documentos sobre su Visita al Gobierno de Nueva España 1563-1565* (México, 1961), pp. 106-107, 114. Montúfar's letters to the King, in which he discusses the Chávez affair, appear in del Paso y Troncoso's *Epistolario*, Vol. 10, docs. 540, 547.
[54] Scholes and Adams, eds., *Cartas del Licenciado Jerónimo Valderrama*, p. 106.
[55] AGN, Inquisición, Tomo 3, exp. 15. See the *Holy Bible, Matthew* 12: 22-28.
[56] AGN Inquisición, Tomo 29, exp. 3.
[57] Ibid., Tomo 8, exp. 5. See the most famous case regarding views on simple fornication in Manuel Toussaint, ed., *Proceso y denuncias contra Simón Pereyns en la Inquisición de México* (México, 1938). See also Henry C. Lea, *The Inquisition in the Spanish Dependencies* (New York, 1908), pp. 198-199.
[58] AGN, Inquisición, Tomo 5, exp. 4.
[59] Ibid., Tomo 8, exp. 1, ff. 5-116.
[60] Genealogical data on the Altamirano is available in AHN, Inquisición, Leg. 1258, exp. 4; AHN, Inquisición, Leg. 1474, exp. 5 and AGI, Audiencia de Méjico, Leg. 114. These documents were consulted by the author in the France V. Scholes collection, Albuquerque.
[61] AGN, Inquisición, Tomo 8, exp. 1, f. 116.
[62] Ibid., Tomo 9, exp. 4, ff. 129-178.
[63] Ibid., f. 133.
[64] *Recopilación de leyes de los Reynos de Las Indias* (4 vols., Madrid, 1681), Lib. I, tít. 19.
[65] AGN, Inquisición, Tomo 3, exp. 2.
[66] ". . . tienen por servir y dar contento a VSR porque le han oido decir a los

THE INQUISITION AND THE CLERGY 157

huespedes que no hay mayor regalo para Vuestra Señoría que un rato de disputa."

[67] Medina, *Primitiva Inquisición*, Vol. II, pp. 279-280, reproduces the letter.

[68] Alonso de Montúfar, *Descripción del Arzobispado de México hecha en 1570 y otros documentos*, Luis García Pimental, ed. (México, 1897), pp. 400-420.

[69] *Ibid.*, pp. 418-420; Medina, *Primitiva Inquisición*, Vol. II, p. 278.

[70] See the letters to Philip II by Chico de Molina and Montúfar, each accusing the other of perfidy in del Paso y Troncoso, *Epistolario*, Vol. IX, docs. 496, 498, 529; and Vol. X, docs. 566, 567, 595.

[71] AGN, Inquisición, Tomo 4, exp. 6.

[72] Scholes and Adams, *Cartas del Licenciado Jerónimo Valderrama*, pp. 162-163, *passim*.

[73] AGN, Inquisición, Tomo 4, exp. 9.

[74] Cuevas, *Documentos*, pp. 250-267.

[75] AGN, Inquisición, Tomo 4, exp. 7.

[76] To what extent the dean's role in the conspiracy has been exaggerated is a moot point. Indeed the extent to which the whole conspiracy was blown out of proportion is a difficult question to resolve. The Franciscan order, in a letter to the King dated August 8, 1566 pronounced the charges against the second Marquis and his cohorts as "frivolous." Bancroft, *History of Mexico*, p. 612; see also the treatment of "The Avila-Cortés Conspiracy 1564-1568," pp. 602-636.

[77] Medina, *Primitiva Inquisición*, Vol. II, p. 230.

Chapter Five

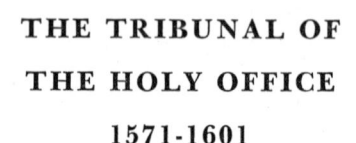

THE TRIBUNAL OF
THE HOLY OFFICE
1571-1601

BY 1571 the episcopal Inquisition had proven itself an unsatisfactory institution in the eyes of the State and the Church. Because the ordinaries had no central direction and their provincial agents lacked adequate training, there had been many abuses of power vis-a-vis both the Indians and the Spanish population. The infiltration of large numbers of heretics pointed to the need for expert prosecutors. But two paramount circumstances impelled the King to found a tribunal of the Holy Office of the Inquisition in Mexico. The first was the feeling that diocesan administrators had used the Holy Office as a weapon in the conflict between the regular and the secular clergy. The second was the deluge of suspicious printed matter from Europe which was entering New Spain. Some competent, apolitical agency, apart from the incumbent religious establishment, had to enforce Counter Reformation orthodoxy in Mexico.[1]

On January 25, 1569 Philip II issued a royal cédula which created two tribunals of the Holy Office in Mexico and Peru.[2] A second cédula of August 16, 1570 delineated the territorial jurisdiction of the Mexican body. Throughout the audiencias of Mexico, Guatemala, New Galicia and Manila all inhabitants of the viceroyalty of New Spain were subject to the tribunal of the Holy Office. Religious administrators suffragan to the Mexican tribunal were appointed in the archbishopric of Mexico and in the bishoprics of Tlaxcala, Michoacán, Oaxaca, Guadalajara, Yucatán, Vera Paz, Chiapas, Honduras and Nicaragua. The entire political machinery of the viceroyalty was charged to assist the tribunal in its work.[3] The inquisitor of Murcia, Dr. Pedro Moya de Contreras, was named the first inquisitor general of Mexico.[4] Licenciado Alonso de Cervantes was designated prosecutor and Pedro de los Ríos assumed the post of notary. By September 12, 1571 the group had reached Mexico City.

The arrival of a powerful tribunal of the Holy Office in Mexico caused some political dislocations, and many of the clergy and their civil counterparts feared loss of prestige. Relations between Moya de Contreras and Viceroy Martín Enríquez were strained. The viceroy arranged that people in the towns along the road from Veracruz to Mexico City gave Moya de Contreras and his staff a warm welcome. But when the tribunal arrived in Mexico City, the viceroy himself received the inquisitor general in a cool, formal manner. Later Enríquez was reprimanded for his conduct. This initial contretemps was but the first clash of viceroys and inquisitors over a period of two centuries. After the tribunal had been suitably housed, it began the business of extirpating heresy on November 2, 1571 with a proclamation which required the entire population of Mexico City to present itself for an installation ceremony on November 4. A solemn procession, staged with great pomp and ceremony, proceeded to the metropolitan cathedral.

Pedro de los Ríos described the event. After the sermon and while the people knelt, he read the King's commands to the viceroy and other secular officials to respect the authority of Inquisitor Moya de Contreras, and he read to the people an edict exhorting them to obey the Holy Office. Enemies of the faith were to be pursued and denounced as "wolves and rabid dogs infesting the souls [of men] and destroyers of the Lord's Vineyard." All major officials swore an oath of obedience to the Holy Office on the book of the mass.[5]

On November 10, 1571 letters were sent by Moya de Contreras to all areas of the viceroyalty commanding that government officials take an oath of obedience to the Holy Inquisition. *Familiares,* or Inquisition police, were appointed in each province to enforce the tribunal's decrees and to make arrests of those guilty of unorthodox conduct. Commissaries were named for each province to investigate heresy and to gather evidence for the central tribunal. With the establishment of the tribunal, there began three decades of energetic effort to combat heresy and immorality within a Counter Reformation framework.[6] Procedures were formalized; permanent and orderly channels for investigation of heresy were established; the rule of law prevailed.[7]

The archive of the tribunal of the Mexican Holy Office from 1571 onward has remained intact. Administrative documents lacking in the episcopal Inquisition records shed much light on Mexico's Counter Reformation mentality between 1571 and 1601. There seems to be little doubt that the colonial population looked upon the tribunal as a benign and popular institution which was protecting religion and Spanish society from traitors and fomenters of social revolution. The tribunal maintained close and voluminous communication with the Council of the Supreme Inquisition in Spain, and the Mexican inquisitors were *au courant* with the changing Iberian intellectual climate and the European political scene.

The correspondence series of documents in Mexico and the registries of letters and reports in Spain show how efficiently the two bodies worked together.[8] From 1572 until the turn of the eighteenth century the tribunal sent periodic reports to the *suprema* recounting the various autos de fé, public and private, staged in the Mexican capital. These *relaciones de causas de fé* contained brief biographical-theological notes on heretics who were punished.[9] Almost inevitably the secretariat of the *suprema* replied to these *relaciones* by the next mail, commenting on the crimes, sentences and procedures meted out and offering advice on how to proceed in the future. The tribunal's contact with the *suprema* was matched by its own meticulous correspondence with its provincial commis-

TRIBUNAL OF THE HOLY OFFICE

saries, especially with the distant functionaries in Guatemala and the Philippines.[10]

Record-keeping and research were two indexes of the professionalism of the Mexican tribunal. Even with a shortage of personnel the judges and the secretary were able to amass impressive data on the religious-social complex of the Mexican colony. When in 1571 an inventory of the library of the episcopal Inquisition was started, the bibliography comprised only one page,[11] while the library of the tribunal between 1571 and the end of the century contained at least fifteen thick legajos of instructions, procedural manuals, data on theological errors and the like.[12] Every effort was made to complete or to reconstruct the records of pre-1571 inquisitorial activities by Moya de Contreras and his staff. The controversial and obscure auto de fé of October 1528 was studied and the events were reconstructed by Licenciado Bonilla in a series of "Testimonies on San Benitos" in 1574.[13] Inquisition papers in the hands of private individuals were reclaimed by the Holy Office as in the cases of the López de Legazpi family archive and the Juan Suárez de Avila fracas with the sons of Gonzalo Gómez in 1572.[14] Lists of reconciled and penanced heretics since 1528 were compiled in chronological order and were indexed alphabetically by the tribunal secretaries during the 1570's.[15] Close checks were made to make sure penances of previous years had been fulfilled. There were retrials of people who had failed to do prescribed penances.[16] The Inquisition jail was revamped and Moya de Contreras gave close supervision to the alguaciles and bailiffs.[17] The tribunal kept record books apart from the trial records on deliberations and actual votes of the judges in each particular conviction.[18] Detailed inventories of property of accused heretics were kept and strict accounting was made of fines and court costs which were entered in a separate set of ledgers.[19]

A study of the administrative documents in the archive reveals that the personnel of the tribunal were more identified with the hierarchy clergy of the viceroyalty than with the Mexican regulars. The diocesan clergy had formal representation on the Inquisition tribunal while the friars served more in the capacity of *califica-*

dores, or expert advisers on canon law.[20] It became clear that the tribunal and the hierarchy were the primary agents of the Counter Reformation after 1571 and that the friars continued to lose doctrinal autonomy. The preponderance of trials of clergy during the last three decades of the sixteenth century were cases of regular clergy. The spectre of Lutheranism was still seen by the hierarchy among their order colleagues.

The prosecution of a Franciscan, Fray Miguel de Bolonia, in 1572 illuminates this trend. Bolonia had claimed, "Each person could achieve salvation in his own way."[21] There were many more trials of regulars than of hierarchy clergy for sexual immorality during this era. The act of soliciting women during confession was the most prevalent offense.[22] Reports of clerical immorality reached Spain through channels other than the Holy Office, and the Council of the Supreme Inquisition gave specific instructions at frequent intervals to the Mexican tribunal to punish the guilty.[23] One is forced to speculate, however, whether the hierarchy were really the "moral" clergy, or whether the friars were being singled out as bad examples of Christian conduct.[24]

I

Corsairs and Judaizantes

In the first twelve months of its operation the tribunal of the Holy Office conducted over 170 trials and investigations. During the twenty-nine-year period to 1601, there were at least a thousand separate trials and several hundred denunciations and investigations which never reached the proceso stage. While bigamy and blasphemy prosecutions outnumbered other charges, the Holy Office tried at least seventy-eight formal heretics and sixty-eight Judaizantes during its first thirty years of existence.[25] There were seven important autos de fé between 1574 and 1596, and many smaller ceremonies in which individual heretics were reconciled.

Thirteen prisoners were released to the secular arm for burning at the stake as a result of the tribunal's activities.

While the tribunal was surely concerned with eradicating groups of Judaizantes in New Spain, during the first decade of its incumbency the judges concentrated on Protestants. The coincidence of the destruction of the Hawkins fleet at San Juan de Ulúa in September 1568, and the establishment of the tribunal of the Holy Office of the Inquisition between 1569 and 1571 dramatized the Counter Reformation role of the Mexican Inquisition. Over a hundred of the raiders had gone ashore near Tampico, and those who were not arrested roamed over Tlaxcala, the Mixteca and central Mexico before they were captured and tried by Moya de Contreras. It seemed appropriate for the tribunal to emphasize Protestantism in the first great public autos de fé of 1574 and 1575.[26] It appears that a great deal of anti-Protestant sentiment was engendered by the ceremonies. One participant, who later wrote his memoirs, recalled that the town crier who led the prisoners through the streets shouted, "See these English Lutheran dogs, enemies of God," and he related that the inquisitors and the familiares exhorted the executioners who were scourging the sailors, "Harder, harder on these English Lutherans." Once the reconciliation and sentencing took place, however, the men seemed to have great mobility. Many of them traveled throughout the entire viceroyalty and often held responsible jobs.

Several of the Inquisition trials of the English corsairs deserve special mention. In point of time the prosecution and punishment of William Collins of Oxford between 1568 and 1574 was the first important trial of the tribunal of the Mexican Holy Office. Collins, a forty-year-old sailor on the "Jesus of Lubeck," was able to escape the San Juan de Ulúa debacle in 1568 and to land with about one hundred others on the Tampico coast. There the survivors had a dreadful time obtaining food and shelter, and fourteen of them were killed by hostile Indians of the area. Finally the corsairs were rounded up and escorted to Mexico City where they were placed in a stockade in the gardens of San Hipólito. Collins, like his compatriot Guillermo Orlando, was able to ingratiate himself with the friars who came to the camp to give the prisoners spiritual care. The Holy Office was swayed by stories of Collins' behavior during the Indian attack when he had exhorted his comrades to pray, even though he confided to a Dominican friar that he was on the verge of taking his own life to escape torture.[27]

Collins was auctioned off as a laborer by the tribunal and he spent several years as a miner and a farm worker in the Taxco area. On September 22, 1572 the priest at Taxco started proceedings against Collins because he had proselytized for Anglicanism and he had talked in a scandalous way about the religious wars in England. On October 7, he was remanded to the Mexico City tribunal for trial. During lengthy interrogations Collins claimed that he had related to others *what the Lutherans said* rather than his own beliefs. He told the Inquisition that he had been a Catholic until the age of twenty-four when he had embraced Anglicanism. He gave details about Anglican worship services on board the Hawkins ships, and he informed the judges of the names of many of his shipmates who were corsairs and desecraters of churches. Only when he arrived in Mexico, and as he was nursed back to health by a Dominican priest, did Collins decide to return to the true faith.

Because the Holy Office felt that Collins had feigned his repentance and his desire to be reconciled with Roman Catholicism, he was charged with sixty-eight counts of heresy, and the judges debated whether to relax him to the secular arm for burning at the stake. Their final sentence was more lenient, but not very. William Collins was to be reconciled, with the loss of all personal property, and he was given the harsh sentence of two hundred lashes and a ten-year term in the galleys. He marched in penitential garb in the auto de fé of February 28, 1574 and then received his whipping. On March 8, 1574 he was sent to Spain to fulfill the galley service. Since the life expectancy of galleymen was rather short, one doubts that William Collins ever emerged from his Inquisition sentence alive.

David Alexander of Surrey was only fourteen years old when the Hawkins raiders were defeated in 1568. After a brief period in jail in Tampico, David was brought to the viceregal capital where he served as a page for Viceroy Martín Enríquez. Later he found work in Tecamachalco and in Guanajuato working for a muleteer named Juan García Vásquez. On December 21, 1572 García Vásquez denounced David to Inquisitor Moya de Contreras as a Protestant. While David Alexander admitted he had followed the Anglican religion as dictated by the Queen of England and his own parents, he insisted that he wished to become a good Catholic.[28] David had been in jail for over a year when the prosecuting attorney formally charged him on January 2, 1574.

Fiscal Avalos pronounced David to be "a notorious Lutheran" who believed in the tenets of mental confession and other heretical dogma. Because of the boy's age and the vagueness of the evidence, Inquisitor Bonilla finally decided to reconcile David Alexander on February 28, 1574. He was to serve a three-year prison term and he was required to wear penitential garb. As soon as possible David was to be exiled to Spain. After a period of incarceration in the Monastery of San Francisco, David was confined in the Hospital of Amador de Díos, first as a patient and later as an orderly. By May 11, 1577 he had fulfilled his sentence, and his confessor wrote the Holy Office that he was "very satisfied" with his conduct and his knowledge of Christian doctrine. While the Holy Office allowed David to go free, he was not permitted to leave Mexico City. By 1584, he had signed on as a member of the Philippine expedition, but when the Holy Office found out about it, he was placed in jail until the ships had sailed. The Inquisition record has a final note on David Alexander on May 25, 1589 when a petition for a pardon was filed on David's behalf. Apparently he was still living in Mexico.

One of the unfortunate corsairs burned at the stake in the auto de fé of February 1574 was George Ribley, a sailor from the "Jesus of Lubeck." Ribley, a native of Gravesend near London, was an outspoken Lutheran. He had been sent to work in the mines of Guanajuato until 1571 when Moya de Contreras ordered him tried. After the inquisitors had satisfied themselves that Ribley was an obstinate heretic who could not be reconciled, a procedure which took over two years, he was relaxed to the secular arm for burning in February 1574. The trial record shows that he was strangled before the cadaver was "reduced to ashes," and his sanbenito was placed in the Metropolitan Cathedral.[29]

John Farenton, a forty-nine-year-old gunner from Windsor who had also been a crew member of the "Jesus of Lubeck," was reconciled in the 1574 auto de fé along with Collins and Alexander. After 1568 Farenton made his way to Zacatecas where he got work in the mines. Interestingly enough, he never learned any Spanish, and in 1572 he needed an interpreter as the Holy Office prosecuted him for Lutheranism. Farenton was condemned to six years in the galleys after his final reconciliation in 1574.[30]

William Cornelius apparently was the ship's doctor on the "Minion," which went aground in Tampico in 1568. His father was sacristan of the cathedral in Cork. Cornelius was able to make his way to Guatemala where he practiced medicine until he was apprehended in 1574. After he refused to recant and ask for reconciliation with the Church, Cornelius was sentenced to the stake in the auto de fé of March 6, 1575. He was garroted and his body was burned in the San Hipólito marketplace in Mexico City on that date.[31]

More is known about Miles Philips than any of the other Hawkins corsairs since Philips wrote memoirs which Richard Hakluyt published in 1589. Philips, also a member of the crew of the "Minion," was submitted to judicial torture before the Holy Office allowed him to be reconciled for Protestantism in the February 1574 auto. After three years of forced labor in a Jesuit establishment, Philips was able to return to England. His description of the auto de fé and the scourgings is the most famous account of the Inquisition in the 1570's.[32] A companion of Philips also had a happy ending to his Mexican venture. Paul Hawkins, the cabin boy of the "Jesus of Lubeck," was probably the nephew of Captain John Hawkins. He was captured at San Juan de Ulúa in 1568, but somehow he got as far north as Sombrerete, Zacatecas, where he worked in the mines until he was arrested in 1572. Finally he was sentenced to three years of labor in a religious house in the auto de fé of December 15, 1577. He was forced to wear the sanbenito for this period and for one year after his release. Documents show that Paul married a mestizo "daughter of one of the conquistadores" after his release, but he was still under surveillance as late as 1589.[33]

Many French corsairs who followed in the path of Nicolás Santour, the Guatemalan reconciliado of 1562, were prosecuted by the Mexican tribunal in the 1570's. Perhaps the most celebrated trial was that of Pierre Sanfoy of St. Vigor who had accompanied the French pirate Pierre Chuetot on the 1570 raid on Cozumel Island off the coast of Yucatán. The raiders were forced ashore on the mainland where ten were killed and another ten were taken prisoner and put in the Mérida jail. Four of the prisoners were executed as war criminals, but Pierre Sanfoy was enslaved and made a servant in a wealthy Mérida household.

On September 13, 1571 Sanfoy was ordered to Mexico City by the Holy Office to stand trial.[34] The viceroy hesitated to hand Sanfoy over to the Moya de Contreras tribunal, and it is evident that Martín Enríquez's first tiff with the inquisitors was still an issue in the capital. Many of the corsairs remained under civil jurisdiction in order to evade Moya's authority. By March 24, 1572 Enríquez had been reprimanded by the sovereign for his reception of the Holy Inquisition six months earlier, and he felt compelled to accede to the religious trial of Sanfoy.

Sanfoy and four of his comrades were indicted as "Huguenots" who had insulted the Pope, eaten meat on Fridays and recited Lutheran prayers and devotionals. Witnesses swore that the men had stolen religious ornaments from the church on Cozumel, using chalices as common drinking cups and desecrating crucifixes and images. They had denied the virginity of the Virgin and they had painted lewd pictures on the walls of the Cozumel church, scenes of men and women embracing and kissing in a lascivious manner. In all, twenty-eight witnesses gave evidence against Sanfoy.

The Holy Office decided to submit Pierre Sanfoy to torture on December 11, 1573. On the rack the corsair claimed he had never been a Lutheran. He merely attended the Protestant services on ship, but under torment Pierre admitted that he had memorized the Lutheran prayers. He claimed to want reconciliation with the Holy Roman Church. The compelling reason for his previous flirtations with Protestantism seemed to be the example of the "Admiral of France" who was a Huguenot, probably Gaspar de Coligny whose scheme to establish French Protestant colonies in America was well known. As the torture session got rougher, Pierre Sanfoy pled for mercy and cited his services in the French army in its campaigns against the Huguenots. In January of 1574 the tribunal voted to reconcile Sanfoy rather than to execute him, but he was given a sentence including two hundred lashes and a six-year stretch as a galleyman. He marched in the penitential garb in the auto de fé of February 28, 1574 along with the English heretics who were punished at the same time.

As the tribunal of the Holy Office finished dealing with large groups of the Hawkins raiders and French corsairs in the first years of its operation, interest in foreign Protestants waned, and since Spanish naval power in the Caribbean was now primed to repulse other raiders, there was not a recurrence of the Hawkins episode in Mexico. The Inquisition kept abreast of corsair movements in the Pacific and there was much interest in the raids on the Peruvian coast. Intelligence documents in the Inquisition archive during the 1580's have detailed information on "the ships of Englishmen, corsairs and Lutherans who are invading the South Seas through the Strait of Magellan and the names of their generals and admirals." The Holy Office relied on its Oaxaca and Guatemalan branches to send in information about pirates and maps detailing their activities on both sides of the Central American land mass.[35] By the decade of the 1590's the Mexican tribunal was more interested in foreign Protestants who were not corsairs, men who had come to New Spain legally on the regular fleets which docked in Veracruz for several months each year. The activities of these men, Germans and Flemings, are the subject of Chapter Six.

After the Hawkins men were tried and sentenced, the Mexican Inquisition entered a twenty-year period when Judaizantes were its primary concern. Several desultory investigations of crypto-

Jews were carried on earlier,[36] but the decade of the 1570's ended with the first execution of a Jew since 1528. García González Bergemero came from Albuquerque, Portugal, to Mexico in 1559. For twenty years he discreetly practiced his Jewish religion although he appeared to the public as an orthodox Catholic. Some members of his family had converted to Catholicism and one of his sons was an Augustinian friar. Because of a periodic letter sent by the Inquisition tribunals of Spain to their Mexican counterpart, it was learned in 1579 that a Bergemero family in Llerena had been tried as Judaizantes, and several of the clan had been burned at the stake. García Bergemero was arrested by the Mexican tribunal on July 6, 1579, and while he admitted that members of the family had been executed as Judaizantes, he insisted that he was a practicing Catholic. All efforts to obtain a confession and thereby to reconcile Bergemero failed, and in light of the evidence he was branded a "Judaizante heretic," obstinate and irreconcilable. He was executed by garroting, and then his body was burned in the auto de fé of October 11, 1579.[37]

Anyone acquainted with the history of sixteenth-century Mexico has heard of the Carvajal family of Nuevo León. The major Inquisition trials of members of that family have been summarized by several scholars.[38] Only recently have the procesos been examined as the social and intellectual history of Mexican Judaism. The story of the Carvajal prosecutions began in 1583, when the Mexican viceroy asked that Luis de Carvajal, governor of the frontier province of Nuevo León, be prosecuted as a Judaizante.[39]

Carvajal, himself an orthodox Catholic, was the son of Portuguese Jews who had converted to Catholicism a generation earlier. The governor had come to New Spain in 1567 as a merchant, and as naval commander of one of the periodic Spanish fleets. In Jamaica he defeated British privateers and thereby impressed Viceroy Martín Enríquez who traveled on Carvajal's flagship. In Mexico Luis became a cattle rancher and a local functionary in Pánuco. It was there that he captured some eighty of the Hawkins raiders in 1568. During succeeding years Carvajal became a famous Indian fighter and a skillful colonizer in the Chichimec-Huastec area. His fame and his competence netted him a royal appointment in 1578 as governor and captain general of the new kingdom of León, and "he was also accorded the privilege of taking with him to Mexico one hundred married or unmarried people without being obliged to ask them for proof that they were Old Christians."[40] When he went to Spain in 1578 to receive his commission, Carvajal brought back to Mexico with him a party of relatives who were new Christians and crypto-Jews.

Two fundamental speculations arise about Governor Carvajal's long trial and incarceration (1583-1590). Why did the Carvajal contract exempt the settlers from the requirement of a limpieza de sangre on the part of the Spanish Holy Office? Seymour B. Liebman feels that Philip II needed the private enterprise type of pacification in the Huastec area, and he was more concerned with pacification than orthodoxy on the frontier.[41] The second perplexing question is whether Governor Luis de Carvajal actually was ignorant of the fact that his sister, her husband and their children, except for one son who was a Dominican friar, were Judaizantes. Although the Inquisition tribunal debated the evidence long and hard, in the end the judges felt constrained to convict the governor of harboring Jewish apostates. He was reconciled in the auto de fé of February 24, 1590.

During the late 1580's the entire family came under Holy Office surveillance and many of them, especially Isabel Rodríguez de Andrade, Luis' niece, and her mother, Francisca Núñez de Carvajal, were tortured. Under stress the women inculpated most of the members of the immediate family living in Mexico and in Spain, as well as other Nuevo León colonists. In all a dozen of Governor Carvajal's family accompanied him in the 1590 auto de fé. Gaspar de Carvajal, his Dominican nephew, did not march in the auto owing to his religious affiliation, but he was chastised for his failure to denounce Judaizers in his family, and he made his abjuration in the Dominican convent in Mexico City.[42] Governor Carvajal's most famous nephew, Luis Carvajal the younger, was reconciled for Judaizing in the 1590 auto, but he was tried a second time and relaxed to the secular arm for burning at the stake along with his mother and his sister in the great auto de fé of December 8, 1596.[43]

The second trial of Luis Carvajal the younger came about because seventeen witnesses offered evidence that Luis had relapsed into Judaism after his 1590 reconciliation. Luis the younger was one of the most remarkable colonists of sixteenth-century Mexico. His faith, a probable mixture of orthodox Judaism and Spanish mysticism, led him to write letters, memoirs and testaments which are priceless documents of social and intellectual history. His writings show the extent of the penetration of Jewish erudition into early Mexican culture. Luis' assumed name of Joseph Lumbroso has led some historians to connect his mentality with Spanish Illuminism,[44] but a modern scholar has traced the name to its correct Hebrew origin.[45]

Unable to withstand the sentence of torture prescribed for him by the Holy Office on February 6, 9 and 10, 1596, Luis Carvajal the younger not only reinculpated his mother and his sisters but also offered the inquisitors four pages of names of Judaizers against whom he would testify if required. There were 116 names on the list.[46] Whether Luis Carvajal actually repented at the eleventh hour so that he might be strangled instead of facing the flames alive is a matter of controversy. In any event a Dominican friar claimed that Luis had confessed and repented before the execution on December 8, 1596, and this intelligence was forwarded to the Council of the Supreme Inquisition in Spain when the Mexican body made its report on the *"Auto Grande"* of 1596.[47]

The Carvajal prosecutions continued into the seventeenth century until all but those members of the family who had not escaped to Peru or elsewhere were completely destroyed.[48] The Counter Reformation tact of the Mexican Inquisition in the trials of the Carvajals is unmistakable. The attempt to intimidate and restrain the growth of Mexican Judaism by the stringent punishment of one clan of Judaizers was probably a failure, since seventeenth-century investigations by the Holy Office showed that the Jewish community of New Spain had continued to grow despite the prosecutions.

II

Faith and Morals in the Colony, 1571-1601

Most of the work of the tribunal of the Holy Office of the Inquisition in Mexico was considerably less dramatic than the trials of corsairs and Judaizantes. Lengthy and tedious investigations of bigamy and blasphemy took up the major part of the tribunal's time. In each auto de fé, whether it was a public ceremony or a private one, those who had violated the teachings of the Church on marriage and the degrees of carnal and spiritual relationships permitted were punished, often severely. While earthiness and angry speech were tolerated by the Inquisition, those who carried their cursing too far, especially if they reviled or insulted the deity, were chastised and punished. From the routine trials of faith and morals before the Mexican Holy Office much is learned about popular speech and ideas as well as patterns of social behavior.

Irreverence was not confined to the humble or lowborn, and many of the trials show glimpses of the aristocracy—including the bawdiness of upper-class ladies. On rare occasions when the family had influence in Spain the decision in blasphemy cases was referred to the suprema. An early instance of such a circumstance was the blasphemy trial of Doña María de Peralta, widow of lawyer and Inquisition functionary Hortuño de Ibarra, who had leverage enough to get her trial transferred to Spain where it was suppressed in 1575.[49] During the first decade of the tribunal's functioning in Mexico there were two hundred and four blasphemy trials and one hundred and ninety-eight prosecutions of bigamists. Many other investigations of bigamy and blasphemy, once initiated, were discontinued for lack of evidence.[50] Many people continued to be tried by the inquisitors for expressing the belief that simple fornication was not a mortal sin.[51] Administrative work of the tribunal required in the prosecution of bigamists and in the framing of genealogies for limpiezas de sangre for those people who were required to prove purity of lineage was exacting and time consuming. The many legajos of genealogies and limpiezas are fertile testimony about the tribunal's knowledge of Mexican society. For the era 1571 to 1573 there are seven large volumes of limpieza documents.[52]

One of the most fascinating dimensions of the Mexican Holy Office was the extirpation of sorcery and witchcraft. Of course the inquisitors had to deal with both Indian and Spanish superstition and wizardry, and as the process of cultural diffusion continued, a fusion of the two.[53] Witchcraft was a different crime from sorcery. The inquisitors were convinced that the "witch has abandoned Christianity . . . has worshipped Satan as God . . . and exists only to be his instrument."[54] Practitioners of black magic were judged to have derived their powers by entering into a pact with the Devil, and in doing so they were accused of inferential heresy. As in previous years the Holy Office tried many women for sorcery and superstition, but the most interesting prosecutions tended to be those of warlocks *(brujos)*.[55] Astrologers began to be tried in 1582,[56] and the Holy Office was harsh in its punishments. In 1583 there began a series of trials of individuals from Puebla who told fortunes through palmistry. The inquisitors collected treatises on palm reading and they required that extensive diagrams be drawn of the palm and ways to interpret "life lines."[57]

In March 1597 Juan Martínez gave the judges considerable evidence about sorcery in the northwest provinces. He told of a palmist who foretold the future in Capotlán, Province of Avalos, and of a Captain Rodrigo Figueroa, on the Vizcaíno voyage to California, who performed incantations to relieve heart trouble.[58] The most severe punishment of a sorcerer by the sixteenth-century Holy Office between 1598 and 1601 was the trial of a young mestizo boy, Juan Luis, who claimed to have entered into a pact with the Devil. Juan Luis was subjected to two hundred lashes and exile to Spain where he was required to wear the sanbenito during a five-year term in the galleys.[59]

The Mexican Inquisition continued to investigate the orthodoxy of the Indian population after 1571, even though jurisdiction over the natives was prohibited to the tribunal and was reserved to the bishop as ordinary.[60] The tribunal adopted a strict construction of the law when it came to defining what an "Indian" was, and Inquisitor Alonso de Peralta made it clear in the 1590's that all mixed bloods were subject to the Holy Office.[61] Meticulous limpiezas de sangre, often based on native records, were constructed to prove that accused sorcerers and idolaters were "pure Indians" rather than mestizos.[62] Bishops and inquisitors often disputed the limpieza of a prisoner, but frequently they remanded mestizos and Indians to the other jurisdiction when there was doubt about blood lines.

An unresolved problem of jurisdiction in Indian cases concerned bigamy and polygamy. Several cases provoked conflict between the Holy Office and the ordinaries in the late sixteenth century with the result that the Mexican tribunal called upon the supreme Inquisition to settle the matter in 1591, but no articulate decision was ever announced from Spain.[63] Indian heresy in remote areas where there were no agents of the ordinary plagued the hierarchy and sometimes the Inquisition intervened in the process. The inquisitors were quick to assert authority in Indian cases where the crime was a mixed civil-religious one, and when the Holy Office or its personnel was the injured party. A case in point was the Mexican tribunal's punishment of Indians who had stolen horses from the inquisitors in 1595.[64] Conflicts of jurisdiction over who should punish delinquent Indians—the friars, the ordinary, the Holy Office or civil authority—led to litigation and a flurry of letter writing to Spain. The Holy Office pondered the problem of recurrent idolatry among the natives, and the judges questioned whether the ordinaries should continue to have exclusive jurisdiction over Indian matters.[65]

III

Conflicts of Jurisdiction and Politics

Colonial officials, civil and ecclesiastical, were reluctant to share jurisdiction, prestige and power with the tribunal from its arrival in Mexico in the fall of 1571, when political conflicts with the viceregency and jurisdictional conflicts with the episcopate and the friars began. The intrusion of a prestigious court of the Holy Office of the Inquisition, empowered by the supreme tribunal of the Inquisition in Spain and directly responsible to that body and to the King, upset the power structure in the viceroyalty of New Spain. Several years of mutual accommodation of operation were required before jurisdictional problems were worked out. Fundamental animosities between competing officials were never eradicated despite commands of the King and the suprema. More than any other type of document, records of administrative squabbles and jurisdictional conflict give day-to-day descriptions of how the Holy Office functioned after 1571.[66] The suprema and the King were called upon to settle most questions of competency in New Spain since the viceroy often was a partisan in the disputes. Repeated commands from Spain were required before the ordinaries and their provisors could be divested of the titles and functions of "Inquisitors Ordinary," and the process was fraught with conflict and unpleasantness. As late as 1585 the Holy Office was sending to Spain complaints about "the excesses of the Ordinary Inquisition" in Central America.[67]

When it came to strife between the tribunal of the Holy Office and the viceroys and oídores, both sides reacted with invective and arrogance. After Viceroy Martín Enríquez gave Dr. Moya de Contreras a proper but cool welcome to the Mexican capital in 1571, each group treated the other with icy formality. The senior inquisitor and the viceroy wrote to Philip II complaining about each other, and on August 21, 1572 the monarch addressed letters to Moya and Enríquez recommending that they make the effort to get along with one another. Philip II told Viceroy Enríquez he was pleased that the populace had greeted the Holy Office with "demonstrations of happiness and contentment," but he expressed the hope that Enríquez would give more support and approbation to Moya's tribunal than he had at the beginning, showing the people and the Indians the respect which civil authority ought to accord the Holy Inquisition.[68]

In his letter to Dr. Moya de Contreras the King counselled the new inquisitor to cultivate good relations with the viceroy, refraining from petty controversies and quarrels. He made it plain that an image of unity between the civil power and the Holy Inquisition was necessary for the good of the colony. Because Moya had complained that the viceroy would not relinquish prisoners to the tribunal, notably Pierre Sanfoy and the French pirates, the King and the Council of the Indies set up procedures for the transfer of prisoners when the nature of the crime was more religious than civil. It was also specified that people employed by the Holy Office, especially the familiares, were not subject to civil jurisdiction. Protocol for civil and Inquisition ceremonies was outlined—in general the same order of precedence for civil and Inquisition personnel that prevailed in Spain.[69]

Viceroy Martín Enríquez and many of his successors found the protocol very irksome and degrading.[70] The civil authorities were required to participate in the autos de fé, and they had their responsibilities assigned them by the Holy Office. The inquisitors designated where the viceroy and his entourage were to sit and stand in the ceremonies. Furthermore, after the viceroy and his staff had marched in the processional and had witnessed the auto, they were obliged to accompany the Holy Office staff back to its headquarters before their official duties were fulfilled. On many occasions the viceroy protested to the Council of the Indies about the arrogance of the tribunal, and he was ever on the alert to take advantage of circumstances which would allow polite revenge on the tribunal. One particular way in which the viceregency retaliated against the inquisitors was in the issuing of Indians for service in *repartimiento*. In 1572 one of the judges of repartimiento assigned twelve Indians to the Holy Office, but the Inquisition staff complained that they were mere boys incapable of the kind of work demanded. The tribunal was incensed because the really good workers were given to other people. Moya decided to try the *juez repartidor,* one Diego de Molina, for affronting the Holy Office. As a result Molina was given a brief jail sentence.[71]

The tribunal got along no better with the oidores of the audiencia of Mexico. Many cases arose where competency to prosecute was debatable. The oidores demanded jurisdiction, and the viceroys usually supported the judges against the inquisitors. There were especially bitter quarrels over jurisdiction between the tribunal of the Holy Office and the audiencia of Guadalajara. As a matter of principle the audiencia invoked every possible technicality of procedural law to maintain its position and to exclude the intervention of the Holy Office.[72] Conflicts of jurisdiction on the local and provincial levels below the audiencia were frequent, and the commissaries of the Holy Office and the alcaldes mayores fought just as vigorously as their higher-echelon counterparts.

In August 1574 the commissary of the Holy Office in Oaxaca became involved in a fracas with the alcalde mayor of Yanhuitlán over the punishment of Indian idolaters and sorcerers.[73] Pedro de Ladrón de Guevara was a tactless administrator of the audiencia of Mexico who cared little for the jurisdictional prerogatives of the Oaxaca ordinary or the Holy Office of the Inquisition. Owing to a dispute which he had with the vicar of Yanhuitlán over Indians under his civil jurisdiction, Ladrón de Guevara had been excommunicated by Fray Hernando Ortíz. This act of ecclesiastical censure seemed to have had little effect on the alcalde and he made a public declaration to the effect that he would enforce royal authority in the Mixteca even if it meant he would remain under the ban of excommunication. Both in Yanhuitlán and Coixlahuaca, Alcalde Ladrón de Guevara demanded that the friars hand over to him those Indians whom the clergy had imprisoned for idolatry. Apparently the Indian juzgado was within the church buildings. Ladrón de Guevara had entered the premises and the sacristy requiring the clergy to remand the natives to him. These actions caused a great scandal and gave the Indians a bad example of defiance of clerical authority, or so the friars complained to Inquisitor Moya de Contreras.

Fray Jacinto de la Serna, author of a famous treatise on Indian idolatry in the early seventeenth century,[74] and Fray Jerónimo de Abrego, who held the title of judge of idolaters in Oaxaca, brought charges against Ladrón de Guevara before the Holy Office. They maintained that the alcalde had ridiculed the friars, saying it was not possible to absolve Indians who had relapsed into paganism through clerical disciplinary action. The two friars accused Alcalde Ladrón de Guevara of having broken down a monastery door to get at an idolater so that he could be placed in the civil juzgado.

A *cause célèbre* between the civil power and the clergy began to develop as a result of Ladrón de Guevara's misconduct. The tribunal of the Holy Office found itself between the two opposing sides. Testimony was gathered from many friars and Indians who had witnessed the events. No doubt Moya de Contreras learned much about civil procedure in the provinces and the apparatus called the *Provisorato de Indios* which had assumed the ordinary's jurisdiction over Indian transgressions against orthodoxy. Perhaps the Inquisition proceso against Alacalde Ladrón de Guevara is incomplete because Bishop Bernardo de Albuquerque in Oaxaca City settled the matter. More likely Dr. Moya de Contreras dismissed the plea because the friars were acting in an inquisitorial capacity in Oaxaca, and he wished to make it clear to them that the tribunal of the Holy Office in Mexico City was the only Inquisition in New Spain. The Oaxaca friars continued to operate a monastic Inquisition in the Mixteca, and the ordinary continued to call himself "Inquisidor Ordinario" until a royal cédula forbade it in 1623. Despite this prohibition the same kind of inquisitorial activity, outside of the tribunal's jurisdiction, continued well into the eighteenth century.[75]

While it tried to assume an apolitical posture, the tribunal of the Holy Office had to contend with denunciations, testimony and trials which were grounded in political jealousy. There can be no doubt that Governor Luis de Carvajal of Nuevo León was denounced for reasons of politics and economic rivalry. Because the governor and Viceroy Conde de Coruña had had a dispute over the control of several villages in the Huasteca, and a priest who served in the area bore Caravajal ill will, the original denunciation against him as a new Christian came about, notwithstanding the fact that he was an orthodox practicing Catholic.[76] The rest of the family who were successful merchants and colonizers earned the animosity of competitors and underlings. Because of the nature of its mission, it was not unusual for the Holy Office to be drawn into provincial controversies and frontier conflicts.

A curious investigation started in Zacatecas during January 1585 when the commissary of the Holy Office began a proceso against the corregidor of Zacatecas, Felix de Zúñiga, and his brother for having reviled the character of visitador Licenciado Pablo de Torres who had uncovered some financial irregularities in Zúñiga's administration.[77] On the morning of January 18, 1585 the visitador found a sanbenito bearing the word "Jew" had been attached to his window during the night. Torres complained to the Zacatecas commissary of the Inquisition who referred the entire matter to Mexico City on January 20. The question immediately arose as to whether the investigation was a matter for the audiencia of Guadalajara or the Holy Office. Until the audiencia proved itself to be partisan and dilatory, the Inquisition agreed to Guadalajara's jurisdiction. By May 1585 the Holy Office had established that Corregidor Zúñiga, his brother and their hirelings were guilty, but it was difficult to punish them since the Guadalajara judges were friendly to the Zacatecas corregidor.

The most publicized altercation over jurisdiction in a trial where political considerations overrode religious issues was that of Francisco de Urdiñola, wealthy New Galicia rancher and miner and a contestant for the contract to colonize New Mexico. In 1593 Urdiñola's wife Leonor had died after a lingering illness while her husband was absent from their ranch at Río Grande, Zacatecas. Soon afterwards one of Urdiñola's factors, Domingo de Lanzaverde, disappeared from the scene and was presumed to have been murdered. During October 1594 Urdiñola had gone to Mexico City to complete his application for the contract to colonize New Mexico. On October 19, 1594 the viceroy was on the verge of granting the commission when the audiencia of Guadalajara brought charges of murder against Francisco de Urdiñola, saying that he had poisoned his wife and had killed her "lover," the factor.

Subsequent investigations proved that Urdiñola was innocent, and modern scholarship has substantiated that the audiencia of

Guadalajara brought the charges against Urdiñola at the behest of New Galicia's first citizen, Juan Bautista de Lomas y Colmenares. His son-in-law Oidor Nuño Núñez de Villavicencio was interested in lessening Urdiñola's chance for the New Mexico contract so that Lomas y Colmenares might get it.[78] When the viceroy was unable to get the Guadalajara proceedings against Urdiñola suspended until the New Mexico contract was let, Urdiñola claimed the Inquisition's fuero since he was a familiar (along with Lomas y Colmenares) of the Holy Office in the Zacatecas area. The tribunal of the Holy Office in Mexico City assumed jurisdiction in the case and the inquisitors commanded the audiencia of Guadalajara to refrain from further action against Urdiñola and to remit what evidence it had to Mexico City.[79] The audiencia of Guadalajara refused to acquiesce, and thus started a momentous battle over competency.

On May 11, 1595 the tribunal of the Holy Office referred the Urdiñola case to the supreme Inquisition in Spain. Meanwhile it sent agents to Río Grande, and to the city of Zacatecas to investigate the audiencia's charges.[80] The Holy Office's representative, Familiar Juan de Morlete, filed a report in which he found no evidence to substantiate the murder charges. On February 21, 1596 the suprema decided that the audiencia of Guadalajara had jurisdiction in the case; and after the decision reached Mexico in June 1597, the audiencia began to reconsider Francisco de Urdiñola's guilt.[81] By then there had been a change of personnel among the Guadalajara judges, and the contract to colonize New Mexico had been given to Juan de Oñate. In September 1598 Francisco de Urdiñola was acquitted of the murder charges. He was fined three thousand ducats and the cost of litigation because it was felt that he was an accessory to the murder of Lanzaverde who probably absconded with some of Urdiñola's funds. In the case of Francisco de Urdiñola the Holy Office of the Inquisition had played a positive role in securing justice and exoneration of an innocent man.[82]

One of the most important administrative concerns of the monarchy and the Council of the Indies in supervising the tribunal of the Holy Office in Mexico was how to circumscribe activities of the Inquisition police. The familiares in Spain, and especially in Aragón, enjoyed vast privileges and in most instances immunity from prosecution by civil authority. They had become a state within a state and abuses of authority were a scandal.[83] As Philip II established the tribunal in Mexico, he determined to lessen the number and the power of familiares in the colony. Since the Inquisition depended on familiares and *comisarios* in the lower echelons of its functions, the judges supported their agents, and the King was only partially successful in limiting their influence.

A royal decree of August 16, 1570 regulated the privileges of familiares in New Spain and held their number to twelve in the viceregal capital, four in cathedral towns, and one in other sizable settlements. Civil authorities were charged to report violations of conduct to the tribunal.[84] Generally these Inquisition police were immune from prosecution by the viceregency for criminal matters, but they were subject to the state in civil suits.[85]

Rather full genealogical data on Mexican familiares, their limpiezas de sangre, their requests for appointment to the familiatura and their disputes with the criminal jurisdiction of the alcaldías mayores and the audiencias are contained in the Inquisition archive.[86] By the decade of the 1580's it became apparent that the familiares had entrenched privileges and positions similar to their Spanish colleagues.[87] The tribunal followed the policy of appointing people to the familiatura who were already wealthy, men who could not be swayed in their duty by bribery and hopes of personal aggrandizement. While the policy was sound in theory, it often broke down in practice when the familiares did further personal goals.

The career of Antonio de Espejo as a familiar of the Mexican Inquisition, who later became an important explorer of Arizona and New Mexico, has been studied by G. R. G. Conway.[88] Espejo was an active agent of Moya de Contreras in the apprehension of the Hawkins raiders between 1572 and 1574. In May 1578 Antonio de Espejo was involved in an economic dispute with the corregidor of Mexico City over a herd of cattle which had been sequestered from him by the municipal authorities. Espejo drew his sword to prevent slaughterhouse officials from killing the cattle. Licenciado Lorenzo Sánchez Obregón, corregidor of Mexico City, had Espejo arrested for obstructing justice, and the civil authority began to inventory and embargo his property before Espejo claimed immunity as a familiar of the Holy Office. What is not clear from the Inquisition records is whether Espejo actually owned the cattle or whether he was acting as a consignee, and for what reason the city confiscated the herd. Since the trial did not continue past the point of the tribunal of the Holy Office's intervention, it is apparent that the familiatura was able to exert influence on Espejo's behalf.

The Espejo episode ended as most controversies over familiar immunity ended in the sixteenth century.[89] Rarely did the local constabulary prevail against the Inquisition police. The honorable intervention of the Holy Office of the Inquisition to protect Familiar Francisco de Urdiñola from the machinations of the powerful Lomas y Colmenares of New Galicia in the 1590's was the exception rather than the rule.

IV

Books and Men

After one views the total documentation of the archive of the Mexican Inquisition from 1571 to 1601, it becomes increasingly clear that the most fundamental obligation of the inquisitors was to control the influx of printed matter which attacked or undermined the religious culture of New Spain. While the spectacular autos de fé of corsairs and Judaizantes often capture the attention of scholars—the combat with heretics rather than heresy—it is apparent from the documents that a relentless daily struggle with unorthodox ideas was the essence of Counter Reformation Mexico. This struggle has not been studied as well as the historians of ideas might wish. After a brief flirtation with Erasmian thought and Renaissance Humanist views of conquest and colonization, the Mexican Church and the viceregency settled down to a rather rigid intellectual milieu within the framework of post-Trentine Catholicism. In the decades before this ambiente evolved into a baroque mentality after the turn of the seventeenth century, the Church and the State in New Spain looked to the Holy Office to maintain the status quo, and to deal with the men, the books and the ideas which threatened to erode orthodoxy.

The tribunal of the Holy Office contrived an entire bureaucracy to cope with censorship. In addition to the appointment of provincial commissaries, who watched their areas for suspicious literature, the tribunal empowered a staff of expert clergy, schooled in canon law, to examine books imported into the colony. These *calificadores* worked very hard and their reports on particular imprints shed much light on the colonial mentality of literate peoples. Of crucial importance were the functions of the Veracruz commissaries who were the first to board ships as they docked at San Juan de Ulúa. A close examination was made of the passports of passengers and sailors, and the commissaries searched their luggage for prohibited books. The volumes were inventoried and sent to the *aduana,* or customs house, pending examination and return to their owners. Books which had not been given clearance in Spain and books on the prohibited list were confiscated.[90]

Merchants who imported books from Spain for sale in Mexico and printers within the colony were subject to close regulations and to censorship on the part of the Church and State.[91] Administrative documents of the Inquisition, and book lists from bills of lading, show that even in the sixteenth century the Mexican colonist had a voracious appetite for books and reading, those which were permitted and those which were not.[92] Hard as it might have tried, the tribunal of the Holy Office was only partially successful in keeping heretical books out of the Mexican colony. In the two succeeding centuries the flood of printed matter from Europe flowed around the Inquisition and into libraries of metropolitan Mexico and the provinces.[93] Hundreds of documents in the Inquisition archive for the era 1571 to 1601 attest to the fact that the tribunal waged a vigorous campaign to keep suspicious books out of New Spain.[94] It would appear that the major part of the correspondence between the tribunal and its provincial commissaries had to do with the book trade. Records show that books were coming into Mexico in increasing number, and the tribunal's lists of books in private hands from Nicaragua to Zacatecas show that the trade was not confined to Mexico City.[95]

In the fall of 1571 Dr. Moya de Contreras set the scene for prosecuting inhabitants of the colony who read prohibited books or had them in their possession. An edict was issued which made it a crime to read books which tended to undermine the faith, and another order commanded that all such books be turned in to the Holy Office.[96] By 1573 an official *Index* of prohibited reading matter was given to the citizenry.[97] The investigations of Moya de Contreras and his successors proved that the people most likely to have foreign books of dubious orthodoxy were the printers. Since many of the printers themselves were foreigners, either Flemings or Frenchmen, the Holy Office kept them under close watch.

Moya felt it important enough in late 1571 to interrupt his corsair investigations to prosecute a French printer named Pedro Ocharte (Ochart) who was suspect in this regard. Ocharte came from Rouen, where he was born in 1532, to Mexico where he became associated with Juan Pablos, Mexico's most famous early printer. He married into the family after Pablos died in 1561, and he continued to operate the business. Two residents of Mexico City denounced Ocharte to the new tribunal of the Holy Office several weeks after it set up operation. Moya de Contreras arrested the printer on January 15, 1572, accusing him of Lutheranism. Ocharte was supposed to have told acquaintances that Miguel de Ecija had "a very good book" which contained the Lutheran doctrine that man ought not to pray to saints but should commune directly with God. Secret testimonies claimed that Ocharte had associated with French Lutherans in Mexico. Ocharte himself testified that Ecija had recommended the book,

> because it described the grandeur, marvels, and mercy of the Lord, . . . and that it was not necessary for men to appeal to

the saints to intercede for them, because the arms of the Lord were open to receive sinners.

Ecija's son later told the Holy Office that all his father's library had been examined by the calificador of the Inquisition, and that his "father was not a man to own prohibited books." Even after Ocharte was tortured by the Holy Office he refused to admit the substance of the allegations against him, and since he had not read the book, he was set free by the tribunal on February 16, 1572.[98]

One of Ocharte's employees was less fortunate in escaping the wrath of the tribunal. Juan Ortíz, born in France and reared in Valladolid, was accused on March 20, 1572 of being a Lutheran heretic. Ortíz was Orcharte's engraver and typesetter. He was charged with proselytizing for Lutheranism and the political system of Protestantism. Ortíz had followed the Lutheran doctrine of salvation through faith alone, and had denied the merit of works for achieving grace. In addition he was not the practicing Catholic he should have been because he ignored many feasts of obligation. Some of his views on miracles smacked of Luther's teachings. Juan Ortíz remained in the Inquisition jail until December 1573 when the Holy Office decided to subject him to judicial torture. Failing to confess and seek reconciliation with the Church, Ortíz was found guilty of Lutheranism. After making public abjuration of his errors in the auto de fé of February 1574 and after he paid the stiff fine of two hundred pesos de oro, Juan Ortíz was banished perpetually from New Spain and the Indies.[99]

As the tribunal of the Holy Office in Mexico approached its climactic auto de fé of 1601, another foreign printer was prosecuted for Lutheranism. Cornelius Adrián César was a native of Haarlem, Holland, and he had entered the printers guild in Leyden before he came to New Spain in 1595 to work for Ocharte's widow. After a time he opened his own print shop, but his press was confiscated when he was denounced as a Lutheran in June 1598.[100] César admitted his Lutheranism to the Holy Office, but upon evidence of his contrition the inquisitors reconciled him in the auto de fé of March 25, 1601. After three years of prison César returned to his trade as director of the press of Diego López Dávalos.

Among the other penitents in the March 25, 1601 auto de fé were thirty-two Lutherans and Calvinists. The campaign of the tribunal of the Holy Office against Calvinist teachings climaxed three decades of the Inquisition's operations.

Notes

[1] For the events leading to the end of the episcopal Inquisition and founding of the tribunal, see Greenleaf, *Zumárraga*, pp. 17-21.

[2] *Recopilación*, Lib. I, tít. 19.

[3] Medina, *Primitiva Inquisición*, Vol. II, pp. 34-36, reproduces the cédula.

[4] For a sketch of the life of the first inquisitor, see Julio Jiménez Rueda, *Don Pedro Moya de Contreras, Primer Inquisidor de México* (México, 1944).

[5] The original relación of Pedro de los Ríos is extracted in Cuevas, *Historia de la Iglesia*, Vol. II, p. 266.

[6] The foremost history of the Mexican tribunal is that of José Toribio Medina, *Historia del Tribunal del Santo Oficio de la Inquisición en México* (second edition; México, 1954). Lea, *The Inquisition*, pp. 191-299, follows the Medina account, as does Cuevas, *Historia de la Iglesia*, Vol. II, pp. 282-304. All three works are lacking in perceptive analysis of the period 1571-1601. Documents cited below have not been consulted by Medina, Lea or Cuevas.

[7] For a résumé of Inquisition procedure, see Greenleaf, *Zumárraga*, pp. 21-25.

[8] Consult AGN, Inquisición, Tomo 223, exps. 1-6, for three decades of administrative correspondence with Spain. See AHN, Inquisición de Méjico, Legs. 1047-1064, for the Spanish side of the correspondence. Particularly valuable for doctrinal matters before the Mexican Holy Office are a series of letters and reports sent to the suprema between 1571 and 1595 in AHN, Inquisición de Méjico, Leg. 2269. A careful study of documents on both sides of the Atlantic dictates that the following evaluation of Lea, *The Inquisition*, p. 203, should be revised: "As communication between the tribunal and the Supreme Council in Madrid was slow and irregular, there was necessity that it should have greater independent authority than allowed to the provincial Inquisitions in Spain. . . ."

[9] AHN, Inquisición de Méjico, Legs. 1064-1067.

[10] See the studies of Ernesto Chinchilla Aguilar, *La Inquisición en Guatemala* (Guatemala, 1953) and José Toribio Medina, *El Tribunal del Santo Oficio de la Inquisición en las Islas Filipinas* (Santiago de Chile, 1889).

[11] AGN, Inquisición, Tomo 72, exp. 30.

[12] Cuevas, *Historia de la Iglesia*, Vol. 2, pp. 287-288n, calls attention to the fact that the "Library that we could call the 'directiva de los Inquisidores' is conserved in its entirety in AGN, Inquisición, Tomos 1477-1486, 1511, 1513, 1514, 1517, 1519."

[13] AGN, Inquisición, Tomo 77, exp. 35.

[14] *Ibid.*, Tomo 72, exps. 29, 32.

[15] *Ibid.*, Tomo 223, exp. 7.

TRIBUNAL OF THE HOLY OFFICE 187

[16] *Ibid.*, Tomo 74, exp. 4.
[17] *Ibid.*, Tomo 72, exp. 37.
[18] One volume of the deliberations has been published for the sixteenth century by the Archivo General de la Nación, *Libro Primero de Votos de la Inquisición de México 1573-1600* (México, 1949).
[19] These financial records have never been studied in a systematic manner. They are contained in the AGN, Real Fisco de la Inquisición, Tomos 1-8, for 1571-1601.
[20] AGN, Inquisición, Tomo 86, exps. 1, 2, 4. See also "Nomina del Tribunal de la Inquisición de Nueva España 1571-1656," *Boletin del Archivo General de la Nación* (México, 1955), Vol. XXVI, pp. 53-90, 293-316; hereafter cited as BAGN.
[21] AGN, Inquisición, Tomo 187, exp. 2.
[22] See a plethora of documents, *ibid.*, Tomos 68, 69, 77, 121, 122, 123, 124.
[23] *Ibid.*, Tomo 223, exps. 1, 3, *passim*.
[24] Documents in AGN, Inquisición, Tomo 71, show how the Holy Office often took a pro-hierarchy position against the regulars.
[25] The count is based on cross tabulations from the "Catálogo de la Inquisición" and the actual Tomos of documents. Using another statistical method, Liebman, *A Guide to Jewish References*, pp. 14-24, estimates that a total of 121 Jews were investigated or prosecuted.
[26] Much has been written about the Hawkins raid and the subsequent trial of the survivors by the Mexican Holy Office: Pablo Martínez del Río, "La Aventura Mexicana de Sir John Hawkins," *Memorias de la Academia de la Historia* (México, 1943), Vol. 2, No. 3; Frank Aydelotte, "Elizabethan Seamen in Mexico and Ports of the Spanish Main," *American Historical Review* (1942), Vol. 58, pp. 1-19; Julio Jiménez Rueda, *Corsarios Franceses e Ingleses en la Inquisición de la Nueva España* (México, 1945); Conway, *An Englishman* (Appendix III contains a list of documents relating to Englishmen and others associated with them who were condemned by the Mexican Inquisition from 1559 to 1575); Baez Camargo has alphabetical lists by century; Julio Jiménez Rueda, *Herejías*, pp. 63-77, summarizes the other literature. Most of the trials are found in AGN, Inquisición, Tomos 50-57.
[27] AGN, Inquisición, Tomo 52, exp. 4, as reproducida en Jiménez Rueda, *Corsarios Franceses e Ingleses*, pp. 307-506.
[28] AGN, Inquisición, Tomo 52, exp. 3, as reproducida en Jiménez Rueda, *Corsarios Franceses e Ingleses*, pp. 231-304.
[29] AGN, Inquisición, Tomo 54, exp. 5. An inventory of Ribley's property appears in Tomo 56, exp. 4.
[30] *Ibid.*, Tomo 53, exp. 2.
[31] *Ibid.*, Tomo 56, exp. 4.
[32] The proceso, no longer extant, is known through a copy by G. R. G. Conway and published as "Proceso contra Miles Philips," BAGN (1949), Vol. 20, pp. 115-172, 255-300. See "Relación escrita por Miles Philips y Publicada por Hakluyt," trans. by Joaquín García Icazbalceta, *Boletin de la Sociedad de Geografía y Estadística* (1869), Vols. I, II; Richard Hakluyt, *The Principal Navigations, Voyages Traffiques and Discoveries of the English Nation* (Hakluyt Society, Extra Series, Glasgow, 1904), Vol. 9, pp. 398-445.

[33] AGN, Inquisición, Tomo 55, exp. 1.
[34] *Ibid.*, Tomo 50, exp. 1, as reproduced in Jiménez Rueda, *Corsarios Franceses e Ingleses*, pp. 3-226.
[35] AGN, Inquisición, Tomo 1A, exp. 67, has data on English corsair visits to the western coast of Mexico in 1587. In Tomo 223, exp. 3, f. 75, the Mexican inquisitors and the suprema exchanged information on the activities of Francis Drake in 1570. Routine investigations of Protestantism in the 1580's are contained in Tomo 126.
[36] See *ibid.*, Tomo 59, exp. 1, for the 1577 trial of an elderly Portuguese Jew, Hernando Alvárez Pliégo, who was reconciled and fined 500 pesos de oro.
[37] *Ibid.*, exp. 6. See also Wiznitzer, pp. 180-181.
[38] The two volumes of Alfonso Toro, *La Familia Carvajal* (México, 1944), complement his earlier work, *Los Judíos* (México, 1932). Wiznitzer, pp. 181-214, synthesizes the known data on the family. The works of Seymour B. Liebman all deal with the family in some way.
[39] AGN, Inquisición Colección Riva Palacio, Tomo 2, as reproduced in the "Proceso Integro de Luis Carvajal el Viejo, Gobernador del Nuevo Reino de León" of Toro, *Los Judíos*, pp. 207-372. Wiznitzer, pp. 181-186, gives a convenient summary in English. See also "Dos Documentos Relativos a Luis Carvajal, El Viejo," BAGN (1951), Vol. XXII, pp. 551-558.
[40] Wiznitzer, p. 182.
[41] Seymour B. Liebman, "Research Problems in Mexican Jewish History," *American Jewish Historical Quarterly* (1964), Vol. 54, p. 178.
[42] Wiznitzer, pp. 186-189.
[43] The trials of Luis Carvajal the younger, his letters to his family and his memoirs are published in AGN, *Procesos de Luis Carvajal, El Mozo* (México, 1935).
[44] Pablo Martínez del Río, *Alumbrado* (México, 1937).
[45] Seymour B. Liebman (ed.), *The Enlightened. The Writings of Luis Carvajal El Mozo* (Coral Gables, 1967).
[46] See Wiznitzer, pp. 211-212, for the list.
[47] AHN, Inquisición de Méjico, Leg. 1064, f. 184.
[48] See AGN, Inquisición, Tomo 225A, pp. 185-187, for sailings of some members of the family to Peru. Liebman, *The Enlightened*, pp. 34, 140-148.
[49] AGN, Inquisición, Tomo 48, exp. 5.
[50] The majority of the bigamy cases for the 1570's are found in Tomos 91-108; and the prosecutions for the succeeding decades are located in Tomos 134-138. For the blasphemies, consult Tomos 143-148.
[51] An entire legajo of trials regarding simple fornication is found in Tomo 70.
[52] *Ibid.*, Tomos 60-67.
[53] For a convenient background to the Mexican occult and the Inquisition, see Manuel B. Trens, *Arte Curativo de las Enfermedades, Farmacia y Hechicería, La Brujería y El Nahualismo en La Nueva España* (Tuxtla Gutiérrez, Chiapas, 1954); and Greenleaf, *Zumárraga*, pp. 111-121.
[54] Lea, *The Inquisition*, Vol. 4, p. 206.
[55] The Holy Office investigations of the occult for the sixteenth century are contained in AGN, Inquisición, Tomos 125, 129-131 and 206-210.
[56] *Ibid.*, Tomo 125, exp. 41; and Tomo 266, exp. 14.

TRIBUNAL OF THE HOLY OFFICE 189

[57] *Ibid.* Tomo 129, exp. 4. Part of this trial, which runs to 280 pages, and several of the diagrams are reproduced in BAGN (1948), Vol. 19, pp. 15-30.

[58] AGN, Inquisición, Tomo 160, exp. 9.

[59] "Proceso de Juan Luis por Hereje y Pacto con el Demonio en el Siglo XVI," BAGN (1933), Vol. 4, pp. 1-70.

[60] *Recopilación*, Ley 35, Lib. VI, tít 1.

[61] AHN, Inquisición de Méjico, Leg. 1049, f. 58r.

[62] Greenleaf, "The Inquisition and the Indians," pp. 149-153.

[63] AHN, Inquisición de Méjico, Leg. 1064, ff. 162v.-165.

[64] *Ibid.*, Leg. 1049, f. 55v.

[65] See Pedro de Feria, *Revelación sobre la Reincidencia en sus Idolatrías de los Indios de Chiapas después de Treinta Años de Cristianos* (México, 1889), for problems of the second half of the sixteenth century.

[66] Most of the major disputes are included in AHN, Inquisición de Méjico, Competencias, Legs. 1734, 1735.

[67] AHN, Inquisición de Méjico, Leg. 1734, exp. 1. See also AGN, Inquisición, Tomo 141, for a legajo of documents on conflicts of jurisdiction in other areas.

[68] AGN, Inquisición, Tomo 223, exp. 6.

[69] *Ibid.*, Tomo 223, exp. 3.

[70] For these matters and other protocol problems, see Medina, *Historia del Tribunal*, pp. 87-91.

[71] AGN, Inquisición, Tomo 75, exp. 12. There is a list of repartimientos included in the trial record. Lea, *The Inquisition*, p. 215, relates this incident from a document in the Royal Library of Munich, Cod. Hispan. 79, Leg. 1, f. 1.

[72] The only scholarly study to touch on the conflict of jurisdiction between the Holy Office and royal audiencias is that of J. H. Parry, *The Audiencia of New Galicia in the Sixteenth Century* (Cambridge, 1948), pp. 173-177. Conflict of jurisdiction between the viceroy of New Spain and the audiencia of New Galicia can be studied in Richard E. Greenleaf, "The Little War of Guadalajara 1587-1590," *New Mexico Historical Review* (1968), Vol. 43, pp. 119-135.

[73] AGN, Inquisición, Tomo 225, f. 188.

[74] Jacinto de la Serna, *Manual de Ministros de Indios para el Conocimiento de sus Idolatrías y Extirpación de ellos* (México, 1892).

[75] Greenleaf, "The Inquisition and the Indians," pp. 144-145, *passim*.

[76] Wiznitzer, p. 184.

[77] AGN, Inquisición, Tomo 139, exp. 13. See the printed proceso in BAGN (1935), Vol. 6, pp. 207-262.

[78] Vito Alessio Robles, *Francisco de Urdiñola y el Norte de la Nueva España* (México, 1931), in Chapters 8 and 9 gives full treatment to Urdiñola's trials before the audiencia of Guadalajara and the Mexican Inquisition. Parry, pp. 177-184, summarizes the Alessio Robles account.

[79] AGN, Inquisición, Tomo 214, exp. 20, and Tomo 215, exp. 14, contain the Inquisition's proceedings in the Urdiñola case.

[80] See the Spanish side of the Urdiñola controversy over competency in AHN, Inquisición de Méjico, Leg. 1734, exp. 5.

[81] AHN, Inquisición de Méjico, Leg. 1049, ff. 7-9, 144v.; AGI 66-6-17.

[82] A highly intelligent and accurate novelesque treatment of Urdiñola and his

defense by the Holy Office is that of Philip Wayne (Powell), *Ponzoña en Las Nieves* (Madrid, 1966).

[83] For the institution of the *familiatura* in Spain, see Lea, *The Inquisition*, Vol. II, pp. 263-283.

[84] "Cédula of Philip II, August 16, 1570, Regulating the Privileges of Familiars in New Spain," Biblioteca Nacional de Madrid, Sección de MSS. X, 159, f. 240, as reproduced in Lea, *The Inquisition*, pp. 536-538.

[85] See *ibid.*, pp. 245-248, for a discussion of the Inquisition fuero in Mexico.

[86] See especially the entire legajo of *nombramientos* in AGN, Inquisición, Tomo 213.

[87] *Ibid.*, Tomo 139, deals with problems of the familiatura in the 1580's.

[88] G. R. G. Conway, "Antonio de Espejo, As a Familiar of the Mexican Inquisition, 1572-1578," *New Mexico Historical Review* (1931), Vol. 5, pp. 1-20.

[89] In 1581 Espejo was again in trouble with civil authority, this time over the slaying of two Indians in Aguascalientes; AGN, Inquisición, Tomo 90, exp. 25.

[90] The foremost authority on the Mexican book trade and the Holy Office is Irving A. Leonard. See his *Books of the Brave, Being an Account of Books and Men in the Spanish Conquest and Settlement of the Sixteenth Century New World* (Cambridge, 1949); the expanded Spanish translation of *Libros del Conquistador* (México, 1953) and *Romances of Chivalry in the Spanish Indies* (Berkeley, 1933); "On the Mexican Book Trade, 1576," *Hispanic American Historical Review* (1949), Vol. 17, pp. 18-34; "On the Mexican Book Trade in 1600," *ibid.* (1941), Vol. 9, pp. 1-40. The last two items use documents from the Notary Archive in Mexico City.

[91] Joaquín García Icazbalceta, *Bibliografía Mexicana;* José Toribio Medina, *La Imprenta en México (1539-1821)* (8 vols., Santiago de Chile, 1912).

[92] A very valuable survey and synthesis of Mexican censorship in the sixteenth century is Elizabeth S. Steele, "Censorship of Books in Sixteenth Century Mexico" (unpublished Master of Arts Thesis, Department of Inter-American Affairs, University of New Mexico, Albuquerque, 1950).

[93] See the excellent "Bibliotecas y Librerías Coloniales," BAGN (1939), Vol. 10, pp. 661-907.

[94] A remarkable collection of these documents, 600 printed pages, is contained in Fernández del Castillo's *Libros y Libreros en el Siglo XVI,* but the compilation is not complete.

[95] See particularly AGN, Inquisición, Tomos 82, 83, 141 and 142 for the provincial side of the attempt to regulate books and men.

[96] Fernández del Castillo, pp. 459-464, reproduces the decrees.

[97] *Ibid.*, pp. 473-497, contains the list followed by a papal brief on the *Index* authored by Gregory XIII.

[98] The trial of Pedro Ocharte is published in Fernández del Castillo's *Libros y Libreros,* pp. 85-141.

[99] For the printed trial record, see *ibid.*, pp. 142-243.

[100] AGN, Inquisición Tomo 165, exp. 5. Fernández del Castillo, pp. 519, 529, gives brief mention to the trial. Many researchers have confused Cornelius Adrian César, the printer, with a pirate who had the same name. Cf. Baez Camargo, pp. 68-72, and Alexander M. Stols, "Cornelius Adrian César, Impresor Holandés en México," BAGN (1957), Vol. 8, No. 3.

Chapter Six

THE MEXICAN INQUISITION AND THE CALVINISTS
1598-1601

BY THE END of the sixteenth century probably there were as many Germans and Flemings in New Spain as there were Judaizantes. The immigration had started during the period 1526-1549, when Charles V permitted his German subjects into the colonies. As the fleet system became a fixed procedure for navigation and trade between Spain and New Spain after 1550, and as foreign equity increased in transatlantic commerce, many Germans came to Mexico.[1] Often they remained only a few months, passing their days traveling and trading from the time the fleets docked at Veracruz in the late spring until they departed in the winter of the next year. Many German sailors and artisans liked Mexico and its people, and they found economic opportunity in the colony. Those who stayed on contributed to the growth of a foreign colony in New Spain, and since northern Europe had become largely Protestant, they were often suspected of heresy.

The Mexican tribunal of the Holy Office undertook to make security files on these foreigners, and the familiares kept them under surveillance. But even after three decades of experience in prosecuting corsairs, the inquisitors had not developed articulate views on what constituted Protestantism, and they had great difficulty distinguishing between Anglicans, Lutherans and Calvinists.

As these foreigners congregated into discernible social and economic groups, the Holy Office viewed them as "Protestants" without any attention to doctrinal variation among them. Between March 1598 and March 1601 more than fifteen of these men were tried by the Mexican Inquisition. Because each had some connection with the others, the Holy Office felt that they were conspirators and dangerous heretics who might lead loyal Catholics into doctrinal error. Perhaps the Mexican's fascination for the northern European, already evident in the late sixteenth century, led the tribunal to use harsh tactics against these visitors, including torture and burning at the stake.

During the investigation of one of the Germans, Simón de Santiago was quoted as saying to a friend that it would be a disaster if Gregorio Miguel were arrested by the Inquisition, since Miguel knew the entire Fleming colony in Mexico and could recount the life histories of all of his countrymen. As it turned out, Gregorio Miguel and his brother Cristóbal Miguel did augment files of the Holy Office on Lutherans and Calvinists in the viceregal capital, and they contributed to evidence which lead to the death of Simón de Santiago at the stake.

I

The Evidence Against Simón de Santiago

On November 26, 1599 Dr. Marthos Vohorques, prosecuting attorney of the Mexican Inquisition, petitioned the judges for the arrest of a Calvinist heretic known in Mexico as Simón de Santiago. Vohorques explained that Simón de Santiago was an unmarried carpetmaker, thirty-six years old, who had worked in Mexico City after he emigrated from Vildeshusen, a district of Bremen in northern Germany, where he had been reared and educated by Calvinists. The attorney said there was evidence that Simón consorted with heretics in Mexico City. Within a week inquisitors Alonso de Peralta and Gutierre Bernardo de Quiróz had seen to the arrest of the accused. He was incarcerated in the secret jail of the Holy Office. All his property, worth a total of seventy pesos, was confiscated and used by the alcalde of the jail to pay for Simón's food.[2]

Inquisition Secretary Pedro de Mañozca proceeded to gather testimony from informants and from the trial records of other Calvinists arrested by the Holy Office. One of these defendants was Andrés Pablo, a thirty-two-year-old cabinetmaker from the city of Danzig. Pablo informed the tribunal that Simón de Santiago had been an employee of Cristóbal Miguel of Otumba where he refined saltpeter and that he helped Miguel with a process which turned silver into gold. Andrés Pablo had gathered some crucial information about both Cristóbal de Miguel and Santiago, and he reported the data to the interpreter of the Holy Office, Enrico Martínez. Santiago had told Pablo that his employer was not a man of good will because he refused to pay his workers properly. Santiago advised Miguel to stay away from the Holy Office when it was rounding up *Flamencos,* and he urged him not to get involved when the Inquisition arrested his own brother Gregorio.

Andrés Pablo relayed information he heard from Santiago about Cristóbal Miguel's career as a German sailor, especially an incident when his ship stopped in Gibraltar and Spanish officials jailed the captain and commandeered the vessel. Cristóbal Miguel and the crew had overpowered the guards and thrown them overboard. Then they assaulted the jail and freed their captain before going on their way. Andrés Pablo quoted Santiago as saying that if the two Miguel brothers left Mexico they could amass a fortune, since one had money and the other had navigational skills which he had learned in the English maritime services. Santiago felt that the brothers ought to recruit other Flemings in Mexico for "trading ventures," presumably piracy in the Caribbean.

When Andrés Pablo expressed the belief to Simón de Santiago that the Miguel brothers should be brought to the attention of the Holy Office, Simón agreed, but he said he did not want anyone to go to prison on his account. He related what Gregorio Miguel had said about the interpreter of the Holy Office, Enrico Martínez.[3]

Martínez, a German Catholic, scientist and engineer, was regarded as an enemy of the Flemings in Mexico and an agent provocateur of the Inquisition. He and Andrés Pablo were friends—and this relationship started the chain reaction which resulted in three years of Protestant investigations after 1598. Pablo insisted that he had counselled Santiago to tell the Holy Office about his employers and about his own religious background because Simón came from the Bremen area, Calvinist country, and not from Cracow, Poland, as he claimed in public.

Simón had replied that he dared not denounce the Miguel brothers to the Inquisition because he had no money to escape from Mexico and their vengeance. Several specific items of theology and religious practice connected Santiago with Calvinism. He told Andrés Pablo he believed in only two sacraments, baptism and the Eucharist. He scoffed at Catholic beliefs, especially those concerning miracles. Simón gossiped about what had happened to monasteries and churches in his homeland after the Catholics departed and the Protestant clergy assumed their places. In addition to the destruction of edifices, he said the Calvinist clergy had repudiated miracular stories of a bleeding Christ in a hermitage near his home. Santiago charged that the friars had staged the entire affair, making the Christ bleed as the host was consecrated.

Andrés Pablo had more to say about the employers of Simón de Santiago to Enrico Martínez who entered the testimony in the trial record. Santiago had told Pablo that Gregorio and Cristóbal were natives of Herderdic in Protestant Holland, one of the first areas to turn Calvinist, even though they professed to be from Hamburg and the Bravant country. He said they had sold their business in Otumba hoping to use the money to escape from the Inquisition, and they were using their desire to study metallurgy as a ruse to get permission to leave Mexico.

Prior to Simón de Santiago's arrest on Friday, November 20, 1599, Inquisitor Peralta hauled Gregorio Miguel before the Holy Office. He had already been in the Inquisition jail for almost a week. Gregorio claimed to be twenty-one years old and a native of Niumeguen in Flanders. He told the judges his profession was that of "extracting gold from silver." The Holy Office apparently frightened him enough to induce him to inculpate not only Simón de Santiago but his own brother Cristóbal Miguel. In early November Simón de Santiago was having dinner in his brother's home when they discussed the passengers from the newly arrived fleet in Veracruz. There were many Germans on the list, but Simón opined that it would be dangerous for them to come to Mexico City because the Holy Office was rounding up Flamencos. Cristóbal Miguel stated that if any of the passengers did visit Mexico City it was the duty of residents to denounce them. Probably Gregorio was hoping to protect his brother by entering this evidence into the record. They proceeded to discuss religion and the sacrament of baptism, and Santiago explained how the ceremony of baptism in Flanders and in Mexico differed. After dinner Cristóbal Miguel confided to Gregorio that it would be better if Simón de Santiago never visited them again, "since he talked too much."

Gregorio informed the Holy Office that Santiago had spent over twenty-five years in Flanders, and only three or four years in Mexico. Therefore he presumed that Simón had consorted with heretics, having traveled all over Poland, Germany and France where a lot of the people were Protestants. Miguel then told the tribunal that Simón de Santiago was on a business trip to Taxco but soon would return to the viceregal capital where he had lodgings with Joseph de la Haya, a lapidary on Donceles Street. Finally he gave a description of the accused. He was medium sized, slim, and fair complexioned; he had a red beard and blue eyes, and he wore a homespun suit and a black cap. Obviously Simón de Santiago was far from inconspicuous.

Further interrogation by Inquisitor Peralta led Gregorio Miguel to admit that Simón de Santiago had been the foreman of Cristóbal Miguel's saltpeter works in Otumba. Many times they had conversed about religion and on one notable occasion, the Feast of San Diego, Simón de Santiago proclaimed that miracles attributed to San Diego were similar to the ersatz bleeding Christ of his youth. The judges insisted Gregorio Miguel defend himself for having neglected to denounce Simón de Santiago and Cornelius Adrián

César, the printer, as Calvinists. Gregorio replied that he had been deceived by the Devil, and being young and foolish, it had escaped his memory.

In June of 1600 Peralta was still extracting testimony from Gregorio Miguel, and it became apparent that Miguel had tried to get Simón de Santiago to leave Mexico because he knew too much about the brothers' affairs and their past history as corsairs. But Gregorio continued to add bits of data to the Santiago denuncia hinting at his Protestantism, quoting Simón's views on the clergy, the sacraments and the veracity of Lutheran teachings. Gregorio claimed Simón de Santiago had converted him temporarily to his own views because he argued so persuasively. Recently Gregorio had seen the error of his ways and he returned to the true faith. His own brother Cristóbal had been instrumental in getting him to repent. Inquisitor Peralta and his colleagues held no less than ten sessions quizzing Gregorio Miguel about the kind of heresy Simón de Santiago believed in. The prosecution learned that Santiago had been arrested on two prior occasions by commissaries of the Holy Office. A clear view of Lutheran and Calvinist doctrines emerged from the testimonies, but some time remained before the accused was labeled a Calvinist.

More details on the background of Simón de Santiago came from a witness named Diego del Valle on November 27, 1599. Del Valle was a twenty-five-year-old tailor from Mideburg in Flanders who had been apprehended for Calvinism. For a time he was the cellmate of Santiago, and del Valle was able to recount data from their conversations before Simón was placed in isolation because he appeared to be a raving lunatic. Simón told Diego he had been in Mideburg and he approved of Calvinist beliefs, and del Valle connected Simón with Joseph de la Haya who had a brother in Mideburg known to all as a Calvinist schoolmaster. Furthermore, the witness said Santiago talked at length about his parents who "would avenge him by killing Spaniards" if the Holy Office harmed him, and he tried to indoctrinate Diego in things of the Calvinist faith, teachings which del Valle already knew and understood. Simón had extremely harsh things to say about Cristóbal and

THE INQUISITION AND THE CALVINISTS 197

Gregorio Miguel who he thought had denounced him to the Inquisition. It was del Valle who first gave Inquisitor Peralta the real name of Simón de Santiago—Zegbo Vanderbec—the name he later gave in his own testimony. He had assumed aliases in Poland and France. Other prisoners from the Inquisition jail substantiated that Simón de Santiago openly talked about his Calvinism. Gómez Ramos, a native of Villanueva in Algarve, Portugal, had heard him affirm his beliefs.

Sometime during December 1599 Simón de Santiago decided to feign insanity. However, the testimonies indicated that he was a clumsy and incompetent actor. He slept well and ate with good table manners, and his personal habits of cleanliness belied the display of deranged conduct he staged for the jailer, the Inquisition physician and the judges. On January 24, 1600 Juan de León Plaza, alcalde of the secret prison of the Holy Office, made a formal report to the tribunal on Simón de Santiago's psychological state. He related how the accused screamed, tore up the furniture of the cell and threw things when the door was opened to bring him his food. As a result of his attack on the guards and other prisoners, he had been placed in manacles and chains. The guards had found it necessary to gag him during the day in order to have some peace and quiet in the jail. When he was alone and thought no one was watching, the jailer said Simón behaved normally and prayed a lot. León Plaza concluded Santiago had not gone mad at all, saying he was merely a "tricky scoundrel." Plaza had placed several prisoners accused of Judaizing in Simón's cell to gain his confidence and to report on his behavior. Manuel Gómez Silvera, Jorge Fernández and Manuel Tavares filed depositions saying Santiago was not insane. Whether the tribunal lightened the punishments of these informers is not known from their trial records. Dr. Gerónimo de Herrera, after talking with Simón about his health and diet, found him to be sane. Andrés Mondragón, barber of the Holy Office, who had attended the accused, swore that Simón de Santiago was in his right mind. The trial dragged on.

The lapidary, Joseph de la Haya of Ghent, Santiago's landlord, gave damaging testimony on December 17, 1600. He and Santiago made several trips to Taxco together and on the road Joseph had learned about the European exploits of Simón. His companion had served in the Calvinist armies of Holland and in the French armies when France was at war with Spain. In these campaigns, where Protestantism was a major issue, Simón desecrated churches and monastic houses and he bragged about having executed Catholics. As a soldier of Count Maurice, son of the Prince of Orange, Santiago supported Calvanism and its political system. On the Taxco trips they had eaten meat on Fridays, and Simón told Joseph de la Haya it was not sinful to break the precept of abstinence; the Calvinists did it all the time. According to Joseph's testimony, Simón and the Miguel brothers often sang Protestant battle hymns and marching songs. When Simón came to Mexico he carried a letter from Pedro de la Haya, Joseph's brother in Rotterdam who was a practicing Calvinist. Joseph assumed that Simón was of the same creed. He was quick to assert, however, that all the rest of the de la Haya family were loyal Catholics.

II

Inquisitorial Proceedings

The foregoing testimonies and miscellaneous data from the procesos of Flamencos arrested after April 1598 provided the Inquisition fiscal, Dr. Marthos de Vohorques, with adequate evidence for the prosecution of Simón de Santiago, and on December 7, 1599 the lengthy trial began. Because the defendant was not fluent in Spanish, the court appointed Enrico Martínez as his interpreter.

Simón de Santiago swore that he was a native of Vildeshusen, some three leagues from Bremen and that he was unmarried and thirty-six years old. He listed his profession as carpetmaker. His parents, Jacob Vanderbec and Anna Reiner, lived in Vildeshusen and Bremen. Simón claimed they were "German people, well born and noble," and they never had any reason to be investigated by the Holy Office of the Inquisition. He knew very little about his grandparents or aunts and uncles. He said he had been baptized by Protestants in Bremen, but he had never been confirmed. Nevertheless, he went to mass, confession and communion in Catholic churches when he could, and he carried a cédula from San Lucar, where the ships embarked from Spain for the new world, saying that he had gone to confession. In New Spain Simón had been a practicing Catholic. He had taken communion in the Franciscan monastery at Otumba, and the very morning of his arrest by the Holy Office he had gone to confession in the Augustinian convent in Mexico City. When the inquisitors questioned him about Catholic belief, Simón exhibited a paltry knowledge of Latin but he was able to recite the Pater Noster, the Ave María, the Credo and the Ten Commandments in German. It was revealing to the inquisitors that Santiago ended the Pater Noster with the phrases "for Thine is the Kingdom, the Power and the Glory for ever and ever," a sure sign of Protestant taint. Simón knew how to read and write. He had gone to school with Lutheran teachers at the insistence of his mother. On the margin of the trial document the scribe wrote, "The mother is Lutheran."

Part of every heresy interrogation included an autobiographical sketch. The data often inculpated the defendant and always provided fuel for additional questioning by the inquisitors. So it was with Simón de Santiago; he had lied about his military career and his coreligionists, and he neglected lacunae in his past which were already known to the tribunal. Simón told the judges he lived at home with his parents until the age of eleven when his father sent him to Danzig in Catholic Poland to work for John Siremberg, a functionary of Prince Bathboda. Then he went to France where he enlisted in the *Catholic* military faction which was allied with Philip II. Simón fabricated an elaborate background of service to the Counter Reformation political figures of his era. To be sure he had traveled among Calvinists in France and Holland and he had been in a Protestant hospital recovering from the wounds of battle, but he had nothing to do with their religious observances. He traced his career to Sevilla where he learned the trade of carpetmaking in an enterprise of the Duke of Medina before he signed on the "Salvadora" and came to New Spain as a sailor and artilleryman with a Genoese Captain Pascual Salicon. They arrived at San

Juan de Ulúa in the fleet of General Pedro Meléndez Márques in September 1597.[4] After that time Simón held odd jobs with Flamencos in Puebla de Los Angeles, and because he fell ill he was unable to sail with the fleet in 1598 for the return trip to Spain. In early 1598 the commissary in Veracruz arrested Santiago and sent him to jail as an "English spy." After several weeks Simón was released and made his way to Mexico City where he got a job with Cristóbal Miguel. In the meantime he had made the acquaintance of Andrés Pablo and Enrico Martínez. Simón de Santiago took advantage of the questioning to insert various pieces of evidence to discredit the Miguel brothers. He said he had gone to confession the morning of his arrest because he feared that they had denounced him to the Holy Office.

There is a curious change in Santiago's testimony in the second and third interrogations from December 1 and 10, 1599. Perhaps by this time he had determined to plead insanity. In any event he cried a great deal and he gave blatantly contradictory evidence. For instance, on December 7 he claimed that he had always been a loyal Catholic, and on the very next day he related he had been a Calvinist for two years. Obviously the mechanism of interrogation terrified him—especially when he was told, "This Holy Office is not accustomed to arrest suspects without considerable information."

Consequently, Simón began to describe Calvinist ceremonies and beliefs from his visits to their churches. He seemed to confuse Lutheran views of the Eucharist and consubstantiation with the Calvinist observance of communion, but he talked at length on subjects that appeared to come from John Calvin's *Institutes of the Christian Religion.* Justification by faith alone, negation of the power of the Pope, denial of purgatory, the attack on images and indulgences, services in German rather than Latin, individual interpretation of scripture—all of these ideas and more emerged from Santiago's testimony. He was careful to state, however, that these were things he had heard and seen on his travels—they were not his own convictions. In a rather crafty way the inquisitors tried to get Santiago to differentiate between Lutheranism and Calvinism, but the suspect, anticipating the pitfalls of the questions, became uncommunicative. Apparently the testimony became more contradictory as Simón de Santiago became more frightened, and as he feigned mental illness in the latter part of December 1599. The more he spoke to the judges, the more he inculpated himself. His frenzied desire to discredit the Miguels and Joseph de la Haya as Calvinists revealed his own heresies. By December 14 Santiago had been given the three required admonitions that he tell the truth in order to avoid stringent punishment and presumably judicial torture. On that morning Simón capitulated and made a full confession. Kneeling and tearful, he begged for mercy and admitted that he had been a Calvinist since he was eight years old, "believing in my heart that [Calvinism] was the way to salvation." Up until this time in his trial Simón had been ashamed to admit his guilt, claiming that he had been deceived by the Devil who kept him from full confession. Now he related his own beliefs about images, mental confession, purgatory and communion. He stated he did not believe that a small piece of bread and a bit of wine could be transformed into the body and the blood of Christ. His denial of the real presence in the Eucharist convinced the Inquisition that he was neither a Catholic nor a Lutheran because he denied consubstantiation as well as transubstantiation. Simón gave details about his military career in Protestant armies and the fact that he had performed acts of desecration of Catholic churches. Had his contrition been more convincing and had he not entangled himself in a web of lies and deceit, Simón de Santiago might have escaped the torture chamber and the stake. But circumstances of procedure and Simón's own equivocation eventually led to both.

III

Indictment and Judicial Torture

On December 31, 1599 Inquisition Prosecutor Dr. Marthos de Vohorques indicted Simón de Santiago on nine major counts as a heretic, apostate and Calvinist. Santiago was accused, with supporting evidence of guilt, of denying the power of the Pope and the faculties of the clergy to absolve sins. His denial of the real presence in the Eucharist and his violation of the precept of abstinence on Fridays were condemned. Simón's views on the veneration of images, miracles, and his denial of the existence of purgatory were pronounced heresy. His service in the armies of Protestant leaders and his refusal to denounce heretics to the Holy Office in Mexico were evidence of his treason to the Spanish Church and the King. The fact that he had perjured himself many times during the Inquisition trial led the attorney to demand the harshest penalty for the accused, and Dr. Vohorques suggested that the tribunal submit Simón de Santiago to judicial torture to get at the truth. Because Simón did not have legal counsel, Inquisitor Peralta appointed a defense attorney, Dr. Juan Núñez de Guzmán, to help him frame answers to the accusations of the fiscal. In a final New Year's Eve session of the tribunal, Simón de Santiago adopted a position of intransigence, refusing to add or subtract from his previous testimony. A perfunctory session of the tribunal was held on January 2, 1600 and Simón was urged to search his memory for more data on his own crimes against the faith, and to refine and elaborate on the testimony he had given about other Calvinists in Mexico.

Almost a year elapsed before the Santiago trial was resumed. During the months from January to December of 1600 the tribunal busied itself with the arrest and trial of other Flamencos, and it used their testimonies as a sounding board to judge the veracity of Santiago's confession. During these months Simón began to build his characterization of instability and insanity. Perhaps he did indeed have mental lapses. But the inquisitors became more convinced than ever that he was a "tricky rogue." Finally on December 20, 1600 inquisitors Peralta and Quiroz held a full-scale review of the case. They employed the assistance of expert consultants Dr. Juan de Cervantes, archdeacon of the diocese who was acting as ordinary, and Drs. Santiago del Riego and Francisco Alonso de Villagrá, judges of the audiencia of México. The panel decided to submit Santiago to judicial torture in order to ascertain if he were really insane, and to see if he could not be induced to confess, recant and seek reconciliation with the Holy Mother Church. As a consequence of this decision Simón was brought before the judges on January 11, 1601 for final interrogation. He refused to amplify his previous confession and he would not admit that he was feigning insanity. As a result the inquisitors signed the order for the torture of the accused, saying that he had only himself to blame if he were mutilated or maimed by the proceedings.

At 9:30 on the morning of January 13, 1601 Simón de Santiago was led to the torture chamber and ordered to undress. Stripped to his underpants he was placed upon the rack and his arms were bound with leather cords. As the questioning continued, the thongs were tightly twisted. Simón cried aloud uttering the name of Jesus, and he told the interrogator that he had lapses of insanity but he was now in his right mind. As the bonds were tightened five times and as Simón screamed in agony, he finally confessed that he had acted crazy in order to escape punishment for being a Calvinist heretic. He begged the tormentors to cease and he implored them to let him convert to Catholicism. After his confession was recorded he was taken down from the rack. On January 15, 1601 Simón de Santiago repeated the confession in court. He signed the document and Enrico Martínez witnessed it.

IV

Climax

After Simón de Santiago's confession, several sessions of the Inquisition tribunal were filled with the publication of testimonies against him. Rather meekly, Santiago heard the evidence and said little in answer to the charges. Maybe the torture proceedings had disoriented him, but it is more likely that he felt there was nothing to be gained from denials, and he had made up his mind on a matter of conscience. It was almost as though he was inviting the death sentence. When Inquisition Secretary Pedro de Mañozca asked Simón to verbalize any doubts he had concerning Roman Catholicism so that they could be explained as a prelude to his conversion, Santiago said he had no doubts left. All he had were firm convictions. He insisted that he was a Christian although he could not accept as truth all that the Holy Roman Church taught. He could not believe that man ought to adore and revere images, nor did he think that the Roman pontiff had the power to forgive sins. Simón Santiago contested the Petrine doctrine of supremacy *(Matthew* 16:18), and he doubted that the Pope was God's vicar on earth. He continued to question the validity of the sacrifice of the mass and that the consecrated host was the body of Christ.

When the inquisitors expressed astonishment at these terse phrases of Simón de Santiago, and as they queried him about his sudden change of attitude, he told them he had always been a *Christian* Catholic but he had never followed the dogmas of *Roman* Catholicism. By saying he was a Calvinist he had meant to imply there were many good things in Calvin's teachings just as the other Protestant faiths had much to offer man on his road to salvation.

The Mexican Holy Office made four separate attempts to reconcile Simón de Santiago before the March 25, 1601 auto de fé. Each time he was admonished to recant and to seek entrance into the body of the Roman Catholic Church; Santiago refused. On two memorable occasions he lashed out at Enrico Martínez saying, *"You* believe in your Pope and revere the images of your Saints because I cannot." He curtly informed his counsellors that he had no wish for Our Lady to intercede for him and "soon he would tell her so." Finally on February 13, 1601 the Mexican tribunal had to vote on a decision in Simón de Santiago's case. The judges pronounced him to be an obstinate Calvinist heretic. They decided to relax him to the secular authority for execution and to confiscate all his properties. On March 8, 1601 at the behest of the tribunal, the Jesuit Dr. Pedro de Morales tried a final time to convert Simón de Santiago to Catholicism. The convicted replied that he did not wish to subject himself to the Roman Catholic Church or its pontiff and he would not adore its images, preferring as he did to remain in his heretical sect.

Inquisition Secretary Mañozca prepared a lengthy relación about the life and theological errors of Simón de Santiago. The document ended by commanding that Simón participate in the auto de fé scheduled for March 25, 1601, and after the ceremonies he was to be remanded to the corregidor of Mexico City for execution. A Dominican friar wrote a graphic description of the auto de fé. The Zócalo was decorated with banners and coats of arms of the Holy Office of the Inquisition. A platform was constructed in front of the *Ayuntamiento* Building for the major focus of the ceremony. It was here among pageantry and velvet trappings that Simón de Santiago would hear his sentence read. At six o'clock on the morning of March 25, 1601 the procession began. Licenciado Juan de Altamirano, knight of the order of Santiago, led the way carrying the standard of the Holy Office. On the platform Dr. Juan de Cervantes, archdeacon of the cathedral, preached his sermon and read the sentence.[5] Of course Simón de Santiago was only one of many who were sentenced in the auto.

After the ceremonies the civil authority took over the task of punishing Santiago. The corregidor of Mexico City, Dr. Francisco Muñoz Monforte, commanded that Simón de Santiago be conducted through the streets of the city on horseback preceded by a town crier who was to inform the citizenry of Simón's crimes against the faith. In the marketplace of San Hipólito he was to be burned alive "until his body crumbled into ashes, and there was left no trace of his being."

Escribano Luis de León witnessed the execution. When the party arrived at the *quemadero* (burning place), many priests begged Simón de Santiago to convert to Roman Catholicism. After he was tied to the stake and a garrote was placed around his neck, the fires were lighted. At this point Simón decided to confess and seek conversion to Roman Catholicism and the garrote was removed. Simón de Santiago begged that they make him an orderly in a hospital where he could serve mankind, and he said, "Death is a bitter thing and life is sweet." At this juncture, seeing Simón de Santiago's contrition, the executioner placed a rope around Santiago's neck and affixed it to the stake.[6] But Simón was straining away from the flames so hard that he strangled himself with the rope. Luis de León's account of the execution varies in one respect from the formal report the Mexican Holy Office sent to Spain in 1601. In this document Inquisitor Peralta said Simón de Santiago "let himself be burned alive."[7]

After Simón de Santiago's execution on March 25, 1601 the commissary of the *real fisco* of the Holy Office, Diego de Briviezca, inventoried a small box of possessions which Simón had left in the jail. He died in New Spain as he had arrived—with nothing save a lust for life.[8]

V

The Other Flamencos, 1598-1601

The confusion of Calvinist ideas and Lutheran doctrine was evident in the trials of Gregorio Miguel and his brother Cristóbal Miguel.[9] From data recorded in the Simón de Santiago trial it became obvious that the brothers were from Calvinist districts of Niumeguen in Flanders. Both Gregorio and the older brother Cristóbal had been corsairs prior to their arrival in New Spain with the fleets of General Luis Alfonso Flores and General Antonio Navarra in 1587. While Cristóbal was accused of Calvinism, the other Miguel was branded a Lutheran. It is evident that ten years of business enterprise in Otumba netted Cristóbal considerable money and many friends.

Both men were reconciled in the auto de fé of March 25, 1601. After the brothers made public abjuration of their errors in the ceremony, the Holy Office confiscated their properties and sent them to jail for a two-year period. After the sentence had been fulfilled, the Miguel brothers again appeared on the Mexico City social scene wearing the sanbenito. Although reconciled heretics had their social lives and their business activities closely circumscribed by the regulations of the Holy Office, Cristóbal Miguel began to prosper. In March of 1602 inquisitors Peralta and Quiróz allowed him to remove his sanbenito. By late 1603 Cristóbal had begun to trade and to dress in violation of the Inquisition's caveats. On June 21, 1604 Cristóbal Miguel was tried a second time by the Mexican tribunal. He was charged with riding horses, bearing arms and wearing silk—things which were forbidden to reconciled heretics.[10]

The fate of the younger brother remains a mystery. On April 17, 1603 Cristóbal petitioned the release of Gregorio Miguel because he had completed his penance.[11] Both Bernardino de la Torre and Enrico Martínez recommended to the Mexican tribunal that the Miguels be allowed to leave New Spain. According to the documents they had shown exemplary conduct during the years of penance and imprisonment. Gregorio asked permission to go to Spain and Cristóbal wanted to return to Holland.[12] Whether the Miguel brothers received lighter sentences and pardons because they cooperated with Enrico Martínez in the Flamenco prosecutions is an interesting speculation.

Before the trials of Simón de Santiago and Cristóbal and Gregorio Miguel, the Holy Office began the investigation of nine other Calvinist heretics. The procesos span the years from the spring of 1598 to the auto de fé of March 1601. All the Flamencos and many others accused of Lutheranism seemed to have been acquainted, and their trial records have data which incriminates one another. The opening phase of the Flamenco campaign began in April 1598 when the tribunal of the Inquisition arrested two Calvinists: Giles of Murbec[13] and Hendrik Montalvo of Hamburg.[14] The evidence showed that Giles came to New Spain on the same ship with Simón de Santiago in 1597. The Inquisition commissary arrested Giles in Tlaxcala and sent him to Mexico City for trial. It developed from his testimony and other Flamencos that Giles had been a Mediterranean pirate before he came to New Spain. In this respect his career paralleled the lives of the

Miguel brothers. Perhaps Simón de Santiago had Giles in mind when he urged Cristóbal Miguel to outfit a corsair crew in the Caribbean. The Calvinism of Giles of Murbec was proven by the fiscal of the Holy Office, and he was condemned to a five-year stretch as a galleyman in the Spanish Navy. He wore the sanbenito and was given two hundred lashes as a part of the punishments meted out after the auto de fé of March 25, 1601.

Hendrik Montalvo had known Cristóbal Miguel in his native Hamburg. After he had endured the rack and the water torture in the Inquisition jail without confessing, Hendrik was commanded to make public abjuration of his Calvinist heresies as part of the auto.

In June of 1598 the Flamenco prosecutions intensified. Juan Guillermo, a seventeen-year-old sailor from Amberes was arrested on June 9. As a result of a severe illness he was incarcerated in the Santo Domingo Monastery where he finally died as a result of an accident. His effigy was carried in the 1601 auto de fé.[15] Martín Díaz from the village of Dist in Flanders was tried on the same day as Juan Guillermo. Finally he was subjected to torture in the same manner as Hendrik Montalvo, but he refused to be intimidated. Because the Holy Office had proof of his background as a Calvinist and a corsair, he was convicted and required to abjure his views along with Montalvo. The Inquisition increased the use of judicial torture in the cases of Alberto de Meyo between June and November of 1598[16] and Jorge de Bruxas, who was arrested in June 1598 and punished in March 1601,[17] but they were unable to get the clear-cut evidence needed for a death sentence.

As the trial of Simón de Santiago started, the lapidary Joseph de la Haya (alias Silva) was inculpated as a probable Calvinist because he was Santiago's close friend and since his family in Rotterdam were known to be Protestants. In December 1599, Joseph de la Haya's own trial began after he had testified in several of the other proceedings.[18] The lapidary was reconciled in the auto of 1601, as was the Calvinist tailor Diego del Valle from Mideburg.[19]

Among the most interesting cases of Calvinists in Santiago's circle was that of Pedro Pedro (or Hugo Pedro) of Argou, Flanders, who arrived in Mexico with Giles of Murbec and Simón de Santiago in 1597.[20] After he had been reconciled for Calvinism in 1601, Pedro was condemned to service in an obraje. He escaped from the sweatshop and made his way to the Philippines before he was apprehended. The Manila commissary returned him to Mexico for punishment, and he participated in the auto de fé of April 20, 1604. The Holy Office was extremely harsh with Pedro Pedro. He was sentenced to life imprisonment and to wear the sanbenito as long as he lived. Before he left Mexico he was given two hundred lashes, and then he was sent to Spain to serve in the galleys for ten years before he could retire to a jail for the rest of his life.

The auto de fé of March 25, 1601 marked the eightieth anniversary of inquisitorial activity in New Spain. One hundred and forty-three heretics were paraded in the auto. Thirty-two of the penitents were Calvinists or Lutherans and four of them were burned at the stake.[21] The pageantry of the auto and the flames of the quemadero, which finally reduced Simón de Santiago's cadaver to ashes, were the epitome of Counter Reformation Mexico.

Notes

[1] Clarence Haring, *Trade and Navigation Between Spain and the Indies in the Time of the Hapsburgs* (Cambridge, 1918), pp. 98-102.

[2] The trial record is found in AGN, Inquisición, Tomo 168, exp. 3.

[3] "Nombramiento de Enrico Martínez, para intérprete del Santo Oficio, 10 de junio de 1598," Fernández del Castillo, pp. 531-532.

[4] Simón de Santiago mentions the name of Meléndez Márques in AGN, Inquisición, Tomo 168, exp. 3, f. 74, and says he arrived "ahora dos años." See "Visita de las Naos que forman la flota llegada a San Juan de Ulúa en septiembre de 1597 a las ordenes del General Pedro Meléndez Márques," Fernández del Castillo, *Libros y Libreros*, pp. 435-437.

[5] Cuevas, *Historia de la Iglesia*, Vol. 3, pp. 171-174, extracts the description from AGN, Inquisición, Tomo 1510, exp. 5.

[6] It was the custom to strangle obstinate heretics who repented at the eleventh hour. See Greenleaf, *Zumárraga*, pp. 24-25.

[7] AHN, Inquisición de Méjico, Leg. 1064, f. 287v.

[8] "Almoneda y otros recaudos tocantes a los bienes confiscados a Simón de Santiago, ocho de Junio de 1602", AGN, Inquisición, Tomo 254A, exp. 5.

[9] AGN, Inquisición, Tomo 167, exp. 6; and Tomo 168, exp. 4.

[10] *Ibid.*, Tomo 274, exp. 8.
[11] AHN, Inquisición de Méjico, Leg. 1049, f. 637r.
[12] AGN, Inquisición, Tomo 168, exp. 4, ff. 4r.-6r.
[13] *Ibid.*, Tomo 164, exp. 5.
[14] *Ibid.*, exp. 9.
[15] *Ibid.*, Tomo 166, exp. 1.
[16] *Ibid.*, Tomo 165, exp. 7.
[17] *Ibid.*, Tomo 168, exp. 5.
[18] *Ibid.*, exp. 5.
[19] *Ibid.*, exp. 2.
[20] *Ibid.*, Tomo 165, exp. 2.
[21] AHN, Inquisición de Méjico, Leg. 1064, ff. 222-288v.

Chapter Seven

CONCLUSIONS

SEVERAL HUNDRED VOLUMES of sixteenth-century manuscripts in the archives of the Mexican Inquisition trace the evolution of a Counter Reformation milieu from an earlier Renaissance mentality. Perhaps the Mexican Counter Reformation was more neo-medieval than anything else, but even within the framework of post-Trentine orthodoxy a vital intellectual atmosphere prevailed. The writings of Alonso de la Vera Cruz, the spirit of his mendicant colleagues, and the activities of many other liberal and reform-minded clergy who ministered to the colonist and the Indian shine through the Inquisition documents and show that the intellectual ambiente of the colony was far from impenetrable.

By the 1560's many of the intellectual and theological characteristics of the baroque, so well described by Irving A. Leonard, are evident in Inquisition proceedings.[1] These included a healthy respect for established form combined with an anarchy of content and a complex conceptualization of the mission of the Church and the structure of orthodoxy.

While the Holy Office of the Inquisition often dealt with orthodoxy on a high level of abstraction, it also left room for the accommodation of a variegated populace of colonists and regional Indians to post-Reformation Catholicism. Punishment of the more vocal dissenter deterred the faithful from proscribed conduct, but one suspects that the blatant culprit was disciplined and the discreet were not. In provincial Mexico and on the northern frontier the zeal to ferret out unorthodoxy diminished. Furthermore the documents suggest that the sixteenth-century Mexican intelligentsia, both clergy and colonist, read, speculated and wrote with a degree of freedom not found in Spain during the same era. Obviously the Holy Office of the Inquisition constrained the colonist to prudence, but evidence is lacking that there was outright intimidation. John Tate Lanning in discussing the same situation in the late eighteenth century gave a characterization of the Holy Office that is equally applicable to sixteenth-century Mexico:[2]

> The Inquisition did not dictate whether there would be an intellectual life, but intellectual life dictated whether there would be an Inquisition. Though they occasionally felt annoyance, professors did not generally feel affected by the commissaries or even the tribunals of the Inquisition.

It is evident that dramatic and spectacular punishment of foreigners in autos de fé was used to encourage the Spanish colonist to remain within the confines of accepted orthodoxy. Since for the most part the harsh sentences were given to foreigners and Indians, the Mexican Spaniard viewed the Inquisition as a benign institution which protected religion and Spanish society from traitors and fomenters of social revolution. Admittedly this is a large statement, but archival data suggest that it reflects the prevailing attitude. Only when political and economic issues eclipsed religious issues did the Inquisition come in for criticism.

The controversy between the Dominican Inquisition and Cortés' supporters, discussed in chapters One and Four, and the somewhat biased position of the Holy Office in the struggle between the regular and the secular clergy all fall into the political category, and the Inquisition was criticized by the Church and State as a result. Certainly the Mexican colony harbored many more Jews and Protestants than appeared in the halls of the tribunal; and while the judges focused on a select number of them and dealt harshly with some, it still seems evident that there was a residuum of the tolerance of the Renaissance church in the latter part of the sixteenth century.

An evaluation of the behavior and effectiveness of the Holy

CONCLUSIONS

Office of the Inquisition in sixteenth-century Mexico is made difficult by reason of the fact that modern historians are prone to disagree on the role of religion in colonial society. The monastic Inquisition (1522-1532) and the episcopal inquisitors (1535-1571) appear to have been less professional and apolitical than the judges on the tribunal after 1571. But the earlier functionaries had to contend with hoary problems—the initial clash of native and Spanish religions and the rapidly changing posture of orthodoxy in European Catholicism and within Iberia itself. Charles V was less sure than Philip II of what to do about Erasmians and other dissenters; and the Mexican Holy Office, successively controlled by friars, bishops and professional judges, reflected the shifting attitudes of Spanish officialdom and of their own restricted groups. It can be argued that these circumstances made the Mexican Holy Office of the Inquisition less of a repressive institution in the sixteenth century than many scholars have imagined.

Notes

[1] Irving A. Leonard, *Baroque Times in Old Mexico* (Ann Arbor, 1959).
[2] John Tate Lanning, "The Church and the Enlightenment in the Universities," *The Americas: A Quarterly Review of Inter-American Cultural History*, Vol. 15 (1959), p. 391.

BIBLIOGRAPHY

INQUISITION MANUSCRIPTS in the Mexican archives have been paginated and rearranged several times. Citations are based on Tomo locations and the *Catálogo de Inquisición,* Volume One, where the enumeration agrees. When the numbers do not coincide, the actual Tomo pagination is used. The bibliography that follows has been arranged in categories of manuscript materials and printed works. Unpublished theses and scholarly manuscripts being readied for publication have been included in the latter section for convenience. Manuscript sources are listed in archival style rather than in chronological or alphabetical order.

I. *Manuscript Materials from Archivo General de la Nación, México (AGN), Ramo de la Inquisición.*

A. Individual Procesos.

Proceso contra Marcos de Acolhuacán por amancebamiento, 1522. AGN, Inquisición, Tomo 1, exp. 1. (No longer extant.)

Primer edicto contra herejes y judíos, 1523. AGN, Inquisición, Tomo 1, exp. 2. (No longer extant.)

Segundo edicto publicado en México contra toda persona que de obra o palabra hiciere cosas que parezcan pecado, 1523. AGN, Inquisición, Tomo 1, exp. 3. (No longer extant.)

Proceso contra Diego Cortés por blasfemo, 1527. AGN, Inquisición, Tomo 1, f. 53.

Proceso contra Rodrigo Rodríguez por blasfemo, 1527. AGN, Inquisición, Tomo 1, f. 54.

Proceso contra Diego de Morales por blasfemo, 1528. AGN, Inquisición, Tomo l, exp. 6.
Proceso contra Diego Núñez por blasfemo, 1527. AGN, Inquisición, Tomo 1, exp. 7.
Proceso contra Hernando de Escalona por blasfemo, 1527. AGN, Inquisición, Tomo 1, exp. 7a.
Proceso contra Juan Bello por blasfemo, 1527. AGN, Inquisición, Tomo 1, exp. 8.
Proceso contra Gil González de Benavides por blasfemo, 1527. AGN, Inquisición, Tomo 1, exp. 9.
Proceso contra Juan Rodríguez de Villafuerte por blasfemo, 1527. AGN, Inquisición, Tomo 1, exp. 9a.
Proceso contra Juan Martín Berenjel por blasfemo, 1527. AGN, Inquisición, Tomo 1, exp. 9b.
Proceso contra Cristóbal Díaz por blasfemo, 1527. AGN, Inquisición, Tomo 1, exp. 9c.
Proceso contra Bartolomé Quemado por blasfemo, 1527. AGN, Inquisición, Tomo 1, exp. 9d.
Proceso contra Alonso de Espinosa por blasfemo, 1527. AGN, Inquisición, Tomo 1, exp. 9e.
Proceso contra Rodrigo Rengel por blasfemo, 1527. AGN, Inquisición, Tomo 1, exp. 10.
Declaración de Gaspar de la Plaza, ante el Provisor Juan Rebollo, por haber escrito una carta sospechosa de herejía, 1539. AGN, Inquisición, Tomo 1, exp. 10a.
Proceso contra Francisco González por blasfemo, 1527. AGN, Inquisición, Tomo 1, exp. 10b.
Proceso contra Diego García por blasfemo, 1527. AGN, Inquisición, Tomo 1, exp. 10c.
Proceso contra Francisco Núñez por blasfemo, 1527. AGN, Inquisición, Tomo 1, exp. 10d.
Proceso contra Gregorio de Monjarrás por blasfemo, 1527. AGN, Inquisición, Tomo 1, exp. 10e.
Proceso contra Alonso de Carrión por blasfemo, 1527. AGN, Inquisición, Tomo 1, exp. 10f.
Proceso contra Diego de Morales por blasfemo, 1524-1525. AGN, Inquisición, Tomo 1, ff. 93-134.
Proceso contra Andrés Griego por herejía, 1528. AGN, Inquisición, Tomo 1, ff. 141-146.
Proceso contra Francisco de Agreda por blasfemo, 1528. AGN, Inquisición, Tomo 1, ff. 151-154.
Proceso contra Reinaldo de Luna por blasfemo, 1527. AGN, Inquisición, Tomo 1A, exp. 14.

Proceso contra Juan de Cuevas por blasfemo, 1527. AGN, Inquisición, Tomo 1A, exp. 15.
Proceso contra Alonso de Corellana por blasfemo, 1527. AGN, Inquisición, Tomo 1A, exp. 16.
Proceso contra Lucas Gallego por blasfemo, 1527. AGN, Inquisición, Tomo 1A, exp. 17.
Documentos relativos a los Corsarios en le costa del oeste de México, 1587. AGN, Inquisición, Tomo 1A, exp. 67.
Proceso del Santo Oficio de la Inquisición y el Fiscal en su nombre contra Gonzalo Gómez, vecino de Michoacán, por judaizante, 1536. AGN, Inquisición, Tomo 2, exp. 2.
Proceso del Santo Oficio contra Gaspar de la Plaza por asegurar que no era pecado estar con una india, 1538. AGN, Inquisición, Tomo 2, exp. 6.
Proceso criminal del Santo Oficio de la Inquisición y del Fiscal en su nombre contra don Carlos indio principal de Texcoco por idolatra, 1539. AGN, Inquisición, Tomo 2, exp. 10.
Proceso contra Dr. Pedro de la Torre, natural de Logroño y vecino de Veracruz, por haber dicho que "Dios y la naturaleza son una misma cosa," 1551. AGN, Inquisición, Tomo 2, exp. 13.
Proceso contra los que resultan culpados sobre palabras que han dicho contra las censuras, 1556. AGN, Inquisición, Tomo 2, exp. 14.
Proceso formado por el Arcediano y Provisor de la Catedral de Valladolid (Honduras) contra Nicolás Santour, natural del ducado de Borgoña en Francia, por luterano, 1560. AGN, Inquisición, Tomo 3, exp. 1.
Proceso de oficio contra el Doctor Chico de Molina, arcediano de la Santa Iglesia de México por proposiciones contra los Sacramentos, 1560. AGN, Inquisición, Tomo 3, exp. 2.
Estas Cosas dijo su Paternidad del padre provincial que entre sabios fueron descuidos y se murmuraron. AGN, Inquisición, Tomo 3, exp. 3.
Proceso criminal hecho de oficio por la Justicia Eclesiástica de la Ciudad de Anteguera contra Mateo de Monjarrás por haber dicho que un fraile dominicano era luterano, 1564. AGN, Inquisición, Tomo 3, exp. 5b.
Proceso hecho de oficio contra Mateo de Monjarrás por hechar mano dentro de la Iglesia, 1566. AGN, Inquisición, Tomo 3, exp. 5c.
Información levantada por Fr. Alonso de Montúfar, Arzobispo de México, sobre ciertas palabras dichas por Fr. Antonio de Velásquez, religioso agustino, en un sermón que predicó en la Iglesia Mayor de México, 1563. AGN, Inquisición, Tomo 3, exp. 15.
Denuncia e información contra Atanasio de Solís, colegial de la Ciudad de México, seguida ante el Provisor y Vicario General por proposiciones heréticas, 1563. AGN, Inquisición, Tomo 4, exp. 1.
Proceso de la inquisición ordinaria contra Juan de Villanueva clérigo presbítero, cura y vicario general de la Villa de San Francisco de Cam-

peche, por mal ejemplo que daba con su conducta y palabras malsonantes, 1563. AGN, Inquisición, Tomo 4, exp. 3.

Información levantada a petición del Doctor Barbosa, Provisor del Arzobispado de México, por haberle acusado el Deán Alonso Chico de Molina de haber dicho ciertas palabras malsonantes en el púlpito, 1564. AGN, Inquisición, Tomo 4, exps. 6, 7.

Información levantada a petición del Padre Maestro Fray Bartolomé de Ledesma contra el Deán D. Alonso Chico de Molina, por haber asegurado éste publicamente que el primero había dicho predicando ciertas palabras heréticas y malsonantes, 1564. AGN, Inquisición, Tomo 4, exp. 9.

Proceso eclesiástico contra Juan Bautista Corvera, natural de Toledo en los reinos de Castilla, por haber hecho versos con proposiciones heréticas, 1564. AGN, Inquisición, Tomo 4, exp. 10.

Proceso contra Juan Bautista Corvera sobre la fuga que hizo de la carcel, 1564. AGN, Inquisición, Tomo 4, exp. 10-bis.

Proceso del Fiscal Diego de Velmar contra Bartolomé Díaz de Piza por palabras malsonantes, 1564. AGN, Inquisición, Tomo 5, exp. 2.

Proceso contra Francisca de la Anunciación, monja profesa, por haber dicho que una religiosa de su convento que se ahorcó no se había condenado, 1564. AGN, Inquisición, Tomo 5, exp. 4.

Proceso de la inquisición eclesiástica contra Bartolomé de Valdespino, clérigo, por haber predicado en la Iglesia de la Villa de la Trinidad, un Día de Todos Santos, cierto sermón en que dijo "que los santos merecían más que nuestra señora la santísima Virgen María y aún algunos de nosotros merecíamos más que ella, 1565. AGN, Inquisición, Tomo 5, exp. 13.

Proceso contra Pedro Pablo de Acevedo, clérigo de Evangelio, natural de la Villa de los Zapotecos, por haber dicho ciertas palabras malsonantes y heréticas contra Jesucristo, 1567. AGN, Inquisición, Tomo 7, exp. 3.

Proceso contra Andrés de Porras, clérigo del curato de la Villa de Tabasco, por haber predicado palabras malsonantes y heréticas en el púlpito, 1568. AGN, Inquisición, Tomo 7, exp. 13.

Proceso de oficio de la autoridad eclesiástica contra Elena de la Cruz, monja profesa del Convento de la Concepción de la Ciudad de México sobre ciertas palabras que dijo contra nuestra santa fé Católica, 1568. AGN, Inquisición, Tomo 8, exp. 1.

Proceso de oficio de la justicia eclesiástica contra Cristóbal de Soria, clérigo cura y vicario de la Villa de San Miguel en el Obispado de Michoacán, por palabras malsonantes contra la Santa Iglesia Católica, 1568. AGN, Inquisición, Tomo 8, exp. 4.

Proceso de oficio de la justicia eclesiástica contra Fr. Andrés de Aguirre de la Orden de San Agustín, por decir que la simple fornicación no era pecado, 1568. AGN, Inquisición, Tomo 8, exp. 5.

Proceso de la justicia eclesiástica contra Fray Alonso Urbano, natural de la Villa de Mondejar en los reinos de Castilla, de la Orden de San Francisco, por palabras malsonantes que dijo en un sermón que predicó en la Iglesia Mayor el día de la Circunsición, 1569. AGN, Inquisición, Tomo 9, exp. 4.

Proceso del Santo Oficio contra don Guillermo de Orlando, inglés natural de Londrés, por haber dicho que "Dios era el Diablo y el diablo Dios," y que "el moriría por su Reyna" que era protestante, 1569. AGN, Inquisición, Tomo 9, exp. 6.

Proceso contra Ruy Díaz por blasfemo, 1532. AGN, Inquisición, Tomo 14, exp. 1.

Sumarea Instruido a Hernando García Sarmiento, por blasfemo, 1527. AGN, Inquisición, Tomo 14, exp. 2a.

Proceso de este Santo Oficio de la Inquisición y del Fiscal en su nombre contra Alonso de Carrión, natural de Córdoba, jugador blasfemo reincidente que había sido penitenciado por Fr. Domingo de Betanzos, 1536. AGN, Inquisición, Tomo 14, exp. 3.

Proceso criminal de Juan Bezos de la una parte contra Alonso Pérez Tamayo, alguacil, sobre lo que dijo contra el libro de la Biblia, 1544. AGN, Inquisición, Tomo 14, exp. 35.

Información que hizo el Inquisidor y Visitador de la Nueva España, Lic. Francisco Tello de Sandoval, sobre lo que había predicado en contra de las bulas de la Santa Cruzada, Fr. Arnoldo de Basancio, francés, Guardián del convento de Zapotlán, 1546. AGN, Inquisición, Tomo 14, exp. 37-bis.

Proceso del Santo Oficio de la Inquisición contra Juan de Avila natural de Zafra en los reinos de España, por blasfemo, 1541. AGN, Inquisición, Tomo 14, exp. 39.

Información sobre la denuncia que hizo Juan Bezos contra Alonso Pérez Tamayo, alguacil de la Carcel de la Ciudad de México, por blasfemo, 1544. AGN, Inquisición, Tomo 14, exp. 44.

Proceso de la autoridad eclesiástica contra Simón Falcón, natural de Portugal, tratante comerciante en la Ciudad de México, por palabras malsonantes, 1558. AGN, Inquisición, Tomo 15, exp. 15.

Proceso de la justicia eclesiástica contra Melchor Martín, indio, vecino de la Ciudad de Santiago de Guatemala, por blasfemo, 1560. AGN, Inquisición, Tomo 16, exp. 11.

Proceso contra el Doctor Pedro de Santander, médico, por blasfemo, 1561. AGN, Inquisición, Tomo 17, exp. 6.

Proceso de la justicia eclesiástica contra Fray Tomás de Chávez por pala-

bras malsonantes en el púlpito, 1562. AGN, Inquisición, Tomo 17, exp. 9.
Proceso contra Francisco de Tijera portugués por blasfemo y escupir a un Cristo, 1564. AGN, Inquisición, Tomo 18, exp. 64.
Proceso contra Hernando Pacheco por blasfemo, 1569. AGN, Inquisición, Tomo 21, exp. 1.
Demanda de divorcio de Francisca López contra Juan Pérez, 1569. AGN, Inquisición, Tomo 29, exp. 1.
Información contra Fray Gregorio Mejía por proposiciones heréticas, 1563. AGN, Inquisición, Tomo 29, exp. 3.
Denuncia contra Fray Francisco de Acosta por decir entre otras cosas que "si estando en contemplación pensaba en la comida daba al diablo la contemplación," 1560. AGN, Inquisición, Tomo 29, exp. 9.
Denuncia que hace Fr. Sebastían de Garcillán Altamirano contra Fr. Concha, Franciscano, por decir que su orden era más perfecta que la de San Agustín, 1562. AGN, Inquisición, Tomo 29, exp. 10.
Proceso contra Alvaro Mateos natural de Medellín, sastre, vecino de México, hijo de cristianos nuevas por judaizante, 1539. AGN, Inquisición, Tomo 30, exp. 9a.
Proceso contra Diego de Morales por decir herejías, 1558. AGN, Inquisición, Tomo 31, exp. 2.
Proceso contra Agustín Boacio por hablar contra el purgatorio, la confesión y por otras herejías, 1559. AGN, Inquisición, Tomo 31, exp. 3.
Proceso contra Roberto Tomson inglés por haber dicho ciertas palabras de la reprobada secta luterana y contra la Santa Fé Católica, 1560. AGN, Inquisición, Tomo 32, exp. 8.
Causa del Santo Oficio de la Inquisición contra Tomás, indio natural de Tecoaloya y María india con quien se había casado antes de la conquista conforme a los ritos de su gentilidad, acusados de mancebía, 1547. AGN, Inquisición, Tomo 34, exp. 6.
Proceso e autos de la Justicia Eclesiástica de esta Ciudad (Puebla) de los Angeles contra Padre Pedro Ortíz de Zúñiga, sobre ciertas cosas que se le opinen en razón de estar amancebado, 1567. AGN, Inquisición, Tomo 34, exp. 8.
Proceso de la justicia eclesiástica contra Antonio Anguiano vecino de México, por amancebado. 1534. AGN, Inquisición, Tomo 36, exp. 1.
Información que el Br. Maraver, Dean de la Iglesia de Oaxaca, presentó en el Santo Oficio de la Inquisición de la Ciudad de México hecha en la Mixteca contra el cacique y gobernadores y principales del Pueblo de Yanhuitlán, por idólatras, 1544. AGN, Inquisición, Tomo 37, exp. 5.
Proceso del Santo Oficio de la Inquisición de México contra Don Alonso y Don Andrés, caciques de Coatlán por idólatras, 1544-1547. AGN, Inquisición, Tomo 37, exp. 6.

BIBLIOGRAPHY

Proceso del Fiscal del Santo Oficio contra Don Francisco y Don Domingo, indios del pueblo de Yanhuitlán por idólatras, 1544-1547. AGN, Inquisición, Tomo 37, exp. 7.

Proceso contra los Indios de Yanhuitlán, 1546. AGN, Inquisición, Tomo 37, exp. 8.

Razón del Proceso que se hizo en el Santo Oficio de la Inquisición contra Don Domingo Cacique de Yanhuitlán, 1545. AGN, Inquisición, Tomo 37, exp. 9.

Probanza del Fiscal del Santo Oficio de la Inquisición contra Don Francisco y Don Domingo y Don Juan, Cacique y Gobernadores de Yanhuitlán, 1546. AGN, Inquisición, Tomo 37, exp. 10.

Acusación contra los caciques de Cuaxtepec por sacrificios humanos, 1546. AGN, Inquisición, Tomo 37, exp. 11.

Proceso del Santo Oficio de la Inquisición contra Don Juan Gobernador del Pueblo de Teutalco, por idólatra, 1546-1547. AGN, Inquisición, Tomo 37, exp. 12.

Proceso del Santo Oficio de la Inquisición y Dr. Rafael de Cervanes en su nombre contra Juan Franco por hechicerías, 1536. AGN, Inquisición, Tomo 38, exp. 1.

Proceso de Oficio de la justicia eclesiástica contra Juan Fernández del Castillo, escribano por acusarle de que había hecho idólatrar a los Indios, 1528. AGN, Inquisición, Tomo 40, exp. 3-bis-a.

Proceso del Santo Oficio de la Inquisición contra Gregorio Gallego y Martín de Aranda, por no haber guardado el secreto que se les recomendó, 1540. AGN, Inquisición, Tomo 40, exp. 6.

Información de la justicia eclesiástica contra Don Pablo Tecatecle, indio del pueblo de Zumpango, por haber hecho "ciertos sacrificios y ceremonias según sus ritos antiguos," 1547. AGN, Inquisición, Tomo 40, exp. 9.

Proceso de la autoridad eclesiástica contra Juan de Jaén, por incestuoso, 1528. AGN, Inquisición, Tomo 42, exp. 13.

Información levantada por Gerónimo Flores, Corregidor del Pueblo de Izucar y dirigida al señor Don Francisco Tello de Sandoval Inquisidor y Visitador de la Nueva España, sobre la acusación presentada contra Tomás Tunalt, 1545. AGN, Inquisición, Tomo 42, exp. 20.

Información levantada en contra de los frailes dominicanos Fr. Andrés de Moguer, Fr. Juan de Olmedo, y Fr. Pedro de Farías por haber burlado las censuras y excomunicaciones del Cabildo Eclesiástico de la Ciudad de Antequera, 1556. AGN, Inquisición, Tomo 42, exp. 28.

Proceso contra Catalina García y contra Domingo Hernández Indio por haber enterrado en el atrio de la iglesia un indio que no estaba bautizado, 1557. AGN, Inquisición, Tomo 43, exp. 1.

Información acerca de un diálogo de la Doctrina Cristiana que en lengua

tarasca escribió Fr. Maturino Gilberti, 1559. AGN, Inquisición, Tomo 43, exp. 6.
Entrega ante notario de los reos Agustín Boacio y Roberto Tomson al Capitan de la Nao Santa María de la Calle para ser conducidos a España, 1560. AGN, Inquisición, Tomo 43, exp. 7.
Copia de una Real Cédula mandando recoger los diálogos en tarasco escritos por Fr. Maturino Gilberti, 1563. AGN, Inquisición, Tomo 43, exp. 20.
Proceso contra Gonzalo López de Avila vicario del pueblo por almorzar antes de decir misa, 1569. AGN, Inquisición, Tomo 44, exp. 4.
Proceso contra Gonzalo Robledo por usurero, 1568. AGN, Inquisición, Tomo 44, exp. 5.
Proceso contra doña María de Peralta viuda de Hortuño de Ibarra por blasfema, 1575. AGN, Inquisición, Tomo 48, exp. 5.
Proceso contra Pierres Anpoy, francés pirata por luterano, 1571. AGN, Inquisición, Tomo 50, exp. 1.
Proceso contra David Alejandre de la Armada de Juan de Haquines, por luterano, 1572. AGN, Inquisición, Tomo 52, exp. 3.
Proceso contra Guillermo Collins, por luterano y blasfemo, por otro nombre Miguel Cabello, de la Armada de Juan Haquines, 1572. AGN, Inquisición, Tomo 52, exp. 4.
Proceso contra Juan Farentón, inglés de la Armada de Juan Haquines por herege luterano, 1573. AGN, Inquisición, Tomo 53, exp. 2.
Proceso contra Jorge Ribli, inglés de la Armada de Juan Haquines, por luterano, 1573. AGN, Inquisición, Tomo 54, exp. 5.
Proceso contra Pablo Haquines de la Cruz, inglés, de la Armada de Juan Haquines, 1573. AGN, Inquisición, Tomo 55, exp. 1.
Proceso contra Guillermo Ricart (alias Cornelius), inglés de la Armada de Juan de Haquines, luterano, 1573. AGN, Inquisición, Tomo 56, exp. 4.
Proceso contra Hernando Alvarez Pliego, por Judaizante, 1577. AGN, Inquisición, Tomo 59, exp. 1
Proceso contra García González Bergemero por Judaizante, 1579. AGN, Inquisición, Tomo 59, exp. 6.
Proceso contra Juan de Viveros, dirigo presbitero, por solicitante y amancebado con Antonia Vargas, 1564. AGN, Inquisición, Tomo 68, exp. 2.
Proceso contra el Doctor Pedro López por desacato a varias imágenes, 1570. AGN, Inquisitión, Tomo 72, exp. 11.
Proceso contra Antón sacristán por haberse robado unos libros prohibidos, 1551. AGN, Inquisición, Tomo 72, exp. 18.
Proceso contra Juan Suárez de Avila o Juan Alvarez Peralta, acusado por

BIBLIOGRAPHY 223

los hijos de Gonzalo Gómez de tratar de infamar su memoria vendiendo papeles escritos, 1571. AGN, Inquisición, Tomo 72, exp. 29.

Pedro López de Salcedo entrega a la Inquisitión de M. papeles y libros del Santo Oficio, que tenía en su poder su suegro, Miguel López de Legazpi, 1571. AGN, Inquisición, Tomo 72, exp. 32.

Visita del Inquisidor don Pedro Moya de Contreras a la Carcel Secreta del Santo Oficio, 1571. AGN, Inquisición, Tomo 72, exp. 37.

Proceso contra Molina, repartidor de los Indios de San Juan, 1572. AGN, Inquisición, Tomo 75, exp. 12.

Autos y diligencias hechas por los Sanbenitos antiguos y recientes y postura de los que sean de relajados por este Santo Oficio, 1574. AGN, Inquisición, Tomo 77, exp. 35.

Memoria de hijos de Quemados en México, c. 1530. AGN, Inquisición, Tomo 89, exp. 38.

Proceso contra Antonio de Espejo familiar del Santo Oficio sobre la muerte de Marcos Ruíz y de otro Indio, 1581. AGN, Inquisición, Tomo 90, exp. 25.

Calificacíon de las proposiciones de Fray Maturino Gilberti. AGN, Inquisición, Tomo 117, exp. 8.

Juan de Beteta se denuncia por practicar la astrología judiciaria, 1582. AGN, Inquisición, Tomo 125, exp. 41.

Declaración de Pedro Juárez de Mayorga acusado de nigromante, 1583. AGN, Inquisición, Tomo 129, exp. 4.

Proceso contra D. Felix de Zúñiga, Corregidor de Zacatecas y D. Francisco de Avellaneda su hermano, 1585. AGN, Inquisición, Tomo 139, exp. 13.

Asuntos de nigromante en la provincia de Avalos, 1597. Fragmento. AGN, Inquisición, Tomo 160, exp. 9.

Proceso contra Simón de Santiago, Natural de Vildeshusen, junto a la Ciudad de Bremen, en Alemania la Baja, Residente en México, mozo, soltero, 1599. AGN, Inquisición, Tomo 168, exp. 3.

Proceso contra Fray Miguel de Bolonia, franciscano, por decir que: "cada uno se puede salvar según su ley," 1572. AGN, Inquisición, Tomo 187, exp. 2.

Información y Proceso contra Francisco de Urdiñola. AGN, Inquisición, Tomo 214, exp. 20.

Información y Proceso contra Francisco de Urdiñola. AGN Inquisición, Tomo 215, exp. 14.

Abecedario de Relaxados, Reconciliados y penitenciados en la Nueva España después que en la tierra se fundó a 4 de noviembre de 1571. AGN, Inquisición, Tomo 223, ff. 711-739.

Información fecha ante el muy ilustre y reverendísimo Señor Inquisidor

General de la Nueva España. Fray Antonio de la Serna contra Don Pedro Ladrón de Guevara, 1574. AGN, Inquisición, Tomo 225, ff. 188-199.

B. Entire Legajos.

Trials for Bigamy 1532-1600. AGN, Inquisición, Tomos 14, 23, 24, 25, 34, 91-108, 134-138.
Blasphemy Trials of Tello de Sandoval, 1544-1547. AGN, Inquisición, Tomos 14, 42, 212.
Early Corsair Prosecutions, 1560. AGN, Inquisición, Tomo 32.
Correspondence between the supreme Inquisition and the Mexican tribunal; Correspondence between the Mexican tribunal and the provincial commissaries to 1600. AGN, Inquisición, Tomos 44, 72, 74, 77, 82, 90, 141, 142, 223, 225.
Trials of Corsairs 1568-1576. AGN, Inquisición, Tomos 50-57.
Genealogies and Limpiezas de Sangre 1571-1600. AGN, Inquisición, Tomos 60-67.
Procesos against Clerical Immorality and Solicitantes, 1564-1600. AGN, Inquisición, Tomos 68-71, 121-124.
Punishment of Sorcery and Superstition, 1580-1600. AGN, Inquisición, Tomos 125, 129-131, 206-210.
Routine Protestant Investigations, 1580-1598. AGN, Inquisición, Tomo 126.
Conflicts of Jurisdiction to 1600. AGN, Inquisición, Tomo 141.
Procesos against Blasphemers 1571-1600. AGN, Inquisición, Tomos 143-148.
Procesos against Calvinists and Lutherans 1598-1601. AGN, Inquisición, Tomos 164-168, 254A, 274, 1510.

II. *Miscellaneous Manuscript Materials from AGN.*

Testamento del Dr. Pedro López. AGN, Tierras, Tomo 3556.
Asuntos Fiscales del Santo Oficio de la Inquisición en México 1571-1600. AGN, Real Fisco de la Inquisición, Tomos 1-6.
Ordenanzas contra blasfemos, 1520. AGN, Hospital de Jesús, Leg. 271, exp. 11.

III. *Manuscript Materials from Archivo Histórico Nacional, Madrid (AHN).*

Información de la genealoxía y limpieza de Martín de Giras abuelo materno de Doña María de Velasco hecha en la Villa de Briones, 1623. AHN, Inquisición, Leg. 1258, exp. 4.

Información de la genealogía y limpieza de linage de Don Juan Altamirano, Caballero del hábito de Santiago, Vecino de la Ciudad de México, 1609. AHN, Inquisición, Leg. 1474, exp. 5.

Registro de cartas y despachos expedidos por el Consejo (de la Suprema Inquisición) para los Inquisidores del Tribunal de Méjico, 1590-1600. AHN, Inquisición de Méjico, Legs. 1047-1049.

Relación de las Causas que se despacharon en el Santo Oficio de la Inquisición de esta Nueva España, que reside en la Ciudad de México, en el Auto Público de la Fé que se celebró en la Plaza Mayor de ella, domingo tercero de quaresma, día de la Encarnación de México de 1601. AHN, Inquisición de Méjico, Leg. 1064, ff. 222-288.

Competencias con la Audiencia de Guadalajara en la causa del capitán Francicso de Urdiñola, Familiar, 1595. AHN, Inquisición de Méjico, Leg. 1734, exp. 5.

AHN, Competencias, Legs. 1734, 1735. Conflictos de jurisdicción.

Cartas al Consejo (de la Suprema Inquisición), expedientes y memoriales, 1573-1600. AHN, Inquisición de Méjico, Leg. 2269.

Censuras escritas por arzobispo Alonso de Montúfar sobre Relectio de Decimis de Fray Alonso de la Vera Cruz, 1558. AHN, Inquisición de Méjico, Tomo 4427, exp. 5.

Gonzalo de Alarcón, clérigo presbitero, en nombre del arzobispo sobre los excesos de Fray Alonso de la Veracruz, 1560. AHN, Inquisición de Méjico, Tomo 4442, exp. 41.

IV. *Manuscript Materials from Archivo General de Indias, Sevilla (AGI).*

Autos del obispo y la Ciudad de Michoacán con Juan Infante, vecino de México sobre que a éste le restituyeran los pueblos de Comanja y Naranja con las Estancias a ellos sujetos que le habían sido encomendados, 1540. AGI, Jústicia, Leg. 130, ff. 969v., 1472-1475, 1494-1495v.

Francisco de Villegas vecino de México con Juan Infante de la misma vecindad sobre el pueblo de Capaquero, 1533-1534. AGI, Justicia, Leg. 138, ff. 83v-112v.

Probanza hecha en la Ciudad de Michoacán sobre razón del mal sitio de la Ciudad de Michoacán y del buen sitio de Pátzcuaro y sobre razón de las demás cosas contenidas en esta dicha Probanza hecha a pedimiento del Rmo. Sr. Don Vasco de Quiroga, Primer Obispo de Michoacán, 1538. AGI, Justicia, Leg. 173, exp. 1, ramo 3.

Información sobre corsarios en Yucatán, 1565. AGI, Justicia, Leg. 1029, exp. 9.

Información de los servicios hechos por Antonio de Villaroel, 1525. AGI, Patronato, Leg. 54, exp. 2.

Información de los méritos y servicios de D. Antonio Huitsimingasi y de su padre Cazonci, rey y señor natural que fue de toda la tierra y provincia de Tarasca, 1553. AGI, Patronato, Leg. 60, exp. 2, ramo 3.
Traslado del título de protomédico general de las Indias del Doctor Francisco Hernández, 1570. AGI, Audiencia de Méjico, Leg. 18.
Información y pedimiento de parte de Don Francisco de Altamirano, 1594. AGI, Audiencia de Méjico, Leg. 114.
Permiso de viajar a la Nueva España por Lic. Pedro López, 1548. AGI, Indiferente General, Leg. 1208, exp. 2.
Información hecha por el gobernador de México sobre ciertas palabras que el presentado Fray Tomás de Chávez dijo ante el arzobispo de la dicha ciudad, 1564. AGI, Indiferente General, Leg. 1217, ff. 1-5v.
Carta a Su Magestad del Arzobispo de México, de cuatro de febrero de 1561. AGI, Indiferente General, Leg. 2978, ff. 650-656.

V. Printed Works.

Adams, Eleanor B., "Before the Buccaneers: Non Spanish Intruders in the Caribbean 1492-1610." (Manuscript.)
————, "The Franciscan Inquisition in Yucatán: French Seamen, 1560." (Manuscript.)
Alessio Robles, Vito, *Francisco de Urdiñola y el Norte de la Nueva España.* México, 1931.
Archivo General de la Nación, *La Vida Colonial.* México, 1923.
————, *Libro Primero de Votos de la Inquisición de México 1573-1600.* México, 1949.
————, *Proceso Inquisitorial del Cacique de Tetzcoco.* México, 1910.
————, *Procesos de Luis Carvajal, El Mozo.* México, 1935.
Aydelotte, Frank, "Elizabethan Seamen in Mexico and Ports of the Spanish Main," *American Historical Review,* Vol. 58 (1942), pp. 1-19.
Baez Camargo, G., *Protestantes Enjuiciados por la Inquisición en Iberoamérica.* México, 1960.
Bancroft, Hubert H., *History of Mexico* (6 vols.) San Francisco, 1883-1889.
"Bibliotecas y Librerías Coloniales," *Boletín del Archivo General de la Nación,* Vol. 10 (1939), pp. 661-907.
Brazil, Blas, "A History of the Obrajes in New Spain 1535-1630." Unpublished Master of Arts Thesis, Department of History, University of New Mexico, Albuquerque, 1962.
Burrus, Ernest J., ed., *Ordenanzas para el Coro de la Catedral Mexicana.* Madrid, 1964.
Carreño, Alberto María, "Luis de Carvajal, El Mozo," *Memorias de la Academia de la Historia de México,* Vol. 15 (1956), No. 1.
————, "The Books of Fray Juan de Zumárraga," *The Americas: A Quarterly Review of Inter-American Cultural History,* Vol. V (1949), pp. 311-330.

BIBLIOGRAPHY

Chinchilla Aguilar, Ernesto, *La Inquisitión en Guatemala*. Guatemala, 1953.
Ciruelo, Pedro, *Reprobación de las Supersticiones y Hechicerías*. Salamanca, 1538.
Cline, Howard F., "The Oztoticpac Lands Map of Texcoco, 1540," *The Quarterly Journal of the Library of Congress*, Vol. 23 (1966), pp. 76-116.
Colección de Documentos Inéditos Relativos al Descubrimiento, Conquista y Colonización de las Posesiones Españolas en América y Oceanía, Sacados de los Archivos del Reino, y muy especialmente del de Indias (42 vols.). Madrid 1864-1884.
Conway, G. R. G., *An Englishman and the Mexican Inquisition*. México, 1927.
―――, "Antonio de Espejo, As a Familiar of the Mexican Inquisition, 1572-1578," *New Mexico Historical Review*, Vol. 5 (1931), pp. 1-20.
―――, "Hernando Alonso, a Jewish Conquistador with Cortés in Mexico," *Publications of the American Jewish Historical Society*, Vol. 31 (1928), pp. 9-31.
Cuevas, Mariano, *Documentos Inéditos del Siglo XVI para la Historia de México*. México, 1914.
―――, *Historia de la Iglesia en México* (4 vols.). México, 1946.
Davis, R. Trevor, *The Golden Century of Spain 1501-1621*. New York, 1965.
de la Serna, Jacinto, *Manual de Ministros de Indios para el Conocimiento de sus Idolatrías y Extirpación de ellos*, México, 1892.
del Paso y Troncoso, Francisco, *Epistolario de la Nueva España* (16 vols.). México, 1939-1942.
―――, *Papeles de la Nueva España*, Vol. I. México, 1905.
Denzinger, Enrique, *El Magisterio de la Iglesia. Manual de los Símbolos, Definiciones y Declaraciones de la Iglesia en Materia de Fé y Costumbres*. Barcelona, 1959.
"Dos Documentos Relativos a Luis Carvajal, El Viejo," *Boletín del Archivo General de la Nación*, Vol. 22 (1951), pp. 551-558.
Ennis, Arthur, *Fray Alonso de la Vera Cruz O.S.A. (1507-1584)*. Louvain, 1957.
Escritos Sueltos de Hernán Cortés. México, 1871.
Feria, Pedro de, *Revelación sobre la Reincidencia en sus Idolatrías de los Indios de Chiapas después de Treinta Años de Cristianos*. México, 1889.
Fernández del Castillo, Francisco, *Libros y Libreros en el Siglo XVI*. México, 1914.
García Icazbalceta, Joaquín, *Bibliografía Mexicana del Siglo XVI*. México, 1954.
―――, *Colección de Documentos para la Historia de México*, Vol. I. México, 1858.
―――, "Los Médicos de México en el Siglo XVI," *Obras*, Vol. I. México, 1896.
―――, trans., "Relación escrita por Miles Philips y Publicada por Hak-

luyt," *Boletín de la Sociedad de Geografía y Estadística*, Vols. I, II (1869).

Gardiner, C. Harvey, *Naval Power in the Conquest of Mexico*. Austin, 1956.

Gay, José Antonio, *Historia de Oaxaca* (4 vols.). México, 1950.

Gibson, Charles, *Tlaxcala in the Sixteenth Century*. New Haven, 1952.

González Obregón, Luis, *México Viejo: Noticias Históricas, Tradiciones, Leyendas y Costumbres*, México, 1959. Revised Edition.

Greenleaf, Richard E., "Francisco de Millán Before the Mexican Inquisition, 1538-1539," *The Americas: A Quarterly Review of Inter-American Cultural History*, Vol. XXI (1964), pp. 184-195.

———, "The Inquisition and the Indians of New Spain: A Study in Jurisdictional Confusion," *The Americas: A Quarterly Review of Inter-American Cultural History*, Vol. XXII (1965), pp. 138-166.

———, "The Little War of Guadalajara 1587-1590," *New Mexico Historical Review*, Vol. 43 (1968), pp. 119-135.

———, "Mexican Inquisition Materials in Spanish Archives," *The Americas: A Quarterly Review of Inter-American Cultural History*, Vol. 20 (1964), pp. 416-420.

———, *Zumárraga and the Mexican Inquisition, 1536-1543*. Washington, 1962.

Hakluyt, Richard, *The Principal Navigations, Voyages Traffiques and Discoveries of the English Nation*. Hakluyt Society, Extra Series, Vol. 9. Glasgow, 1904.

Haring, Clarence, *Trade and Navigation Between Spain and the Indies in the Time of the Hapsburgs*. Cambridge, 1918.

Holy Bible. (Various editions.)

Icaza, Francisco A., *Diccionario Autobiográfico de Conquistadores y Pobladores de Nueva España* (2 vols.). Madrid, 1923.

Jiménez Moreno, Wigberto and Salvador Mateos Higuera, *Códice de Yanhuitlán*. México, 1940.

Jiménez Rueda, Julio, *Corsarios Franceses e Ingleses en la Inquisición de la Nueva España*. México, 1945.

———, *Don Pedro Moya de Contreras, Primer Inquisidor de México*. México, 1944.

———, *Herejías y Supersticiones en la Nueva España*. México, 1946.

Jones, William B., "Evangelical Catholicism in Early Colonial Mexico: An Analysis of Bishop Juan de Zumárraga's Doctrina Cristiana," *The Americas: A Quarterly Review of Inter-American Cultural History*, Vol. 23 (1967), pp. 423-432.

Lanning, John Tate, "The Church and the Enlightenment in the Universities," *The Americas: A Quarterly Review of Inter-American Cultural History*, Vol. 15 (1959), p. 391.

Lea, Henry C., *A History of the Inquisition of Spain* (4 vols.). New York, 1908.

———, *The Inquisition in the Spanish Dependencies*. New York, 1908.

Leonard, Irving A., *Books of the Brave, Being an Account of Books and*

BIBLIOGRAPHY

Men in the Spanish Conquest and Settlement of the Sixteenth Century New World. Cambridge, 1949.

―――, *Baroque Times in Old Mexico.* Ann Arbor, 1959.

―――, *Libros del Conquistador.* México, 1953.

―――, "On the Mexican Book Trade, 1576," *Hispanic American Historical Review,* Vol. 17 (1949), pp. 18-34.

―――, "On the Mexican Book Trade in 1600," *Hispanic American Historical Review,* Vol. 9 (1941), pp. 1-40.

―――, *Romances of Chivalry in the Spanish Indies.* Berkeley, 1933.

Liebman, Seymour B., *A Guide to Jewish References in the Mexican Colonial Era.* Philadelphia, 1964.

―――, "Hernando Alonso: First Jew on the North American Continent," *Journal of Inter-American Studies,* Vol. 5 (1963), pp. 291-296.

―――, "Research Problems in Mexican Jewish History," *American Jewish Historical Quarterly,* Vol. 54 (1964), pp. 165-180.

―――, ed., *The Enlightened. The Writings of Luis Carvajal El Mozo.* Coral Gables, 1967.

Longhurst, John E., *Erasmus and the Spanish Inquisition: The Case of Juan de Valdés.* Albuquerque, 1950.

―――, *Luther and the Spanish Inquisition: The Case of Diego de Uceda.* Albuquerque, 1953.

López de Gómara, Francisco, *Cortés, The Life of the Conqueror By His Secretary.* Berkeley and Los Angeles, 1964. Lesley B. Simpson, translator and editor.

Malkiel, Yakov, "Hispano-Arabic *Marrano* and Its Hispano-Latin Homophone," *Journal of the American Oriental Society,* Vol. 68 (1948), pp. 175-184.

Mariel de Ibáñez, Yolanda, *La Inquisición en México durante el Siglo XVI.* México, 1945.

Martínez del Río, Pablo. *Alumbrado.* México, 1937.

―――, "La Aventura Mexicana de Sir John Hawkins," *Memorias de la Academia de la Historia,* Vol. 2 (1943), No. 3.

Medina, José Toribio, *El Tribunal del Santo Oficio de la Inquisición en las Islas Filipinas.* Santiago de Chile, 1889.

―――, *Historia del Tribunal del Santo Oficio de la Inquisición en México.* México, 1954. Second edition revised.

―――, *La Imprenta en México (1539-1821)* (8 vols.). Santiago de Chile, 1912.

―――, *La Primitiva Inquisición Americana 1493-1569* (2 vols.). Santiago de Chile, 1914.

Millares Carlo, Agustín and J. I. Mantecón, *Indice y Extractos de los Protocolos del Archivo de Notariás* (2 vols.). México, 1945.

Miranda, José, *España y Nueva España en la Época de Felipe II.* México, 1962.

Montúfar, Alonso de, *Descripción del Arzobispado de México hecha en 1570 y otros documentos.* México, 1897. Luis García Pimental, editor.

"Nómina del Tribunal de la Inquisición de Nueva España 1571-1646,"

Boletín del Archivo General de la Nación, Vol. XXVI (1955), pp. 53-90, 293-316.

Padden, Robert C., "The Ordenanza de Patronazgo 1574: An Interpretative Essay," *The Americas: A Quarterly Review of Inter-American Cultural History,* Vol. XII (1956), pp. 333-354.

Pallares, Eduardo, *El Procedimiento Inquisitorial.* México, 1951.

Parry, J. H., *The Audiencia of New Galicia in the Sixteenth Century.* Cambridge, 1948.

Paz y Melia, A., *Papeles de Inquisición: Catálogo y Extractos.* Madrid, 1947.

Pérez Martínez, Héctor, *Piraterías en Campeche (Siglos XVI, XVII, XVIII).* México, 1937.

Primer Libro de las Actas del Cabildo de la Ciudad de México. México, 1889.

"Proceso de Juan Luis por Hereje y Pacto con el Demonio en el Siglo XVI," *Boletín del Archivo General de la Nación,* Vol. 4 (1933), pp. 1-70.

"Proceso contra Miles Philips," *Boletín del Archivo General de la Nación,* Vol. 20 (1949), pp. 115-172, 255-300.

Recopilación de leyes de los Reynos de Las Indias (4 vols.). Madrid, 1681.

Remesal, Antonio de, *Historia de la Provincia de San Vicente de Chyapa.* Guatemala, 1932.

Ricard, Robert, *Études et documents pour l'historie missionaire de l'Espagne et du Portugal.* Louvain, 1930.

———, "Notes sur la biographie de Fr. Alonso de Montúfar, second archeveque de México," *Bulletin Hispanique* (July-September, 1925), pp. 242-246.

———, *The Spiritual Conquest of Mexico.* Lesley B. Simpson, translator. Berkeley and Los Angeles, 1966.

Rubio Mañé, J. Ignacio, *Archivo de la Historia de Yucatán,* Vol. III. México, 1942.

Rumeu de Armas, Antonio, *Los Viajes de John Hawkins a América (1562-1595).* Sevilla, 1947.

Scholes, France V. and Eleanor B. Adams, eds., *Cartas del Licenciado Jerónimo Valderrama y otros Documentos sobre su Visita al Gobierno de Nueva España 1563-1565.* México, 1961.

———, *Don Diego de Quijada Alcalde Mayor de Yucatán 1561-1565* (2 vols.). México, 1938.

———, *Ordenanzas del Hospital de San Lázaro de México: Año de 1582.* México, 1956.

———, *Proceso contra Tzintzicha Tangaxoan el Caltzontzin formado por Nuño de Guzmán, Año de 1530.* México, 1952.

———, *Relación de las Encomiendas de Indios hechas en Nueva España a los Conquistadores y Pobladores de ella, Año de 1564.* México, 1955.

Scholes, France V. and Ralph L. Roys, *Fray Diego de Landa and the Problem of Idolatry in Yucatán.* Washington, D.C., 1938.

Simpson, Lesley B., *The Encomienda in New Spain.* Berkeley, 1950.

BIBLIOGRAPHY 231

Somolinos d'Ardois, Germán, *Vida y Obra de Francisco Hernández*. México, 1960.
Spores, Ronald M., *The Mixtec Kings and Their People*. Norman, 1967.
Steele, Elizabeth S., "Censorship of Books in Sixteenth-Cenutry Mexico." Unpublished Master of Arts Thesis, Department of Inter-American Affairs, University of New Mexico, Albuquerque, 1950.
Stols, Alexander M., "Cornelius Adrián César, Impresor Holandés en México," *Boletín de la Biblioteca Nacional de México*, Vol. 8 (1957), No. 3.
Suárez de Peralta, Juan, *Noticias Históricas de la Nueva España*. México, 1949.
Toro, Alfonso, *La Familia Carvajal* (2 vols.). México, 1944.
―――, *Los Judíos en la Nueva España*. México, 1932.
Toussaint, Manuel, *Pátzcuaro*. México, 1952.
―――, ed., *Proceso y denuncias contra Simón Pereyns en la Inquisición de México*. México, 1938.
Trens, Manuel B., *Arte Curativo de las Enfermedades, Farmacia y Hechicería, La Brujería y El Nahualismo en La Nueva España*. Tuxtla Gutiérrez, Chiapas, 1954.
Vasco de Puga, *Provisiones, Cédulas, Instrucciones de Su Magestad, Ordenancas de Difuntos y Audiencia Para la Buena Expedición de los Negocios y Administración de Justicia y Gobernación de esta Nueva España, y Para el Buen Tratamiento y Conservación de los Indios Desde el Año de 1525 Hasta este Presente de 1563* (2 vols.). México, 1878.
Warren, F. Benedict, "The Carvajal Visitation: First Spanish Survey of Michoacán," *The Americas: A Quarterly Review of Inter-American Cultural History*, Vol. XIX (1963), pp. 404-412.
―――, "The Conquest of Michoacán, 1521-1530." Unpublished Master of Arts Thesis, Department of History, University of New Mexico, Albuquerque, 1960.
―――, *Vasco de Quiroga and His Pueblo-Hospitals of Santa Fé*. Washington, D.C., 1963.
Wayne (Powell), Philip, *Ponzoña en Las Nieves*. Madrid, 1966.
Wiznitzer, Arnold, "Crypto-Jews in Mexico During the Sixteenth Century," *American Jewish Historical Quarterly*, Vol. 41 (1962), pp. 168-214.
Zulaica Garate, Román, *Los Franciscanos y La Imprenta en México en el Siglo XVI*. México, 1939.

INDEX

Abrego, Fray Jerónimo de, 177
Acevedo, Pedro Pablo de, 127
Acosta, Fray Francisco de, 127
Adams, Eleanor B., 92
Adrian VI, 25
Agreda, Francisco de: trial, 39
Aguirre, Fray Andrés de, 133
Agundes, Diego de, 104
Ahumada Sámano, Pedro de, 132
Albornoz, Auditor Rodrigo de, 52, 63
Albuquerque, Bishop Bernardo de, 178
Aldama, Alonso de, 78
Alexander, David: trial, 164-165, 166
Alonso de Puerto Rico, Bishop, 33
Alonso, Hernando, 26, 27, 32, 39, 45, 46; trial, 33-37
Altamirano, Lic. Juan Gutiérrez, 32, 134, 135, 136, 205
Alvarez de Espinosa, Alonso: witness, 60-61
Andreas of Rhodes. *See* Griego, Andrés
Anguis, Provisor Luis Fernández de, 91, 105, 119, 121, 123, 129, 130, 142, 143, 145, 147, 149, 151, 153
Anglicans. *See* Heretics
Antón, the Tarascan, 102
Anunciación, Nun Francisca de: trial, 133-134; family, 134
Aranda, Martín de, witness, 52, 58, 62, 66; convicted, 69

Arévalo, Sedeño, Mateo, 130
Arias, Francisco: witness, 54
Arias, Fray Juan de, 98-99
Arriaga, Fiscal Sebastián de, 14, 15, 16, 20, 22, 24
Arvallos, Pedro: witness, 17
Audiencia: First, 48, 68; Second, 48-49; of Guadalajara, 177, 179-180; of Guatemala, 110, 158; of Manila, 158; of Mexico, 130, 131, 140, 148, 158, 176-177, 202; of Michoacán, 112; of New Galicia, 158; of Santo Domingo, 9
Augustinians, 169; conflict with Montúfar, 131, 141, 144, 148; conflict with Quiroga, 124-126, 127; control of Inquisition, 120; in Michoacán, 120
Autos de fé, 17, 160, 162, 172, 176, 182, 212; Oct, 1528, 26-40, 45, 71, 108, 109, 161; Mar 17, 1560, 86, 92; Feb 28, 1574, 163, 164, 165, 166, 168, 185; Mar 6, 1575, 163, 166; Dec 15, 1577, 167; Oct 11, 1579, 169; Feb 24, 1590, 170; Dec 8, 1596, 171; Mar 25, 1601, 6, 185, 186, 204, 205, 206, 208, 209; Apr 20, 1604, 209
"Auto Grande," 171
Avalos, Fiscal, 165
Avila, Alonso de, 55, 58
Avila-Cortés conspiracy, 14, 113, 133, 152

233

234 MEXICAN INQUISITION

Avila, Fray Jorge de, 67
Avila, Juan de, trial, 71
Avila, Juan Suárez de, 161
Ayala, Alonso de: witness, 87, 88, 89

Barbosa, Dr. Rodrigo, 119, 130, 142, 149; trial, 150-151
Basancio, Fray Arnoldo de, 82
Bello, Juan: trial, 13-14; witness, 21
Benavente, Lic. Cristóbal de, 48, 49, 59, 77
Berenjel, Juan Martín: trial, 14-15
Berri, Martín de: witness, 29, 35
Betanzos, Domingo de, 9, 27, 40; and blasphemers, 11-25, 46
Bezos, Juan de, 81
"Black Order," 143. *See also* Dominicans
Blanco, Attorney Miguel, 103, 104
Boacio, Agustín: trial, 86-92, 99; younger brother of, 87, 89
Bolante, Juan: witness, 23
Boloña, Fray Miguel de, 66
Balonia, Fray Miguel de, 162
Bonilla, Lic. Antonio, 70, 161, 165
Books: 182-186; prohibited, 94, 102, 123, 124, 135, 183, 184, 185; suspicious, 143, 158, 183, 184. *See also* Index of prohibited books
Bruxas, Jorge de: trial, 208

Caciques, 74, 76, 78, 80
Caltzontzin of the Tarascans: trial, 10; torture, 46
Calvinists. *See* Heretics
Calvin, John, 200
Campos, Martín de, 50, 71, 78
Canseco, Lt. Gov. Alonso, 28
Cárdenas, Fray Tomás de, 108, 109, 110
Carlos Chichimecatecuhtli of Texcoco: trial, 74-75, 79
Carmona, Antón de: witness, 65, 66
Carmona, Marcos de: witness, 61, 63
Carriago, Francisco de, 132
Carrión, Alonso de: trial, 18, 69; witness, 48, 51, 61, 63, 69

Carvajal family: persecutions, 169-171, 178-179
Carvajal, Francisca Núñez de: trial, 170-171
Carvajal, Gaspar de, 170
Carvajal, Gov. Luis de, 169-170, 178; trial, 170
Carvajal, Luis, the younger: trials, 170-171; witness, 171
Casa de Contratación, 35
Castellano, Eugenio Fernández: witness, 106-107
Castillejo, Francisco de, 62-63
Castillo, Juan Fernández del: trial, 39
Castillo, Pedro del, 29; trial, 39
Cerezo, Gonzalo de, 85, 86
Cervanes, Rafael de, 58-59, 61, 64, 65, 66
Cervantes de Salazar, Maestro Francisco: witness, 149
Cervantes, Dr. Juan de, 202, 205
Cervantes, Leonel de, 27
Cervantes, Leonor de: witness, 29, 30
Cervantes, Lic. Alonso de, 159
César, Cornelius Adrián, 195-196; trial, 185
Charles V, 2, 11, 16, 36, 50, 75, 81, 191, 213
Chávez, Fray Tomás de: trial, 129-131
Chico de Molina, Dr. Alonso, 128, 132; controversy with Montúfar, 141,152; relationship with Cortés, 152; trials, 141-149, 151-152
Chirinos, 13, 16, 19
Clergy: attacking theory of church on sexual morality, 132-133, 150, 172; conflict between regular and secular, 116-157; dangerous interpretation of scripture, 143; heresy in sermons of, 124, 126, 127, 128, 129, 131, 132, 137, 140, 141, 147, 150; immorality and discipline of, 126, 128, 162; trials of, 162. *See also* Nuns, heresy of
Coligny, Gaspar de, 168
Collins, William: trial, 163-164, 166
Colmenares, Pedro de: witness, 97, 98

INDEX

Contreras, Fray Pedro de, 32
Conway, G. R. G., 85-86, 181
Copete de Figueroa, Juan: witness, 108-109
Córdoba, Fray Pedro de, 8, 10
Corellana, Alonso: trial, 19
Cornelius, William: trial, 166
Corona, Escribano Diego de, 24
Corsairs, 2, 82, 98, 162-172, 182, 184, 191, 193, 196, 206, 208; English, 163, 166; French, 82, 93, 95, 167, 168, 176
Cortés, Diego: trial, 19
Cortés, Hernán, 10, 13, 14, 15, 16, 18, 19, 21, 39, 45, 60, 63, 66; army, 33, 38; controversy, 23; enemies, 11, 12, 19, 20, 22-23, 31, 35; estate, 132, 134; family, 134, 152; on Honduras expedition, 13, 15, 19; ordinances against blasphemy, 9, 19, 27; supporters, 5, 12, 13, 14, 15, 19, 39, 68, 150, 212; witness, 24. *See also* Avila-Cortés conspiracy; Cortés-Narvaéz struggle
Cortés, Martín, conspirators, 149
Cortés-Narvaéz struggle, 13
Coruña, Viceroy Conde de, 178
Council of Florence, 143
Council of the Indies, 75, 119, 130, 140, 176, 180
Council of Supreme Inquisition, 75, 82, 124, 125, 142, 145, 148, 160, 162, 170, 171, 174, 175, 180
Council of Trent, 111, 116, 117, 125, 135, 137, 139, 142, 143, 146; doctrines of, 117, 118, 143
Counter Reformation, 3, 4, 5, 6, 74, 81, 82, 111, 153, 158, 160, 162, 163, 171, 182, 199, 209, 211; Mexican, 152-153, 211; prosecutions, 82
Cruz, Elena de la: trial, 133, 134-137
Cruz, Fray Domingo de la, 123
Cruz, Sor Juana Inéz de la, 135
Cuevas, Juan de: trial, 19

Damian, Fernando: witness, 17
Dávila, Pedrarias, 47
Delgadillo, Lic.: informer, 48, 51, 61
Díaz, Cristóbal: trial, 15-16

Díaz de Aguero, Attorney Pedro, 106, 107
Díaz del Castillo, Bernal, 36
Díaz de Piza, Bartolomé: trial, 126
Díaz de Real, Juan: witness, 17
Díaz, Martín: trial, 208
Díaz, Ruy: trial, 40
Domingo, Don, 76, 77, 79; trial, 78
Domingo, Fray, 139
Dominicans, 8, 9, 52, 56, 78, 108, 119-120, 122, 126-127, 128, 131, 144, 147, 148, 153, 164, 170, 171, 205, 212; abuse of inquisitory functions, 40, 121; against Augustinians and Franciscans, 141; attitude toward Indians, 129; in control of Mexican Inquisition, 13-14, 24-40; as inquisitors, 12-13, 16, 18, 23, 29, 37, 39; in politics, 146, 150; as witnesses, 22, 32, 98, 99

Ecija, Miguel de, 184-185
Ennis, Fr. Arthur, 125
Enríquez, Viceroy Martín, 97, 99, 159, 165, 167, 169, 175, 176
Erasmism, 122, 135, 153, 182-183, 213
Escalona, Hernando de: trial, 14
Espejo, Familiar Antonio de, 181-182
Espinosa, Alonso de: trial, 15; witness, 29
Estrada, Gov. Alonso de, 32, 34, 49

Falcón, Antonio Gómez: denouncer, 84, 85
Falcón, Simón, 92; trial, 83-85
Familiares. *See* Inquisition, Mexican, general: police
Farenton, John: trial, 166
Farías, Fray Pedro de, 127
Figueroa, Capt. Rodrigo, 173
Flemings (Flamencos), 168, 184, 191, 192, 193, 194, 195, 198, 200, 202, 206-209
Flores, Dr. Manuel, 60
Flores, Gerónimo, 80
Franciscans, 8, 10-11, 52, 57, 78, 119-120, 122, 124, 147; in conflict with

Montúfar, 122-124, 131, 137-141, 148; in control of Mexican Inquisition, 24, 40, 120; as investigators, 82; punishing Indians, 119; as witnesses, 32
Francisco, Don, 76, 77; trial, 78
Franco, Juan: trial, 65; witness, 65
Fuenleal, Sebastián Ramírez de, 37
Fuensalida, Fray Luis de: witness, 22, 24-25

Gallego, Gregorio, 69; witness, 51, 58, 62
Gallego, Lucas: trial, 19
Gallegos, Vicar Rodrigo de, 81
García Bergemero, González: trial, 169
García, Catalina, 101; witness, 102
García, Diego: trial, 15
García Vásquez, Juan: denouncer, 165
Germans, 168, 191, 192, 194, 195, 198. *See also* Santiago, Simón de
Gilberti, Fray Maturino, 122, 124
Giles of Murbec: trial, 207-208
Godoy, Antonio de: witness, 53-54, 57, 58, 62, 63, 64
Godoy, Juan de, 64
Gómez, Amador, 70
Gómez, Antonio, 70, 71
Gómez, Beatriz, 47, 56, 61, 66, 70
Gómez de Maraver, Dean Pedro, 76, 77, 78
Gómez, Francisco (brother of Gonzalo): informer, 52, 58
Gómez, Gonzalo, 49, 50; trial, 46-48, 50-69; family, 70-71, 161
Gómez, Juan (merchant), 47, 56, 60, 61, 62, 64-65
Gómez, Juan (illegitimate son of merchant), 62
Gómez, Juan (son of merchant), 70, 71-72
Gómez, Melchor, 48, 61
González de Benavides, Gil, 13; trial, 14
González, Francisco: trial, 14
González Obregón, Luis, 4
Gonzalo, Fray: witness, 22

Granada, Fray Luis de, 135, 136
Griego, Andrés: trial, 38
Grijalva, Juan de, 13, 38
Guerrero, Luis, 75
Guillermo, Juan: trial, 208
Guisado, Juan: witness, 17, 18
Gutiérrez de Aguilar, Juan: denouncer, 106
Guzmán Ballesto, Juan de: witness, 27, 28, 29, 31
Guzmán, Diego de: witness, 28
Guzmán, María de Morales: witness, 28, 29
Guzmán, Nuño de (president of first audiencia), 63, 68; trial, 40, 46

Hakluyt, Richard, 166
Hawkins, Capt. John, 166
Hawkins, Paul: trial, 166-167
Hawkins raiders, 97, 99, 163, 164, 165, 166, 168, 169, 181
Haya, Joseph de la, 195, 196, 201; trial, 208; witness, 197-198
Haya, Pedro de la, 198
Heresies. *See* Inquisition, Mexican, types of cases
Heretics, 158, 160; Anglicans, 164, 165, 191; Calvinists, 186, 191-210; Huguenots, 167, 168, 184; Indians, 173-174, 177; Jews, 168-169, 171, 179; Judaizantes, 162, 163, 168, 169, 170, 172, 182; lists of, 161; Lutherans, 85, 87, 90, 91, 94, 95, 97, 104, 105, 123, 127, 162, 163, 164, 165, 166, 167, 168, 184, 185, 186, 192, 196, 199, 201, 206, 207, 209. *See also* Clergy; Lutheranism; Nuns, heresy of
Hernández de Mesa, Diego: witness, 93, 95
Hernández, Domingo: burial of father, 101-102; witness, 84-85
Hernández, García: witness, 28
Herrera, Fray Alonso de, 56
Hinojosa, Fray Diego: witness, 22
Holy Office. *See* Inquisition, Spanish
Hoyos, Francisco de, 93, 95
Huguenots. *See* Heretics

INDEX

Hurtado, Francisco, 98

Ibarra, Diego de, 86
Ibarra, Hortuño de, 172
Ibarreta, Notary Juan de, 130, 147
Illuminism, Spanish, 171
Index of prohibited books, 184. *See also* Books
Indians: books about, 177; cases under Inquisition, 74-81, 101, 120-121, 173, 174, 177, 178; disputes over, 176, 177, 178; harsh sentencing of, 212; leaders of, 74; nature of, 102, 124, 129; Mayan, 102; Tarascan, 10, 102, 124
Infante, Juan, 48, 49, 63
Inquisition Archives, 3, 8, 9, 37, 48, 51, 100, 126, 128, 160, 161, 165, 167, 168, 181, 182, 183, 193, 212
Inquisition: episcopal, 5, 7-8, 9, 74-115, 158, 159, 160, 161, 213; monastic, 8, 12, 177-178. *See also* Augustinians; Dominicans; Franciscans
Inquisition Index, 5
Inquisition, Mexican, general: abuses in, 46, 120-121; apolitical role, 68; civil intervention in, 23, 35, 39; conflict with civil authority, 159, 167, 174-182; edicts of, 36; establishment of, 163, 181; first decade, 7-44; first trial, 10; fugitives from, 14; and medical profession, 103-107; and political involvement, 5, 7; police, 160, 163, 176, 180, 181, 182; purpose of, 1, 2; protocol for, 176; records as revelation of folk culture, 1-2, 172, 173, 211; security files, 191-192; Tribunal of, 4, 5, 72, 81, 102, 141, 153-154, 158-186, 195, 197, 202, 204, 207
Inquisition, Mexican, types of cases: assumption of priestly powers by laymen, 22, 23, 34, 51, 54, 56, 101-102, 108; bigamy, 40, 75, 100, 162, 172, 174; blasphemy, 2, 9, 11-26, 39, 40, 54, 59, 69, 71, 75, 83, 100, 101, 102, 103, 104, 108, 110, 111, 128, 162, 172; clerical heresy, 133-137, 158, 162; concubinage, 10, 17, 22, 32, 40, 81, 100, 113, 128; desecration of churches, 20, 22, 25, 52, 53, 54, 58, 164, 167, 198, 201; desecration of crucifixes, 16, 17, 18, 22, 27, 29, 31, 33, 52, 53, 54, 56-57, 58, 61, 64, 106, 107, 109, 167; doubt or denial of church tenets, 105, 194-195, 200, 201-202; eating meat on Fridays, 10, 18, 36, 80, 167, 198, 201, 202; failure to attend church, 17, 51, 54, 59, 80, 185; idolatry, 10, 20, 22, 39, 76, 77, 78, 79, 80, 101, 102, 124, 174, 177; paganism, 75, 76, 101, 178; performing "Jewish" rites, 18, 34-35, 36, 51, 53, 54, 59, 64, 106, 108, 111, 169; polygamy, 174; proselytizing, 164; quackery, 103; reading prohibited books, 87, 88, 135, 158, 182-184; sacrifice (human and animal), 10, 76, 77, 78, 79, 80, 81, 102; sexual immorality, 10, 20, 23, 39, 100, 104, 109, 110; sorcery and occult arts, 80, 81, 104, 173, 174, 177; treason, 202; usury, 111-113
Inquisition, Mexican, types of sentences: abjuration and reconciliation, 29, 30, 35, 37-38, 48, 51, 52, 61, 85, 86, 90, 92, 96, 104, 110, 136, 163, 166, 167, 170, 185, 206, 208; alms for poor, 25, 31; ban on preaching, 141, 145; burning, 121, 166, 169, 192, 205; burning at stake, 16, 26, 31, 32, 33, 36, 163, 165, 169, 170-171, 206; capital punishment, 16, 26, 31, 32, 36, 37, 166, 169; confiscation of property, 16, 25-26, 30, 36, 55, 88, 91, 96, 164, 193, 204, 206; excommunication, 67-68; execution and burning, 75, 204; exile, 86, 90, 104, 152, 165, 185, 209; fines, 13, 15, 16, 25, 32, 67, 80, 81, 85, 90, 101, 104, 105, 110, 185, 193; forbidden to bear arms, 96, 207; forbidden to ride horses, 207; forbidden to wear silks, jewels, or silver, 96, 207; imprisoned in jail, 4, 14, 15, 18, 19, 27, 36, 39, 48, 50, 55, 65, 85, 88, 90, 96, 104, 105, 109, 110, 121, 135-136, 152, 165, 167, 185, 193,

194, 206, 208; imprisoned in monasteries, 25, 38, 67, 165, 208; pay costs of trials, 14, 18, 32, 38, 85, 110; pilgrimage, 13, 14, 15, 85; provide wax for church, 15, 19, 101; public humiliation, 14, 15, 25, 26, 31, 39, 67, 85, 86, 93, 94, 96, 110, 205; service in galleys, 164, 166, 168, 173, 208, 209; service in sweatshops, 164, 165, 166-167, 209; spiritual penance, 15-16, 18, 67, 85, 105, 136; tongue piercing, 12, 39; torture, 192, 208; torture by rack, 30, 94-95, 121, 166, 167, 168, 171, 185, 201-203, 208; torture by water, 208; wear sanbenitos, 32, 36, 38, 65, 71, 86, 92, 96, 164, 165, 166, 167, 168, 173, 207, 208, 209; whipping, 163, 164, 166, 168, 173, 208, 209
Inquisition, Sevillian, 61, 99, 123, 148
Inquisition, Spanish, 12, 24, 125. See also Council of Supreme Inquisition
Isidro, Fray Antonio, 144

Jaén, Juan de: trial, 39
Jaso, Juan de: witness, 71
Jesuits, 3, 153, 166
"Jesus of Lubeck" (ship), 163, 165, 166
Jews, 3, 17, 70, 109, 134, 169, 171, 212; burning of, 17, 26, 33, 36, 40; Crypto-Jews, 81, 169, 170; edicts against, 8; influence on Mexican culture, 171. See also Judaizantes
Jiménez Rueda, Julio, 5
Jofre, Martín: witness, 52, 63
Juan Luis: trial, 173
Juan (Xual), Don, 76, 78
Judaizantes, 106, 107-111, 162-172, 182, 191, 197; definition, 3, 30; trials of, 12, 36-37, 48, 67, 69, 70, 107-111. See also Heretics; Jews

Ladrón de Guevara, Pedro: trial, 177-178
Landa, Diego de, 102
Lanning, John Tate, 212
Lanzaverde, Domingo de, 179, 180
Las Casas, Bartolomé, 128

Las Casas, Domingo de, 79
Las Casas family, 79
Las Casas, Francisco de, 78
Las Casas, Fray Vicente de, 32-33, 36
Last Judgment, painting of, 51, 52, 53, 57, 59, 60, 67, 69
Lea, Henry C., 4, 12
Ledesma, Fray Bartolomé de, 37, 96, 119, 123, 125, 130, 133, 134, 135, 136, 137, 141, 142-143, 147, 148, 150, 153
Leo X, 8, 10, 11, 25
Leonard, Irving A., 211
Léon, Escribano Luis de, 205-206
Leyva, Damaso de, 137-138
Liebman, Seymour B., 170
Lomas, Juan Bautista de, 86, 87, 88, 90
Lomas y Colmenares, Juan Bautista de, 180, 182
López Dávalos, Diego, 185
López de Legazpi family, 161
López de Legazpi, Miguel, 37, 71, 77, 80
López, Dr. Pedro, 105-107; sisters of, 105; founder of hospitals, 106
López, Francisca: trial, 100-101
López, Juan: witness, 69
López, Martín, 33
Lovera, Ovejon de: informer, 22
Lozano, Attorney Nicolás, 90
Lugo, Fiscal Cristóbal, 77
Lumbroso, Joseph. See Carvajal, Luis, the younger
Luna, Reinaldo de: trial, 19
Luque, Gabriel de: witness, 38
Lutheranism, 81-99, 104-105, 153, 162, 163, 165, 166, 167, 168, 184, 185, 186, 199; defined, 82; identified with Erasmism, 153; identified with Protestantism, 82; in Great Britain, 88-89; trials for, 86-92, 96. See also Heretics
Luther, Martin, 126, 153, 185

Maldonado, Dr., 148
Mañozca, Secretary Pedro de, 193, 204, 205
Manso, Bishop Alonso, 8, 31

INDEX

Marcos of Acolhuacán: trial, 10ff
Marmolejo, Diego de, 27
Marquéz, Leonor, 30
Marroquín, Bishop, 27, 108
Martín de Chemanal, Alonso, 102
Martínez, Enrico, 193-194, 198, 200, 203, 204, 207
Martínez, Juan, 173
Martínez, Pedro: witness, 106
Martín, Melchor, 102
Medina, José Toribio, 4
Mejía, Fray Gregorio: trial, 131, 132
Melchor, Fray, 22
Mendinilla, Pedro de, 55, 71
Mendoza, Baltazar de: witness, 24
Mendoza, Fray Diego de, 137, 138-139
Mendoza, Jorge: witness, 84, 85
Mercado, Friar Tomás de, 130
Mexía, Judge Alonso, 94-96
Mexican Church Councils, 122, 123, 153
Meyo, Alberto de: trial, 208
Miguel, Cristóbal, 193, 194, 195, 196-197, 198, 200, 201, 207; trials, 206-207; witness, 192
Miguel, Gregorio, 192, 193, 194-195, 197, 198, 200, 201, 206, 207, 208; trial, 206-207; witness, 192, 195-196
Millán, Francisco: trial, 70
"Minion" (ship), 166
Moguer, Fray Andrés de, 127
Molina, Diego de: trial, 176
Molina, Fray Pedro de, 80
Mondragón, Andrés, 197
Monjarrás, Gregorio de: trial, 16
Montalvo, Hendrik: trial, 207, 208
Montúfar, Alonso de, 82-83, 85, 86, 99, 111, 112, 113, 122, 123, 126, 128, 130, 135, 140, 142, 153; character, 118-119; control of books, 122; Erasmian ideas, 122; investigation and prosecution of clergy, 116-157; Quiroga probe, 124
Morales, Diego de: trials, 9, 26-29, 35, 38, 39, 108, 109
Morales, Gonzalo de, 31, 45, 46; burned for heresy, 26, 27, 29, 32, 37, 39, 108; trials, 27, 32, 35, 38; witness, 36
Morales, Hernando de, 30
Morales, Bartolomé de: burned at stake, 16
Morisco (Moor), 109, 135; defined, 30
Morlete, Familiar Juan de, 180
Motolinía, Fray Toribio de, 10-11, 14, 25-26, 35
Moya de Contrerar, Dr. Pedro, 70, 71, 159, 160, 161, 163, 165, 167, 175, 176, 177, 178, 181, 184

Nava, Doña Magdalena de: witness, 150
Narvaez, Pánfilo de, 13, 33
Narvarro, Fray Miguel, 137, 138
Núñez de Villavicencio, Oidor Nuño, 180
Núñez, Diego: trial, 16-18
Núñez families, 15, 46; of Sevilla, 34
Núñez, Francisco, 16; trial, 15
Núñez, Lic. Alonso, 152
Nuns, heresy of, 133-137. *See also* Cruz, Elena; Anunciación, Francisca
New Mexico: colonizing, 179, 180; exploring, 181

Ocaña, Diego de, 11, 35; trial, 26, 27, 31, 35-37, 38
Ocaña, Leonor Suárez de, 35
Ocharte, Pedro: trial, 184-185
Olarte, Fray Diego de, 147, 148
Olid Biedma, Presbyter Luis de, 133
Olmedo, Fray Juan de, 127
Olmos, Rev. Pedro de, 76
Oñate, Juan de, 180
Orbaneja, Lic., 123
Ordaz, Beatriz de, 34
Orlando, Guillermo de, 163; trial, 96-99
Ortego, Attorney Juan de, 11, 49
Ortíz de Matienzo, Judge Juan, 48
Ortíz de Zúñiga, Alonso: witness, 22
Ortíz, Fray Hernando, 177
Ortíz, Juan: trial, 185
Ortíz, Luis, 98

Ortíz, Tomás, 9, 11, 19, 20, 22, 40
Osorio, Fray Diego de, 123, 142, 143, 146, 147-148
Ovilla, Andrés, 99

Pablo, Andrés: witness, 193, 194, 200
Pablos, Juan, 184
Pacheco, Hernando: trial, 51, 101
Pacholero, Juan Gómez, 48, 61-62, 64-65
Palma Zapata, Francisco de la: witness, 28, 31
Pasillas, Alonso de, 112
Pazillas, Alonso de, 127
Paz, Rodrigo de, 15
Pedro Pedro of Argou, Flanders: trial, 208-209
Peñafiel, Francisco: witness, 69
Peña, Fray Pedro de la, 129
Peralta, Alonso de, 174, 192, 194, 195-196, 197, 202, 206, 207
Peralta, Doña María de: trial, 172
Pereira, Lic., 84
Pérez, Alonso, 11; witness, 84-85
Pérez, Friar Diego, 54
Pérez, Hernán, 29-30.
Pérez, Iñigo: witness, 28
Pérez, Juan, 100-101
Pérez Marañón, Bachiller Alvaro, 146-147
Pérez Tamayo, Alonso, 81
Philip II, 2, 96, 117, 119, 120, 126, 131, 139, 141, 150, 152, 153, 158, 159, 170, 175-176, 181, 199, 213
Philips, Miles: memoirs, 166; trial, 166
Pinto, Gaspar: witness, 87-88, 89
Pius V, 117, 120, 125, 131, 135, 139
Plaza, Attorney Gaspar de la, 23, 24
Plaza, Juan de León, 197
Ponce de la Fuente, Constantino, 122-123
Ponce, Visitor Luis, 13, 19
Porras, Bartolomé: witness, 23
Portillo, Judge Estéban de, 97, 106, 137, 140, 141, 142
Pravia, Fray Pedro de, 130, 131
Protestants, 3, 6, 12, 81, 163, 165, 166, 167. See also Heretics
Protestantism. See Heretics; Protestants

Quemado, Bartolomé: trial, 16
Quiñones, Catarina: witness, 106
Quiroga, Vasco de, 45, 49, 54, 56, 61, 68, 123, 124, 127, 130
Quiróz, Gutierre de, Bernardo, 192, 202, 207

Ramírez, Gaspar: witness, 17
Ramos, Gómez, 197
Rebollo, Juan de, 29
Remesal, Antonio de, 8
Renaissance, 4, 5, 12, 74, 211, 212; Humanist beliefs, 116, 183; Mexican, 152-153
Rengel, Rodrigo: trial, 19-26
Ribley, George: trial, 165-166
Ricard, Robert, 124
Riobo y Sotomayor, Gonzalo de: witness, 54
Ríos, Notary Pedro de los, 72, 159
Rivera, Diego de, 60
Rivera, Don Bartolomé de, 90
Riverol, Lic. Vicencio de, 59, 64, 79, 149
Robertanillo, Francisco, 90
Robledo, Gonzalo, 112-113
Rodríguez de Andrade, Isabel, 170-171
Rodríguez, Rodrigo: trial, 19
Rodríguez, Violánte: witness, 24
Roldán, Fray Antonio, 36
Romero, Rev. Bartolomé: denouncer, 103
Ruíz, Anton, 31, 32-33
Ruíz de Aguilar, Isabel de, 34
Ruíz, Fray Diego: denouncer, 108

Salazar-Chirinos usurpation, 19
Salazar, Gonzalo de, 13, 16, 36
Salcedo, Lic., 37
"Salvadora" (ship), 199
Sánchez, Alonso, 17
Sánchez, Fiscal Juan, 93, 94
Sánchez Obregón, Lic. Lorenzo, 182

INDEX

Sanctuary, right of, 101
Sandoval, Gonzalo de, 22, 34
Sanfoy, Pierre, 176; trial, 167-168
San Miguel, Fray Juan de, 66
Santa María, Fray Bernardo de, 78
Santa María, Vicente de, 9, 11, 29, 30, 31, 32, 33, 34, 36, 37, 38-39, 40
Santander, Dr. Pedro de: trial, 104-105
Santiago, Simón de: trials: 192-206, 207, 208; witness, 200-201
Santillana, Hernando de: witness, 29, 61
Santour, Nicolás, 94, 167; trials, 92-96
Sarmiento, Hernando García: trial, 19
Saucedo, Bartolomé, 66
Sauzo, Lic., 30
Sayavedra, Lope de, 52, 62, 66
Serna, Fray Jacinto de la, 177
Solís, Gonzalo and Francisco de: witnesses, 22, 144
Sorio, Diego de: witness, 24
Sosa, Bernabe, 108
Sosa, Pedro de, 51, 52, 53, 57, 62
Soto, Amador de, 101
Soto, Fray Domingo de, 143
Sotomayor, Riobo de, 62
Suárez, Juan de Avila, 70, 71; family, 70-71
Suárez, Fray Juan: witness, 22
Suárez, Hernán García, 35, 36

Tecatecle, Pablo: trial, 81
Téllez, Lic. Francisco, 59, 77, 78
Tello de Sandoval, Francisco, 75-81, 111. *See also* Indians
Terrazas, Francisco de, 17
Thomistic theology, 144, 153
Tirado, Juan: witness, 22-23
Toledo, Attorney Cristóbal de, 83, 84, 91
Tomson, Robert, 99; trial, 85-86, 91, 92
Toral, Bishop Francisco de, 121
Toro, Alfonso, 34
Toro, Dr. Francisco de: denouncer, 103
Toro, Juan de: witness, 84

Torre, Dr. Pedro de la: trial, 103-104
Torre, Juan de la, 23
Torres, Antonio de: witness, 21
Torres, Lic. Pablo de, 179
Tunalt, Tomás, 80

Urbano, Fray Alonso: trial, 137, 138-141
Urdiñola, Francisco de, 179-180, 182
Urdiñola, Leonor, 179
Usury. *See* Inquisition, Mexican, types of cases

Valderrama, Cristóbal de, 49, 50; denouncer, 46, 50, 51, 61, 62, 63, 64, 69
Valderrama, Visitador Jerónimo de, 130-131, 151, 153
Valdés, Alfonso de, 153
Valdespino, Bartolomé de, 128
Valencia, Martín de, 8, 10
Valle, Diego del: trial, 208; witness, 196-197
Vanderbec, Zegbo. *See* Santiago, Simón de
Vargas, Alonso de, 65
Vargas, Pedro de: witness, 60
Vasco de Puga, 130, 148
Vásquez de Coronado, Juan, 109
Velasco, Viceroy Luis de, 132
Velásquez, Fray Antonio de: trial, 131, 132
Vellerino, Lic. Juan, 136
Vera Cruz, Fray Alonso de la, 124-126, 145, 147, 211
Vergara, Pedro de, witness, 28
Viezma, Father Francisco de, 93-94
Vigue, Attorney Fulgencio, 98, 136
Villafranca, Attorney Juan Torres de, 17, 18
Villafuerte, Juan Rodríguez de: trial, 16, 18-19
Villagómez, Juan de, 88
Villalobos, Oidor, 130, 148
Villa of San Francisco de Campeche, priest of: trial, 127-128
Villegas, Francisco de: witness, 57, 60, 63

Vohorques, Dr. Marthos, 192, 198, 201-202

Warren, F. Benedict, 49

Xighy, old Indian: 101-102

Zarate, Martín de, 130
Zuazo, Lic. Alonso, 47
Zumárraga, Juan de, 8, 11, 37, 39, 40, 46, 47, 48, 50, 53, 54, 55, 56, 58, 59, 61-62, 65, 66, 67, 68, 69, 74, 78, 79, 81, 111, 118, 119; campaign against Judaizantes, 70; conflict with Montúfar, 122-123; consecration as bishop, 8, 74; criticism of, 77; Erasmism, 122; and Indian trials, 74-75; loss of title of apostolic inquisitor, 75; writing of 1544 tract, 123

Zuñiga, Felix de, 179